THE
HISTORY of HEALTH,
AND THE
Art of Preserving it:

This is a volume in the
Arno Press collection

AGING AND OLD AGE

Advisory Editor

Robert Kastenbaum

Editorial Board

Joseph T. Freeman
Gerald J. Gruman
Michel Philibert

See last page of this volume
for a complete list of titles.

THE HISTORY of HEALTH,

AND THE

ART of PRESERVING IT

JAMES MACKENZIE

ARNO PRESS
A New York Times Company
New York • 1979

Publisher's Note: This book has been reproduced from the best available copy.

Editorial Supervision: Joseph Cellini

Reprint Edition 1979 by Arno Press Inc.

Reprinted from a copy in the Duke Medical Center Library

AGING AND OLD AGE
ISBN for complete set: 0-405-11800-7
See last pages of this volume for titles.

Manufactured in the United States of America

Library of Congress Cataloging in Publication Data

MacKenzie, James, 1680?-1761.
    The history of health and the art of preserving it.

  (Aging and old age)
  Reprint of the 3d ed. printed in 1760 for W. Gordon, Edinburgh.
    1. Health--Early works to 1800. 2. Smallpox--Preventive inoculation--Early works to 1800. I. Title. II. Series.
RA775.M15 1979   613   78-22208
ISBN 0-405-11822-8

A Note About This Book

MacKenzie was a Fellow of the Royal College of Physicians in Edinburgh who wrote "an account of all that has been recommended by Physicians and Philosophers, towards the preservation of health, from the most remote antiquity to this time" and added a review of the principal rules and reasons for his objective. In this edition he discusses the value of innoculation for smallpox. The book, dedicated to the Bishop of Worcester, is in two parts. Part 1 discusses the rules for ailment and other hygienic conditions of medical historians as far back as biblical times. MacKenzie traces the history of food and the prevention of health deterioration through all of antiquity up to and including writers from Greece, Rome, Arabia, Italy, England, France, and other parts in order to include all notable figures who had contributed importantly to the subject. In Part 2 he takes up every phase of physiology, health regeneration, diseases and longevity as they were known in the middle of the 18th century up to his times. The book is an invaluable and interesting collection of citations about the entire subject of aging in a most readable and interesting form. No major author was neglected; no important contribution to regimen was skipped; and all serve as a most effective way of summarizing the history of the subject beyond the period of the Industrial Revolution. It is a compendium of the major historical works on aging and a comprehensive text of what was known about aging and its management up to the middle of the 18th century.

THE HISTORY of HEALTH,

AND THE

ART of PRESERVING IT:

OR,

An Account of all that has been recommended by Phyficians and Philofophers, towards the Prefervation of Health, from the moft remote Antiquity to this Time. To which is fubjoined, a fuccinct Review of the principal Rules relating to this Subject, together with the Reafons on which thefe Rules are founded.

By JAMES MACKENZIE, M. D.
Phyfician lately at Worcefter, and Fellow of the Royal College of Phyficians in Edinburgh.

By furfeiting many have perifhed, but he that taketh heed prolongeth his life. ECCLUS.

The THIRD EDITION:
To which is added, a fhort ana clear Account of the Commencement, Progrefs, Utility, and proper Management of Inoculating the SMALL POX, as a valuable Branch of the Prophylaxis.

EDINBURGH.
Printed for WILLIAM GORDON Bookfeller in the Parliament Clofe.

M. DCC. LX.

THE CONTENTS.

PART I.

THE introduction, exhibiting the Plan of the work — page 1

CHAP. I.

Of man's food before the fall — 17
Mofes the beft hiftorian of remote antiquity — 19
Probable ufe of the tree of life — 21
Early advances towards the improvement of man's food by hufbandry — 27
Why loft in fome countries — 29
Longevity of the firft generations infers the wholefomnefs of their diet — 33

CHAP II.

Food of the firft inhabitants of Greece — 35
Arcadians the moft noted fhepherds — 37

The

iv CONTENTS.

The golden age.—Wherein confifted
  its felicity 39
Aliment of the Greeks improved by
  hufbandry 40
Benefit of the arts, and gratitude to the
  inventors of them 41
Bread and milk the firft mild and wholefome aliment found out by man 43

CHAP. III.

Firft permiffion to eat flefh 44
This opinion controverted 45
Invention of wine and beer 51
The various forts of aliment ufed by
  men from the creation to the time of
  Mofes 53

CHAP. IV.

Of the writers on aliment 54

CAHP. V.

Neceffity invented every branch of phyfic 62
Firft rudiments of it among the Babylonians and other nations 64
Cures recorded in the temple of Æfculapius 65

Egyptian

CONTENTS.

Egyptian method of preserving health 67
Firſt inſtances of the Gerocomicè 69
Pythagoras firſt recommended modera-
    tion and temperance as conducive to
    health 72
Herodicus inventor of the medicinal
    gymnaſtic 73
Plato's abſurd cenſure of this invention 74
Herodicus not the author of the three
    books on diet, publiſhed among the
    works of Hippocrates, as Le Clerc 78
    conjectures.

CHAP. VI.

Of Hippocrates 80
His general and particular precepts re-
    lating to the preſervation of health 82

CHAP. VII.

Of Polybus 128
Of Diocles Caryſtius 130
Of Cornelius Celſus 133
Of Plutarch 146
Of Agathinus 162

CHAP.

CHAP. VIII.

Of Galen 165
Such of his rules of health as were but slightly touched upon before his time 167

CHAP. IX.

Of Porphyry, Dr. Cheyne, and those who condemn the use of animal food 190

CHAP. X.

Of Oribasius 199
Aetius 200
Paulus Ægineta 201
Of Actuarius and others, as Friar Bacon and Lord Verulam, who imagined that health might be preserved, and life prolonged, by antidotes and panaceas ibid.

CHAP. XI.

Of the Arabian physic 212
Its commencement 213
Return of physic from the East to Europe 220
Of Rhases 214

CONTENTS. vii

Of Avicenna 216
Of the Tacuin or Elluchaſem Elimithar 221

CHAP. XII.
Of the Schola Salernitana, Caſtor Durante, Dr. Armſtrong, and thoſe authors who wrote of the preſervation of health in verſe 222

CHAP. XIII.
Of Marſilius Ficinus and others who joined aſtrology with phyſic for the preſervation of health 228
Of Platina Cremonenſis 234

CHAP. XIV.
Of Lewis Cornaro, Leſſius, and ſome who, in order to preſerve health, were ſo curious as to weigh their aliment 235

CHAP. XV.
Of the phyſicians who wrote on health in the ſixteenth century before Sanctorius, as,
Thomas Philologus of Ravenna 245
Vidus Vidius 246

Hieronimus

Hieronimus Cardanus	247
Alexander Trajanus Petronius	251
Levinus Lemnius	252
Jason Pratensis	253
Antonius Fumanellus Veronensis	ibid.
Joannes Valverdus de Hamusco	254
Gulielmus Gratarolus	ibid.
Henricus Ranzovius	255
Æmilius Dusus	ibid.
Ferdinandus Eustachius	ibid.
Oddi de Oddis	256

CHAP. XVI.

Of Sanctorius	257
His useful discovery of insensible perspiration, and remarks upon it	258
Of those who adapted his method to their respective climates, as	
Dodart in France	260
Keil in Britain	ibid.
De Gorter in Holland	261
Rogers in Ireland	262
Bryan Robinson ibid.	263
Linin in Carolina	ibid.

Of

CONTENTS.

Of their aphorisms relating to the preservation of health — 265
Of inhalation by the reforbent veins, treated on by Jones — 287

CHAP. XVII.

Of foreign writers concerning health after Sanctorius, as
Rodericus a Fonseca — 291
Aurelius Anselmus — 292
Franciscus Ranchinus — ibid.
Rodolphus Goclenius — 293
Claudius Deodatus — ibid.
Joannes Johnstonus — 294
Petrus Lotichius — ibid.
Bernardin Ramazzini — 295

CHAP. XVIII.

Of the British writers on health, *viz.*
Sir Thomas Elliot — 299
Dr. William Bulleyn — 300
Thomas Coghan — 301
Edmund Hollyngs — 304
William Vaughan — ibid.
Thomas Venner — 305
Andrew Boorde — 307

CONTENTS.

Edward Mainwaring   308
Thomas Phayer   309
Francis Fuller   310
Dr. George Sibbald   311
Dr. Wainwright   312
Dr. Welsted   314
Dr. Burton   315
Dr. Arbuthnot   317
Dr. Lynche   320
Dr. Mead   322

PART II.

CHAP. I

A Short view of concoction or the mechanism by which our aliment is digested   331
Of the circulation of the blood and its consequences   348
From both these it will be obvious to perceive the ground and reason of the rules laid down for the preservation of health, and the expediency of observing them.   358

CHAP.

CONTENTS.

CHAP. II.

A summary of the rules of health proper to be observed with regard to

Air	367
Aliment	370
Exercise and rest	377
Sleep and wakefulness	383
Repletion and evacuation	385
The passions and affections of the mind	388
Some other general rules	393

CHAP. III.

Of the different temperaments of the human body, with the rules of health adapted to them respectively, *viz.*

The choleric	397
The melancholic	398
The phlegmatic	ibid.
The sanguine	ibid.

CHAP. IV.

Of the different periods of human life, with precepts of health peculiar to each of them, *viz.*

Infancy	402

Youth

Youth. 405
Manhood 410
Old age 412

C H A P. V.
Of the various circumſtances and conditions of men, with ſuitable directions to all of them, conſidered as
Robuſt or delicate 415
Free or ſervile 417
Wealthy or indigent ibid.

C H A P. VI.
Of the prophylaxis, or ways to prevent approaching diſtempers 419
Of inoculating the ſmall-pox 426

C H A P. VII.
Of longevity
The natural marks of it 454
The means of attaining it 455
The riſe and fall of the transfuſion of blood from one animal into another 460
The concluſion 463

THE INTRODUCTION

Addressed to the

Right Reverend

ISAAC

Lord Bishop of Worcester.

My Lord,

WHEN I found it expedient to retire from business, your lordship was pleased, affectionately, to remind me, "That we are obliged to do good in every "station and period of life, and that a phy-"sician of long experience may contrive "some method of being useful even in re-"tirement."

I was not surprised at any instance of humanity from your lordship: I had long known your sympathy with the distressed, and your zeal to relieve them, having been the first to whom you thought proper to communicate your noble defign of eftablifhing an infirmary at Worcefter, which, in fpite of many difcouragements, has flourifhed for feveral years; and will, I hope, long flourifh, to the glory of God, the relief of the helplefs, and your own perpetual honour. I knew alfo, that your lordfhip's advice to me was no unmeaning compliment, and did not proceed from any partiality in my favour, becaufe you made the fame benevolent reprefentation to another phyfician who had lately declined practice.

Prompted thus by your kind admonition, and animated by your example, I revolved in my mind which way I might be ufeful in my prefent fituation. My age rendered me unable to purfue the painful practice of a country phyfician. I could not ride long journies to remove diftempers: I determined therefore to endeavour, in fome meafure, to prevent them, by acquainting thofe that will reftrain their appetites, and hearken to reafon, with the moft effectual rules

rules to preserve health: For certain it is, that from men's ignorance or contempt of such rules, thousands never arrive at that period of life which their strength of constitution would have reached with proper care.

Should I succeed in this endeavour, it was no unpleasing reflection to do some good beyond the grave. And should I not succeed, yet still my subject afforded me an agreeable amusement.

That I might add a greater weight and authority to these rules, I resolved to trace them from their sources, by giving the history of the whole art of preserving health, from the most remote antiquity down to the present time. But so few and short are the records we have of the first ages of the world, that it is no easy matter to collect facts from them, which have any relation to this subject.

Six things are known to be necessary to the life of man, commonly called the Six Non-

NON-NATURALS*, namely, *aliment, air, exercise* and *rest, sleep* and *wakefulness, repletion* and *evacuation*, together with the *passions* and *affections* of the *mind;* in the proper use and regulation of which the art

* The very sound of the epithet NON-NATURAL, when applied to *aliment, air, sleep,* &c. so essential to the subsistence of mankind, is extremely shocking; nor is the long continuance of this ill fancied appellation, which arose merely from the jargon of the Peripatetic schools, less surprising. The origin of it appears in a passage, where Galen divides things relating to the human body into three classes: Things which are NATURAL to it: Things which are NON-NATURAL; and things which are EXTRA-NATURAL. I shall subjoin his own words from the vulgar Latin version, Clafs. vii. lib. de ocul. partic. tertia, cap. 2. " Qui sanitatem vult restituere decen-
" ter debet investigare septem res NATURALES, quæ sunt *ele-*
" *menta, complexiones, humores, membra, virtutes, spiritus,*
" et *operationes.*----Et res NON-NATURALES, quæ sunt sex,
" *aer, cibus, potus, inanitio* et *repletio, motus* et *quies, som-*
" *nus* et *vigilia, et accidentia animi.*----Et res EXTRA-NA-
" TURAM, quæ sunt tres, *morbus, causa morbi,* et *acciden-*
" *tia morbum comitantia.*" From this fantastical distinction the epithet NON-NATURAL first arose, and has been retained in common use to this day, tho' it cannot be understood without a commentary, by which physicians seem to make an apology for the impropriety of it. Hoffman, for instance, and some others, when they apply the appellation NON-NATURAL to *air* and *aliment*, are obliged to subjoin the following explanation: " A veterbus hæ res NON-NATURALES appellan-
" tur, quoniam extra corporis essentiam constitutæ sunt."
Dissertatio 3. Decadis 2.

of

of preserving health principally consists. Among these six, *aliment* is the only one of which mention is made before Pythagoras*, or (as some think) Herodicus †, who joined *exercise* with *aliment*, in order to preserve health. For this reason, no more should be expected from me, in looking over the first and obscure ages of the world, than to throw all the light I can collect upon that single article of the *Aliment of mankind*, until the gradual improvement of arts opens a more extensive scene.

The Samian philosopher made some small advances toward the conservation of health: Iccus and Herodicus proceeded a little farther; but it was the masterly hand of Hippocrates that (to use Galen's expression) first opened the way ‡ to this and every other

* Pythagoras flourished about 530 years before Christ.

† Herodicus was one of the preceptors of Hippocrates.

‡ Omnem ad medicationem viam aperuisse mihi videtur Hippocrates, sed ita tamen ut ea curam diligentiamque ad absolutionem desideret. Gal. de method. medend. lib. 9. cap. 8. Thoma Linacro Anglo interprete.

branch

branch of the medical art, tho' in most branches it has been greatly improved since his time.

And here it may be asked, since all the learned seem to agree, that Hippocrates was the father of physic, Why should I not begin my history with him? And to what purpose do I trouble the reader and myself with impertinent conjectures about what passed in the dark ages of the world? To this, my lord, I answer, That as Hippocrates * flourished within 430 years of the Christian æra, it is not an unreasonable curiosity to enquire, if nothing was done with regard to the preservation of health for upwards of 3500 years from the creation. The gradual advances made by the human mind in cultivating the sciences, is a very entertaining subject, and the more interesting health is, the more one is amazed, that it should lie so long neglected. And we shall find, in the course

* See the most learned dean Prideaux's connect. part 1. book 6. page. 396.

of

of this history, that the first men were obliged to alter and improve their diet, and that the prefervation of health was actually studied many ages before Hippocrates, tho' the extreme difficulty of attaining any confiderable knowledge therein, rendered its progrefs very flow; and the want of records †, to tranfmit what was truly valuable among the productions of the Greeks, has, in a great meafure, deprived us of the benefit of their experience. But farther, we learn from Hippocrates himfelf, whofe authority is decifive in this point, that the medical art was actually cultivated to a great degree before his time*. And furely it was not foreign to my

† We are informed by Pliny, (lib. 7. cap. 56.) that Pherecydes of Scyros firft taught the Greeks the compofition of difcourfe in profe: And that Cadmus of Miletus was the firft who taught them to write hiftory; and yet both thefe authors flourifhed but about 113 years before Hippocrates. How was it poffible therefore, that any accurate account of what was done in phyfic by the Greeks before that time, fhould be tranfmitted to us? See Sir James Stewart's excellent defence of Sir Ifaac Newtown's chronology, p. 107, 108.

* At vero in medicina jampridem omnia fubfiftunt, in eaque principium et via inventa eft, per quam præclara multa *longa temporis*

my purpose to search whether or no the branch I treat of, had received any improvement.

But to return, tho' Hippocrates has given us excellent precepts on all the *six articles necessary to life,* yet those precepts lie scattered throughout his works, with so little connection, that to render them universally useful, it was necessary to bring them under one regular view, which, so far as I know, was never attempted before.

Celsus and Plutarch are the only valuable writers we have on the subject of health in that long interval of time between Hippocrates, who was contemporary with the Persian Xerxes; and Galen, who lived under the reign of Marcus Aurelius Antoninus.

temporis spatio sunt inventa, et reliqua deinceps invenientur, si quis probe comparatus fuerit, ut ex inventorum cognitione, ad ipsorum investigationem feratur. De prisc. medic. p. 8. lin. 42. versionis Fœsii.

Galen

GALEN (if we throw aside his Peripatetic rubbish) has written one of the fullest and best treatises * on the preservation of health that we have at this day; but it was expedient to contract his exuberance, and for preventing repetitions, to retrench what he has copied from Hippocrates.

THE latter Greek physicians, the Arabians, and indeed all who have treated on this subject, from Galen to Sanctorius, have done little more than copy Galen, except a few whimsical Authors; among whom, some have recommended a total abstinence from animal food; some a very spare diet, weighing temperance by the balance; some depended for health on panaceas, and some on the stars.

AMONG the more modern physicians, who wrote before the discovery of the circula-

* Galeni liber extat de tuenda sanitate, quem omnibus aliis qui hodie supersunt, præferimus. Conringii introductio, cap. 13. thes. 7.

tion, Sanctorius deserves to be named with honour; who, by an amazing application, and a method little thought of before, has not only confirmed the observations of the ancients with regard to health, but has also added many valuable rules of his own. His method has been pursued by some physicians of different nations, that have, with great industry and judgment, accommodated many of his aphorisms to their respective climates.

LATE writers on this subject, enlightened by the knowledge of the circulation, have rather illustrated and enforced the precepts laid down before, than made any new or important discoveries; and yet some of them address the public with such an air of superiority, as if themselves had invented the rules which they only transcribe. Of this number is Frederick Hoffman, (in many respects a physician of great merit) who in a dissertation, which he calls *The seven rules of health*,

health*, after borrowing five of the seven from Hippocrates, and one from Galen, as your lordship will see at the bottom of the page, subjoins this curious rule of his own, viz.

* Septem leges sanitatis. Hoffm. Differt. 3. Decad. 2.

Lex prima. Omne nimium, quia naturæ est inimicum, effuge. Hoffm.----*Omne nimium naturæ inimicum.* Hippoc. Aphor. 51. Sect. 11.

Secunda. Ne subito muta assueta, quia consuetudo est altera natura. Hoffm.----*A multo tempore consueta, etiamsi fuerint deteriora, insuetis minùs turbare solent.* Hippoc. Aphor. 50. Sect. 11.

Tertia. Animo hilari ac tranquillo esto : quia hoc optimum longæ vitæ et sanitatis præsidium. Hoffm.----*Lætis diffunditur per universum corpus calor, atque plus foras ejus motus fertur, unde major fit merito pulsus.* Gal. de caus. puls. lib. 4. cap. 3. version. latin.

Quarta. Aerem purum et temperatum vehementer ama, quia ad corporis et animi vigorem multum confert. Hoff.----*Mortalibus aër, tum vitæ, tum morborum, causa est ;---morbi raro aliunde nascuntur quam ab aëre, cum is morbidis inquinamentis corpus subierit.* Hipp. de flatib. pag. 296. edit. Fœsii.

Quinta. Quam maxime seligo alimenta corpori nostro congrua, et quæ facilius solvuntur et corpus transeunt. Hoff. ----*Cibi ad sanitatem optimi sunt qui parce ingesti, fumi et siti sufficiunt, et moderatè per alvum secedunt.* Hippoc. de affect. pag. 527.

Sexta. Mensuram semper quære inter alimenta et motum corporis. Hoff.----*Si inventa fuerit ciborum mensura et laborum ad unamquamque naturam, ita ut excessus neque su-*

viz. " Avoid phyſic and phyſicians, if you have any value for your health." Theſe ſix rules of health are undoubtedly good, and ſo much the more to be depended on in practice, as they are unanimouſly recommended both by the *ancients* and *moderns;* but ſtill the knowledge which we learn from our predeceſſors, ought rather to excite gratitude than arrogance.

Some writers of reputation upon the art of preſerving health I could not find, tho' carefully ſearched for by my friends at London and in Holland, and by myſelf in the immenſe libraries of Oxford. Others again, who advance nothing new in matter or method, I have omitted; but ſhall gladly make mention of either when I can meet with the former, or be convinced of any miſtake with regard to the latter. Syſtematical writers in phyſic I ſeldom take notice of, as moſt of them touch but very ſlightly on my ſubject.

pra neque infra modum fiat, inventa erit exacta hominibus ſanitas. Hip. de diæt. lib. 1. pag. 341.

Septima. Fuge medicos et medicamenta, ſi vis eſſe ſalvus. Hoff.

Upon

Upon the whole I have endeavoured to diftinguifh and felect fuch precepts as may be of fome ufe at this time, from a large mixture of exploded cuftoms and needlefs digreffions, which are frequently met with in feveral ancients and moderns that wrote concerning health; and I have laboured to reduce thofe precepts to a proper method, with all the perfpicuity and precifion in my power, preferving the fpirit and fenfe of my authors, rather than a clofe tranflation of their words. But after all, repetitions are unavoidable, where various authors treat on the fame fubject, and fucceeding writers have interwoven the fentiments of thofe who went before them with their own.

When, in order of time, I mention an author that recommended any particular regimen of health, I join with him the principal writers who adopted his notions, tho' they were born many ages after him: Thus, for inftance, I join doctor Cheyne with the philofopher philosopher Porphyry; and lord Verulam with the Greek physician Actuarius. Lastly, I have in the second part, for the ease of the reader, collected into a narrow compass those general and particular rules which are most conducive to health in the several periods and circumstances of life.

If it should be asked, why I address a medical treatise to your Lordship? I answer, in the first place, that the preservation of health is an important branch of that *preventive wisdom*, which you so earnestly and constantly recommend. In the next place, it is a *philosophical* as well as a *medical* subject. Plutarch has composed an elegant dialogue upon it; Porphyry, Cornaro, Lord Verulam, Addison*, and other philosophical gentlemen, have recommended some parts of it. The clergy also have contributed their assistance; a pope † and a cardinal ‡

---

* See Spect. No. 115. and 195.
† John XXI. formerly Petrus Hispanus,
‡ Vitalis de Furno.

wrote

wrote concerning health, and we have few better treatiſes on temperance than Leſſius's Hygiaſticon. Beſides; all men are concerned to take care of their health. It is uſeful towards the diſcharge of our duty, and without it every other enjoyment is inſipid. When the body is in pain, ſays Democritus, the mind has no reliſh for the exerciſe of virtue; but *health enlarges the ſoul* *. In ſhort, ſince health is apt to be impaired by the labours of the mind, it is principally for ſuch as your Lordſhip I write; for thoſe, who think themſelves in duty obliged to preſerve their health for the good of the public, and recommend to others a due regard to that invaluable bleſſing.

* "Αυξέλαι δὲ ῥόος παρέϋσης ὑγίείας.
       Epiſt. ad Hippoc.

         THE

THE HISTORY
OF
HEALTH, &c.

PART I.

CHAP. I.

Of man's food before the fall.-----Moses the best historian of remote antiquity.-----Probable use of the tree of life.-----Early advances toward the improvement of man's diet by husbandry.-----Why lost in some countries.-----Longevity of the first generations infers the goodness of their aliment.

GOD was pleased to create man in such a manner that he could not subsist without a daily supply of aliment; and all the ancient writers of every denomination, who touch on this subject, agree that fruits, seeds, and herbs, just as they grew,

grew *, and prefented themfelves to the hand, were the food of the firft men.

But when we come to inquire into the nature of this fort of food, we find that, tho' it is very proper for cattle, whofe organs are adapted to fuch aliment, it could not be quite agreeable to man, who was made of a more delicate frame. The moft delicious fruits are cold, and afford but little nourifhment. Seeds, without a previous dreffing, are flatulent and hard to digeft; and herbs ftill more harfh and crude. Nor is this a controverted point, but the fettled opi-

---

* " And God faid, behold I have given you every herb bearing feed, which is upon the face of all the earth, and every tree, in the which is the fruit of a tree yielding feed; to you it fhall be for meat." Gen. i. 29.

I am of opinion, fays Hippocrates, that in the beginning man made ufe of the *fame food* with the beafts. Lib. de prifc. medic.

Volgivago vitam tractabant *more ferarum.* Lucret. lib. 5.

And as to the firft pair before the fall, one may venture to fay, that the drudgery of providing utenfils, and dreffing victuals, was not very fuitable to a life of paradifiacal happinefs.

nion

hion of phyficians in all ages and climates, Greeks*, Arabians †, Germans ‡.

WE are not from hence to infer, that man, at his firſt production, was treated worſe than the beaſts of the field; ſuch partiality was inconſiſtent with the attributes of the deity, ever perfect in wiſdom and goodneſs, tho' we cannot always comprehend the reaſon of his diſpenſations. We ſhould rather conclude, as man was endowed with nobler faculties, that he was alſo diſtinguiſhed with higher marks of favour; and that the pleaſures, even of the animal life, were beſtowed in greater profuſion upon him, while he preſerved that innocence of which he muſt neceſſarily have been poſſeſſed, when he came out of the hands of his creator.

MOSES is the only hiſtorian§ who gives an account of this tranſaction worthy of the
ſupreme

---

* Hippocrates, Galen. † Avicenna. ‡ Melchior Sebizius.

§ The heathen hiſtorians having themſelves no knowledge of the true God, repreſent man (without alledging any cauſe for ſuch uſage) as in a moſt wretched condition, ſprung up
by

supreme Being, which, in my humble opinion, is an argument of the truth of his history, and of the preference it deserves.

He by *chance*, by *fate*, or by *nature*, (words which convey no distinct idea) destitute of all aid or resource, except from his own sagacity, which, according to them, must have been very pitiful, since it had not, in many ages, found out the necessary use of the plough, or the sheep-fold.

Sanchoniatho, in the fragment we have of him, (Euseb. præp. Evang. lib. 1. cap. 10.) says, that "the first men " consecrated the plants shooting out of the ground, and judg- " ed them gods, and worshipped those deities upon whom they " themselves lived."

Diodorus Siculus, from the Egyptian records (Bibl. histor. pag. 11. edit. Westlingii) tells a lamentable tale concerning the first race of men, " who perished in great numbers thro' " want of knowledge in providing themselves food, cloaths, " or houses against winter."

Pliny also, enumerating the calamities of this proud and helpless lord of the earth, peevishly remarks, that " it is " hard to determine, whether nature deserves to be called " a kind parent, or a cruel step-mother," lib. 7. hist. nat. in proœm. The truth of it is, Moses had a much better opportunity of knowing the transactions of the first ages than any pagan historian could possibly have; being himself a descendent from Abraham, between whom and Adam there interveened but two persons, Methusalem and Sem, through whose hands an account of facts, in which themselves were concerned, might be very faithfully transmitted. And indeed, where very long-lived families mingle so little with strangers, as the ancestors and posterity of Abraham did, family

He allots indeed to Adam, before the fall, the same sort of aliment* which other historians do to the first men; but then he informs us, that the tree of life grew in the midst of the garden †, of which men might freely eat ‡, until he forfeited his right to immortality, was driven out of paradise; and the reason of his expulsion assigned, " lest " now he put forth his hand, and take also " of the tree of life, and live for ever §."

Now, a tree intended to secure immortality to man, would likewise secure perpetual health, as the means leading to that end; and

---

mily traditions, especially of important facts, are not easily lost. " On ne compte que deux tetes (says Berruyer) entre " Adam le premier des hommes et Abraham appellé de Dieu " a fonder un peuple nouveau; scavoir Methusalem, mort " l'année même du deluge, et Sem, mort vingt cinque ans " seulement avant Abraham. En sorte qu' Abraham a du " apprendre l' histoire du monde devant et apres le deluge, " de Sem avec qui il a vécu cent cinquante ans; Sem de Me- " thusalem avec qui il a vécu quatre vingt dix-huit ans; et " Methusalem d' Adam lui même avec qui il a vécu deux cens " quarante trois ans." Hist. du peuple de Dieu, livr. 1.

* Gen. i. 29. † ib. ii. 9. ‡ ib. ii. 16. § ib. iii. 22.

would

would consequently prevent, or immediately remove, every inconveniency which might arise from the insalubrity of his common diet. Does it not seem absurd to imagine, that neither Adam nor Eve ever tasted this fruit, tho' they had an unlimited permission to partake of so great a blessing? If prudence or curiosity did not prompt them, would not the natural effects of their ordinary food oblige them to make so necessary an experiment? Besides, it is evident from the nature and mechanism of the human body, that man was originally created mortal, and that there was no* possibility (while he continued the same creature) of making him immortal in this world, but by means of the tree of life, or some such panacea, contrived by in-

---

* " Corpus bene sanum, (says Boerhaave) per actiones a
" vita sana inseparabiles sensim ita mutatur, ut tandem mors
" senilis accidat inevitabilis. Instit. med. sect. 1053.-----
And some of our great divines are of the same opinion. See Clark's sermons, vol. 8. serm. 14. where the doctor says, that " Adam was not (as some have, without any ground from
" scripture, imagined) created *actually immortal*, but by the
" use of the *tree of life* (whatever is implied under that ex-
" pression) he was to have been preserved from dying."

finite

finite wifdom, and miraculoufly interpofed, to prevent ficknefs, old age, and death.

To have an univerfal remedy always at hand, which could not only remove every inconveniency that the natural qualities of their common food, or any excefs or other miftake, might bring upon them, but alfo in a moment renew their ftrength and youth, which otherwife, by the very ftructure of the animal machine, muft perpetually tend to decay. To enjoy fuch a privilege, I fay, infured their living for ever, and to be excluded from it, configned them over to death, or, in other words, permitted nature to take her courfe: And thofe who confider the pernicious effects which the fruit * and leaves of fome trees have upon animal life, will, from a parity of reafon, eafily imagine the renovation of health that might be inftantly

---

* A fimple water diftilled from the leaves of the lauro-cerafus, from the kernel of the black cherry, or from the bitter almond, given to a dog, kills him in a moment. " Quam " multa fieri non poffe, priufquam funt facta, judicantur." Plin. lib. 7. cap. 1.

received

received from a tree or fruit of contrary qualities. Give me leave to add, that as St. John, speaking of the tree of life, alludes to its use of healing, this allusion seems to strengthen the former opinion, and to shew what its original destination was. "On ei-
"ther side of the river was the tree of life,
"which bare twelve manner of fruits, and
"yielded her fruit every month; and the
"leaves of the tree were for the † healing
"of the nations."

SEVERAL learned and worthy men are, indeed, of opinion, that the food appointed for Adam, in his state of innocence, was not only delicious, but in every respect perfectly agreeable to the human constitution; and support their opinion by what Moses says, that "out of the ground made the Lord
"God to grow every tree that was pleasant
"to the sight, and good for food.*" That God made to grow every tree which was

† Rev. xxii. 2.   * Gen. ii. 29.

good

good for food, does not contradict any thing I have advanced, for several kinds of fruit were then, and always will be *good for food* with a proper preparation. For my part, I am as far from depreciating the paradisiacal happiness as any person, but cannot see why the extraordinary virtues communicated to the tree of life, and the permission to mingle it with every other sort of food which might have any inconvenient quality, should not as clearly demonstrate the beneficence of the Deity, and the felicity of man, as an appointment of various sorts of food in themselves delicious and wholesome. And perhaps the perpetual access which man had to this supernatural gift, might be a proper means to remind him of his constant dependence on the hand by which it was bestowed. Nor does the curse denounced against the earth seem to imply an essential change in the nature and quality of its productions, but only that the ground was less fertile, and required more culture than before; for some culture was necessary, even in the *happy garden*

garden of Eden, into which the man was put *to drefs it* *. The great difference feems to have been, that what was a pleafing a-mufement before the fall, became a painful toil after that fatal period.

THUS far I have ventured to touch upon the nature of man's aliment before the fall, being obliged, according to my plan, to inquire into his manner of fubfiftence from the beginning; but fince Mofes, my only guide in this narrative, has been fo fhort upon it, I fhall purfue it no farther.

AFTER man became ungrateful, and rebelled againft his maker, it was but a gentle and neceffary punifhment ‡ to remove him from thofe pleafures of which he had made a bad ufe; and to leave him amidft the fpon-

---

* Gen. ii. 15.

‡ Punifhment feems to be the only effectual means of reclaiming perverfe minds, as well as the beft expedient to deter the innocent from purfuing bad courfes; for it is not to be imagined, that the deity would punifh any creature, from indignation or revenge, as men frequently do.

taneous

taneous productions of the earth in a fruitful foil, to provide his food by his own induftry, and drefs it by his own fagacity, and growing experience. He might alfo, and no doubt did, receive fpecial * inftruction from God concerning things, above his own capacity, which were neceffary to his fubfiftence, fince it is evident, from the hiftory of Cain and Abel, that all immediate intercourfe between God and man was not ceafed; but it is probable, that for the moft part, he was left to draw thefe helps from reafon, which the brutes did from inftinct. Guided accordingly by his reflection and good fenfe, Adam in a few years reaped the fruit of his induftry, and lived on the produce of his flocks and fields; for we find his fons inftructed

* The greateft men of antiquity thought that the interpofition of the Deity was neceffary to the invention of arts; I fhall at prefent only cite Pliny, who fays, " Quod fi quis illa " forte ab homine excogitari potuiffe credit, ingrate deorum " munera intelligit.----Quod certe cafu repertum fit, quis " dubitet?----Hic ergo cafus, hic eft ille qui plurima in vita " invenit Deus." Lib. 25. cap. 2, 3.

both

both in pasturage and agriculture: " Abel
" was a keeper of sheep, but Cain was a
" tiller of the ground *."

And here we may observe, that mere
necessity invented the first rudiments of the
art of preserving health, since Adam was
obliged, after he lost his panacea, to contrive some method of dressing the fruits of
the earth, in such a manner as to make them
agree better with him, than they had done
quite crude and unprepared.

To this opinion it has been objected, that
bread is expresly named by God himself upon the fall: " In the sweat of thy face thou
" shalt eat bread ‡." But it may be answered, That the word *bread*, mentioned there,
cannot mean bread, in contradistinction to a
more crude aliment, because, " Thou shalt eat
" the herb of the field," goes immediately
before it, but must be intended to mean food

* Gen. iv. 2. ‡ Gen. iii. 19.

or suſtenance in general, as we have it in the lord's prayer, and many other * paſſages of ſcripture.

How ſome nations came totally to loſe the knowledge of huſbandry, and live for many ages, in a ſavage manner, on acorns and other wild fruits and plants, it is not eaſy to clear up, unleſs we ſuppoſe (which ſeems to be the truth of the matter) that huſbandry was at all times cultivated in the fertile and champaign provinces of Aſſyria and Egypt; but that the people who firſt tranſported themſelves into Greece (perhaps to avoid oppreſſion or puniſhment) being deſtitute of every aid and implement of huſbandry, were obliged to live on the ſpontaneous produce of the woods and fields ſo long, that their poſterity might forget to have heard of any ſuch art as huſbandry in the world, and might conſequently themſelves imagine, and perſuade others who were not acquainted with the Jewiſh hiſtory, that the

* As in Gen. xxviii. 20.----xxxix. 6.----xliii. 32. Exod. ii. 20. Prov. xii. 19.----xxxi. 27. Lam. v. 9.

firft generations of mankind, every where, had lived after the manner of their own rude and ignorant anceftors. And as we have almoft all our ancient hiftories from the Greeks, it was natural that their notions fhould prevail before the writings of Mofes were publifhed *.

INFLUENCED by this national prejudice, Hippocrates gives it as his opinion, that "in "† the beginning man made ufe of the fame "food with the beafts, and that it was the "many diftempers brought upon him by "fuch indigeftible aliment, which taught "him, in length of time, to find out a dif- "ferent diet, better adapted to his conftitu- "tion;" and he was probably in the right with refpect to his own country. But with refpect to mankind in general, that, from their firft production, they lived miferably,

* They were not tranflated into Greek, and confequently could not be known to the world before the time of Ptolomy Soter, about 300 years before Chrift. See Prideaux's connections, part 2. book 1. page 45.

† De prifc. medic. pag. 9. edit. Fœfii.

and

and in a wretched ignorance of the common conveniencies of life, Hippocrates, who was so great a lover of truth, would doubtless have entertained a different opinion of them, had he been acquainted with the rational and confiftent hiftory of Mofes.

It is amazing that the Greek and Latin writers, who admit the longevity of the primeval generations, fhould, at the fame time appoint no better food for them than that of the beafts, *viz.* the fpontaneous and crude productions of the earth; which, according to Hippocrates, and, indeed, according to common fenfe, muft rather have fhortened, than lengthened their lives.

That the tradition of this longevity has run through all antiquity without controul, we learn from Jofephus, who had the good fortune to fee many works intire, of which we have now but a few fcattered fragments. He affirms, that all the writers of antiquities, as well Greeks as Barbarians, admit the longevity

gevity of the firſt ages, and ſubjoins theſe words: " * Manetho who wrote the Egyptian hiſtory, Beroſus who wrote the Chaldean, Mochus, Heſtiæus, and Jerom the Egyptian, who wrote the Phenician antiquities, give their concurrent teſtimony to this truth. Heſiod alſo, Hecatæus, Hellanicus, Accuſilaus, Ephorus and Nicolaus, relate, that among the firſt race of men, ſome lived to a thouſand years."

Lucretius alſo, (that we may cite one teſtimony out of many among the Latin poets) aſſents to the longevity of the firſt men, and ſays that they were hardy, " becauſe the hard earth produced them:"

———————tellus quod dura creaſſet.

———————validis aptum per viſcera nervis ;.
Nec facile ex æſtu, nec frigore quod caperetur :
Nec novitate cibi nec labi corporis ullâ.
Multaque per cœlum ſolis volventia luſtra
Volgivago vitam tractabant more ferarum.

The nerves that join'd their limbs were firm and ſtrong,
Their life was healthy, and their age was long,

* Antiq. Jud. lib. 1 cap. 3.

Returning years still saw them in their prime,
They wearied e'en the wings of meas'ring time.
CREECH.

NOTHING can be more obvious than that the awowed longevity of the primeval race necessarily infers the salubrity of their food. And in fact, we find that bread, milk, and the fruits of the earth, dressed in a plain and simple manner, together with water to drink, were the aliment of Adam's family; which sort of aliment, to healthy persons, accustomed to it from their infancy, is perhaps as wholesome as any we have at this day; and by the experience of all ages of the world, found proper to prolong life * : And there is no reason to doubt that Adam's posterity was well acquainted with this diet before their migrations into transmarine countries; and it was, perhaps, to the sa-

---

* This is evident from the long lives of the first Hermites, who subsisted on bread and water with a few fruits and sallads, plainly dressed. See also Gemelli's account of the late Aurenzebe, who, from his usurpation of the throne, never tasted flesh, fish, nor strong liquors, and lived in good health to near a hundred years.

lubrity of this simple diet, as well as to the strength of their stamina, and the temperature of the seasons, that, in a great measure, they owed their extraordinary longevity. It is also insisted upon by some learned men, that the antediluvians were no strangers to animal food and fermented liquors, which opinion shall, in its proper place, be discussed.

CHAP. II.

Food of the first inhabitants of Greece.----The golden age.----Wherein consisted the felicity of it.----Arcadians the most noted shepherds. ----Aliment of the Greeks improved by husbandry.----Benefit of the arts.----Bread and milk, the first mild and wholesome food found out by man, as well in Europe as in Asia.

WHEN Adam lost his innocence, he lost also the benefit of the tree of life, but the same common food was continued after his transgression which he made use of before it, " and thou shalt eat the
" herb

"herb of the field*." Happily, however, by his own fagacity, under the kind direction of providence, he and his family foon became acquainted with hufbandry, which fupplied them with the neceffaries of life, in a plain and comfortable manner.

It was not fo with the firft inhabitants of Greece, who having left the fertile countries of Afia, and being deftitute of the implements and fupports of hufbandry, lived, like the beafts, on the fpontaneous productions of the woods and fields. This account we have from their own hiftorians, of whom it will be neceffary to remark, that they fpeak of their earlieft Grecian anceftors, as if they had been the firft generations of mankind.

Diodorus Siculus † writes, that "the firft men ranged over the fields and "woods in fearch of food like the beafts,

* Gen. iii. 18.   † Bibl. hift. lib. 1. fect. 8.

"eating

"eating every mild herb they could find,
"and such fruits as the trees produced of
"their own accord."

Ælian * affirms, that "the diet of the
"primeval race differed according to the
"different products of their respective coun-
"tries: The Arcadians having lived on a-
"corns, the Argives on pears, the Athe-
"nians on figs, &c." Plutarch † relates,
that "the first Argives, led by Inachus,
"searched the woods for wild pears to sup-
"port them." ‡ Among the Roman writers also, Pliny laments the savage condition of the first ages, "which subsisted on
"acorns."

* Var. hist. lib. 3. cap. 39.

† 'Αχράσι διατραφῆναι λέγυσι,

The same author, in his life of Artaxerxes Longimanus, tells us, that much later than the time we speak of, this unwary prince led a great army against the Cadusians, a robust and warlike people, whose inhospitable country produced neither corn nor good fruit, so that the natives were forced to live on pears and apples, which grew wild and spontaneous.

‡ Hist. nat. lib. 16. in princip.

AND

AND Galen seems to think all these accounts true; for he assures us ‡, " that a-
" corns afford as good nourishment as ma-
" ny sorts of grain; that in ancient times
" men lived on acorns only; and that the
" Arcadians continued to eat them, long
" after the rest of Greece had made use of
" bread-corn."

THIS account Galen probably learned from Herodotus *, who relates, that " up-
" on the death of Lycurgus, the Lacedemo-
" nians, meditating the conquest of Ar-
" cadia, were told by the oracle, that
" there were many brave † acorn eat-

‡ Gal. de aliment. facult. lib. 2. cap. 38. And he means the acorns of the beech, as well as those of the oak.

* Clio, cap. 66.

† It should seem that the Arcadians might continue in their primitive state longer than their neighbours, merely because they were shepherds, for property of lands did not begin so early among them, as among those addicted to agriculture. This appears from what is said in Genesis xiii. 9. concerning the people of Palestine, who allowed Abraham and Lot to feed their cattle on the neighbouring grounds; whereas the Egyptians had their lands in full property, until Joseph bought them for Pharaoh; Gen. xlvii. 20.

" ers

"ers (Βαλανηφάγοι ἄνδρες) in that country, who would repel them in cafe they attempted to carry their arms thither, as it afterwards happened."

The Poets are of the fame opinion with the hiftorians, concerning the food of the firft inhabitants of the earth: Hefiod fings*,

-----καρπὸν δ' ἔφερε ζείδωρος ἄρεα
Αὐτομάτη πολλόν.

<blockquote>
The fields, as yet untill'd, their fruits afford,
And fill a fumptuous and unenvied board.

COOKE.
</blockquote>

And Ovid, (for it would be tedious to cite all the poets) to the fame purpofe fays, in the firft book of his metamorphofis:

<blockquote>
Contentique cibis nullo cogente creatis,
Arbuteos fœtus, montanaque fraga legebant,
Cornaque et in duris hærentia mora rubetis,
Et quæ deciderant patula Jovis arbore glandes.

Content with food which nature freely bred,
On wildings, and on ftraw-berries they fed;
Cornels and bramble-berries gave the reft,
And falling acorns furnifhed out a feaft.

DRYDEN.
</blockquote>

*Oper. et dier. lib. 1. lin. 117.

Those ages, neverthelefs, are by fome philofophers and poets called the *golden ages* of the world: But this notion muft have arifen, either from fome obfcure tradition they had concerning paradife, or from the fuppofed integrity of men's lives, while they fubfifted in common on what the woods and fields fupplied, and while there was yet no property or private intereft to raife difputes and animofities, and tempt them to violence or fraud; for fuch a *fplendid appellation* could not, with any propriety, be given with refpect to the comforts and conveniencies of life, which have been enjoyed in a much higher degree by fucceeding ages, inftructed in the knowledge of arts and fciences.

After this celebrated æra, in which, whatever peace the mind might enjoy, the body was but indifferently provided for, and man could juft preferve his exiftence from day to day, the firft approach towards a more mild and wholefome diet among the Greeks,

Greeks, and towards a fund of plenty for all seasons of the year, was made by tilling the ground and sowing corn.

Hesiod * ascribes this invention to Ceres, by his admonishing the husbandman to pray to Jupiter and to *her*, before he enters upon his labour, in the season of tillage:

Εὔχεσθαι δὲ Διὶ χθονίῳ, Δημήτερι θ' ἁγνῇ.
Pray to terrestrial Jove, and *Ceres* chaste.

The Roman Poets do her the same honour more expresly:

Prima Ceres unco glebam dimovit aratro,
Prima dedit fruges, alimentaque mitia terris.
Ovid.

Pliny attributes not only the invention of the plough, but of grinding corn also, and making bread to Ceres; and adds, that " divine honours were paid her in Attica, " Italy, and Sicily on this account ‡." And

* Oper. et dier. lib. 2. lin. 83.

‡ Ceres frumenta invenit, cum ante glande vescerentur; eadem molere et conficere in Attica, Italia, et Sicilia; ob id dea judicata. Hist. nat. lib. 7. cap. 25.

indeed

indeed, if fhe had any fhare in fuch a noble and ufeful invention, fhe deferved all the reafonable encomiums which they could beſtow.

When we confider that the moſt polite nations on earth have formerly lived as the moſt favage and barbarous do at this time, we have reafon to extol the difcernment and induſtry of our anceſtors, in cultivating the arts and fciences. It would be endleſs to enumerate the advantages we derive from them. How many conveniencies and pleaſures of life have their fagacity and addreſs put us in poſſeſſion of! How much labour, inquietude, and mifery have they delivered us from! And perhaps the munificent author of nature has himſelf, in a great meaſure, directed their refearches both for ufe and ornament. Does not Mofes feem to favour this opinion, when, defcribing the work of the tabernacle, he tells us, that God faid, " And in the hearts of all that are wife " hearted I have put wifdom *?" And fo grateful were the ancient inhabitants of Italy

F to

* Exod. iii. 1, 2, 3, 4, 5, 6.

to their benefactors, that they conferred immortal honours † even on Stercutius the fon of Faunus, for his invention of improving land, by fpreading dung over it.

And have we not reafon to admire the genius and generofity of Hippocrates, who has fo greatly improved and communicated to mankind, an ufeful fcience, which feemed, in his days, to be wholly confined to himfelf and his family? And fhould we not be thankful to providence, when we fee the art of healing brought fo near to perfection in our time, and daily receive fo great benefit from it?

As to the other great branch of hufbandry, or the management and ufe of flocks and herds, it is probable that this was recovered in Greece, about the fame time with agriculture, and that the Arcadian fhepherds

† Italia fuo regi Stercutio, Fauni filio, ob fimi inventum immortalitatem tribuit. Plin. lib. 17. cap. 9. See Rollin's introduction to his hiftory of arts and fciences.

might

might teach their skill in pasturage to the other provinces, and from them, in return, learn agriculture.

From what has been said, it appears probable, that as bread, milk, and various simple preparations of mild fruits and herbs, were the first kindly and healthful food found out by Adam and his family, and used by his posterity in Asia, until they became acquainted with animal food; so likewise the same seems to have been the first wholesome aliment, revived by the Greeks, after it had been lost by their ancestors.

CHAP III.

First permission to eat flesh.——This opinion controverted.——Invention of wine and beer.——The various sorts of aliment used from the creation down to Moses.

THE next step to improve man's aliment, was the permission given him to eat flesh, upon account, perhaps, of the scarcity and bad condition of the fruits of

the

the earth, after it had undergone fo great a change, by being fo long and fo deeply covered with the waters of the deluge. " E-" very moving thing that liveth fhall be " meat for you; even as the green herb " have I given you all things *." This opinion, however, has been ftrenuoufly controverted. Some learned men affert, that Adam was permitted to eat the flefh of animals, or, at leaft, that his pofterity did eat it, with or without permiffion, long before the flood. Others, on the contrary, maintain that Noah was the firft who had a permiffion to eat, or did eat any animal food.

THE former, in fupport of their opinion, affert that the *dominion* ‡ given to Adam over the brute creation, implies a permiffion to kill animals for food; and that the *Skins* †, of which GOD made coats for the firft pair, fhew that a proper ufe was made of fuch a permiffion: That no good reafon can be affigned, why the Almighty fhould give a

* Gen. i. 28. ‡ Gen. i. 28. † Gen. iii. 21.

more

more unlimited authority over the brutes after the deluge, than before it; and since animal food affords a more strengthening nourishment than the vegetable kind, we ought to conclude, that it was allowed from the beginning: That the clean beasts being taken in by sevens, and the unclean only by two, the male and his female, it may be presumed, that the surplus of the clean was intended for provision to Noah's family, during their abode in the ark: That the appetites of the antediluvians must have been pampered with flesh meat, and their passions inflamed with strong liquors, to incite them to commit such great wickedness as provoked the Creator to destroy the whole species, except one family; since bread, milk and water could never stimulate them to that excess of violence: And this argument is farther confirmed by observing, that carnivorous animals, as lions and tigers, are more fierce than those which live on herbage. And lastly, that as the sacrificing of animals (which was a most early institution) might have

have given occasion first to the tasting, and afterwards to the eating of dressed flesh, which (to a hungry stomach especially) sends forth no unsavoury odour, we can easily account for the commencement of this food. And as most of the antediluvians were under no restraint of conscience, to prevent their using that kind of food, supposing it had not been expresly permitted, there is little reason to doubt that flesh became a part of common aliment long before the deluge.

THOSE on the opposite side deny, that the *dominion* given to Adam over the brutes implies a power to kill them; it is cruel, say they, to infer such a power from an ambiguous expression. Isaac gave Jacob *dominion** over his brethren. The Philistines had *dominion* † over Israel, which did not imply a right to destroy them. Man's *dominion* over the brutes seems to have consisted in the use which he might make of their milk, wool, honey, feathers, &c. and of their assistance and service for carriage, agri-

* Gen. xxvii. 40. † Judg. xiv. 4.

culture,

culture, and defence. It does not follow, becaufe animal food affords a more ftrengthening nourifhment, that therefore it muft have been allowed from the beginning; for we find, fay they, that tho' blood ‡ is as nourifhing as flefh, yet it is prohibited, not only to Noah † and the Jews ‡, but alfo to the ftranger*, under pain of death; and fince blood is prohibited in every place where flefh is permitted, it follows, that the prohibition and permiffion muft have been promulged at the fame time, *i. e.* after the flood.

NOAH did not take in the clean animals by fevens, with a view that the furplus fhould become food for his family during their abode in the ark, becaufe their food was, by GOD's exprefs orders, laid up for

‡ Galinarum ac columbarum fanguine nonnulli vefcuntur, maximè altilium, qui fuûm fanguine haudquaquam eft inferior, neque voluptate, neque coctionis facultate. Gal. clafs. 2. De aliment. facult. lib. 3. cap. 23. Homerus quoque caprarum fanguinem in cibo jucundum effe non ignoravit. Ibid. cap. 18.

† Gen. ix. 3, 4.   ‡ Lev. xvii. 10, &c.   * Deut xii. 23, 24.

them before they went in *. *Take unto thee of all food that is eaten, and thou shalt gather it to thee; and it shall be for food for thee and for them* †. From this text, by the way, it seems pretty plain, that the produce of the earth was the aliment, as well of man, as of the beasts before the deluge. The clean animals were surely taken into the ark by sevens, (as Moses himself informs us) *to keep seed alive upon the face of all the earth* ‡.

As to the argument, That the sons of violence before the deluge, must have been stimulated by high food and strong drink, to perpetrate so much wickedness; the opposite side maintains, that mens morals are corrupted rather, through want of discipline, than by the nature of their food; and that men of healthy and robust constitutions, (as the antediluvians most certainly were) under no restraint from laws human or divine, are the most violent and mischievous savages of

---

* I was favoured with this remark by my learned and judicious friend, the reverend Doctor Greenwood, rector of Solyhull.

† Gen. vi. 21. ‡ Gen. vii. 3.

nature,

nature, let their aliment be what it will: That, in fact, the nations of the earth moſt addicted to lewdneſs, rapine, and murder at this day, are frugal in their diet, and forbid wine by their religion, particularly the pirates of Barbary, and the wild Arabs. And even in Britain and Ireland, that thoſe who live on bread, milk, cheeſe, cabbage, and potatoes, are, perhaps, no leſs diſpoſed to rapine and violence than ſuch of the community as have good drink and fleſh meat in abundance. Nor is a wild bull that eats graſs leſs furious than a lion that feeds on fleſh. And we daily ſee ſome birds, that live on grain, fight and tear each other with amazing animoſity.

THEY urge farther, that as we have no genuine account of the primeval ſtate of man from any hiſtorian but Moſes, and ſince he informs us that vegetable food was expreſly appointed for man before the flood* in two different periods, and animal food immediately after it †, we have no authority to aſſert the contrary, unleſs we can ſhew that

* Gen. i, 29.——iii. 18. † Gen. ix. 3.

we

we know the transactions of those times better than the Jewish historian: And why should a direct explicite permission to eat animal food after the deluge, as he had done *the green herb before it*, be given to Noah, if the same permission had been given to Adam?

BESIDES, the most eminent historians *, physicians †, and philosophers ‡ of antiquity agree, that the first generations of men did not eat flesh.

LASTLY, in reference to the first who ventured to destroy animals for food, they affirm, that the attempt to tear and devour creatures so like himself was the most sa-

* Moses, Sanchoniatho, Diodorus Siculus.
† Hippocrates, Galen.
‡ Pythagoras, Empedocles, Plato lib. 6. de republica. Porphyr. de abstin. ab esu animalium. Plutarch de esu carn. See also Diog. Laërt. de vit. philosoph.

" Enimvero, (says Pliny) rerum omnium parens nullum animal ad hoc tantum ut pasceretur, aut alia satiaret, nasci voluit. Nat. hist. lib. 21. cap. 13.

vage

vage and unnatural thought which ever entered into the heart of man, and that nothing lefs than an exprefs permiffion from the Deity could either induce or juftify the firft who made the cruel experiment, to take fuch a bold ftep, let his appetite be never fo keen, or the odour of burnt offerings never fo fragrant.

ANOTHER great improvement of man's aliment was the invention of wine, which well deferves the encomium beftowed upon it by Plutarch †, of being " the moft no-
" ble of all liquors, the moft palatable me-
" dicine, and of all delicacies the moft
" grateful to the ftomach *. Noah began
"to

† Præcept. de fanit. tuend.

* Aretæus alfo, a phyfician of the firft rank among the ancients, commends wine no lefs for the cures which it performs. I fhall cite his own words from the elegant Latin verfion of the learned Dr. Wiggan. De morb. acut. curat. lib. 1. cap. 1.
" Sed quum metus fit; ne in vaporem humiditatemque homo
" diffolvatur, unicum fubfidium vinum eft: celeriter enim fub-
" ftantiam alendo inftaurat: et quoquoverfus ad extremitates
" ufque permeat, robori apponit robur, et fpiritum torpentem
" experge-

"to be a huſbandman, and he planted a vineyard, and he drank of the wine and was drunken ‡." This good man being a ſtranger to the qualities of his new liquor, reaſon and humanity required that he ſhould try what effect it might have upon himſelf, before he would recommend it to his family; but had the misfortune to be, for a while, deprived of his reaſon by the trial, like a thouſand other curious enquirers into nature, who have generouſly expoſed themſelves to danger for the benefit of mankind. Noah had doubtleſs taſted grapes before, and found them harmleſs; and it was impoſſible he ſhould know (until experience taught him) that *fermentation* gives an *inebriating quality* to liquors, or would produce a ſpirit in the juice of the grape which it did not contain before.

"expergefacit, frigiditatem calore temperat, laxantem madorem aſtringit, extrorſum erumpentia atque diffluentia coërcet, olfactu ſuavi delectat: vires demum fulcire ad vitam prorogandam poteſt."

‡ Gen. ix. 20, 21.

Not long after wine, it is probable that beer was difcovered; for Herodotus informs us, that in the corn provinces of Egypt, where no vines grew, the people drank a fort of wine made of barley*, οἴνῳ ἐκ κριθέων πεποιημένῳ. And this feems ‡ to be the ftrong drink mentioned, together with wine, in many places of the old teftament †.

In fhort, the feveral improvements made with refpect to the different forts of aliment ufed by men in different periods of time from the creation to Mofes, feems to have proceeded nearly in the following order, *viz.* fruits, feeds, herbs, bread, milk, fifh, flefh, wine, ale, to which may be added, butter, honey, oil olive, eggs and cheefe. But as aliment came in procefs of time to be improved to fuch a high degree, that a tho-

---

* Euterpe, fect. 77.

‡ Diftilled liquors were not heard of in any part of the world, known to Europeans, for many centuries, after the time of Mofes and the other writers of the old teftament.

† Lev. x. 9. Numb. vi. 3. 1 Sam. i. 15. Mic. ii. 11.

rough

rough difcuffion of it would take up too much room here, I fhall only point out the principal authors who have treated on this article.

CHAP. IV.

Of the Writers on Aliment.

THE neceffity of food, which fupports life, contributes to reftore health, and adminifters pleafure, has induced fome eminent men, in moft ages and nations, to confider it, and to form the beft rules they could to direct people in the choice of it, under the various circumftances of life. It is amazing to think what myriads of vegetables and animals the munificence of the creator has provided on the earth, and in the waters, for the ufe of man. From this immenfe ftore, Mofes * was the firft, who with great judgment felected fome of the animal kind

---

* Mofes, according to the reverend and learned Mr. Shuckford, was born A. M. 2433. Connect. vol. 2. lib. 9. pag. 376. octavo.

for food to the Jews, and in his history mentions several vegetable productions used by that people; which vegetables and animals make the principal part of the sustenance of mankind, in all nations of the world, to this time, *viz.* bread, wine, milk, honey; quadrupeds that divide the hoof, and chew the cud; all the feathered kind, a few only excepted; and fishes that have fins and scales.

NEXT to him, though at the distance of more than eleven hundred years, came Hippocrates †, who marks the qualities of several sorts of aliment with regard to health, and whose rules of diet (especially in acute distempers) are among the best we have at this day.

CORNELIUS CELSUS, who flourished in the time of Tiberius, has concisely, indeed,

† The most learned dean Prideaux says, that Hippocrates flourished in the time of the Peloponnesian war, which Mr. Shuckford reckons to have happened about the year of the world 3570. Connect. vol. 7. lib. 9. pag. 414.

but

but with his ufual elegance and propriety, treated on this fubject from the beginning of the eighteenth chapter to the clofe of his fecond book.

XENOCRATES, who lived alfo under the reign of Tiberius, wrote a treatife on fifhes, which was in fome eftimation with Galen, and is publifhed in the collection of Photius; but I cannot fay that it will now be of great ufe to mankind.

DIOSCORIDES, who feems, by what himfelf fays* in the beginning of his work, to have been phyfician to one of the Roman armies in Nero's Time, has difperfed his obfervations upon different aliments throughout his materia medica, but has chiefly thrown them into his fecond and fifth books.

CÆLIUS APICIUS†, about the time of Trajan, wrote ten books on the art of cook-

* Nofti noftram militarem vitam.   Verfio commun.

† This was not the famous Epicure Apicius, of whom we are told fo many extraordinary ftories by Pliny and Athenæus.

ery:

[57]

ery: Whether his manner of dreſſing food might be to the taſte of his contemporaries, I ſhall not determine; but will venture to ſay, that he has ſtudied health very little in his diſhes. Among his other refinements he has quite ſpoiled the ſimple and wholeſome ptiſan of Hippocrates, by his addition* of dill, hogſlard, ſavory, coriander-ſeeds, vetches, peeſe, beets, fennel, and mallows.

Galen follows next, he flouriſhed in the reign of Marcus Aurelius Antoninus; and in his books concerning the nature of aliments, and in ſome other tracts †, gives ſuch a rational account of the various kinds of food uſed in his time, and of their effects on different conſtitutions, that his writings are the baſis, and model of almoſt all that has been advanced on the ſame ſubject ſince his time.

---

* De re culinari, lib. 4. cap. 4.

† De ſuccor. bonit. et vitio. De attenuante victus ratione.

After

After him Oribafius, archiater to Julian the apoftate, beftows upon aliment the whole fourth book of his fynopfis, three books of his collections, and feveral chapters of his directions to Eunapius.

Aetius, who lived in the latter end of the fifth century, treats this fubject in the fecond book of his firft Quaternion.

Paulus Ægineta wrote in the feventh century, and gives an epitome of the nature of aliments in his firft book, from the feventy-third to the ninetieth chapter inclufively.

Simeon Sethi, the copier of Michael Pfellus, lived in the eleventh century, under the reign of Michael Ducas, and dedicates to that emperor a treatife on the nature of aliments.

And the laft Greek, Actuarius, who practifed phyfic with good reputation at Conftantinople

ftantinople in the thirteenth century, touches the article of aliments flightly.

AMONG the Arabians, Ifaac Ifraelita, the adopted fon of Solomon king of Arabia, (which princely author has been commented upon by Petrus Hifpanus, afterwards pope John XXI.) Serapion, Rhafes, Avicenna, and Averrhoes, have handled this fubject.

SEVERAL Italians, French and Germans, have written upon aliment: Arnoldus de villa nova, Mich. Savanarola, Carolus Stephanus, Ludovicus Nonnius, Petrus Caftellanus, &c. It has alfo been treated of in verfe by the Schola Salernitana, Caftor Durante; and fome forts of fifh have been elegantly defcribed by Aufonius in his Mofella.

The three exotick liquors alfo, tea, coffee, and chocolate, fo much in common ufe among us; and tobacco, which has no fmall influence

influence on health, have been severally treated of by various authors: Tobacco by king James I. Simon Pauli, and Joannes Neander Bremensis: Chocolate by Doctor Chub of Warwick: and tea by the learned doctor Short of Sheffield, and others.

But as it would be too tedious to give a detail of all that have laboured in this search into the nature of aliments, I shall only recommend to the curious some of the most eminent, whose works seem to have exhausted all that is valuable in this branch of knowledge. These are Galen, Joannes Bruyerinus Campegius de re cibaria, Julius Alexandrinus salubrium, sive de sanitate tuenda, Melchior Sebizius de alimentorum facultatibus; and to the English reader (who must mind rather the sense than the stile) " Health's improvement, or rules compriz- " ing the nature and manner of preparing " all sorts of food used in this nation," by doctor Mouffet, and enlarged by the famous Christopher Bennet, author of the Theatrum Tabidorum:

Tabidorum: Or, if he chufes a fhort, ufeful, and entertaining difcuffion of this fubject, let him confult the learned and ingenious doctor Arbuthnot's excellent effay concerning the nature and choice of aliments.

HAVING thus mentioned the high degree of falubrity and elegance given by time and induftry to man's aliment, which was the only one of the fix things neceffary to animal life known to the firft and moft remote ages of the world, let us next examine the gradual improvements made in the remaining five: Or, in other words, let us enquire into the firft rudiments and progrefs of the art of reftoring, but efpecially of preferving health among mankind.

C H A P.

CHAP. V.

Neceſſity invented every branch of phyſic.——— Firſt rudiments of it among the Babylonians and other nations.———Egyptian method of preſerving health.———Earlieſt inſtances of the care of old age.———Pythagoras the firſt who recommended temperance and moderation, as conducive to health.———Herodicus inventor of the medicinal gymnaſticks. ———Plato's abſurd cenſure of this invention.———Herodicus not the author of the three books on diet, publiſhed among the works of Hippocrates.

HIPPOCRATES is of opinion, that mere neceſſity compelled men to invent both the art of preſerving health, and the art of reſtoring it when loſt: As to the former, he remarks particularly, that " the " diſtempers * ariſing from the coarſe ali- " ment which men at firſt made uſe of, ob- " liged them to ſtudy the moſt proper me-

* De priſc. med. ſect. 1. pag. 9. line 37. edit. Fœſii.

" thods

" thods of preparing bread from grain, and
" of dreſſing other vegetables in ſuch a man-
" ner as ſhould render them more whole-
" ſome:" And as to the latter, " One cauſe
" (ſays he) which made it neceſſary to ſtu-
" dy the art of reſtoring loſt health, was
" the great difference to be obſerved be-
" tween the diet of the healthy and that
" of the ſick." People * had frequently
ſeen, that what agreed with the ſtrong, did
hurt to the infirm, and therefore it was in-
diſpenſably requiſite, that different rules of
diet, as well for the reſtoration of the ſick
and infirm, as for the preſervation of the
ſtrong and healthy, ſhould be eſtabliſhed.

But this required time and experience,
and, in fact, a long time it took to eſtabliſh
ſuch rules; for tho' the beginning † of the

* De priſc. med. pag. 9. line 31. et. ſeq.

† Medicina quondam paucarum fuit ſcientia herbarum, quibus ſiſteretur fluens ſanguis, vnlnera coirent: paulatim deinde
in hanc pervenit tam multiplicem varietatem.—Non minus
quam cæteræ artes, quarum in proceſſu ſubtilitas crevit. Senec.
epiſt. 95.

medical

medical art muſt have been very antient, the progreſs was exceeding flow, and many ages elapſed before it could properly be called a ſcience. We learn from Herodotus *, that the Babylonians obliged themſelves by an expreſs law to carry their ſick into places or ſtreets of publick reſort, and to enquire of all who paſſed by, whether they ever had, or ſaw any ſuch diſtemper as the ſick perſon preſent laboured under, and what was done to remove it? It is obvious that the progreſs of phyſick muſt be very flow under this regulation, tho' it really was νομὸς σοφότατὸς, " a moſt prudent inſtitution," as the author calls it, and the beſt which could be contrived at that time. It was undoubtedly a proper method to gain experience, and in proceſs of time to bring to maturity a ſcience which was then in embryo. Hippocrates ſeems to have been of this opinion, for in his ſhort book of precepts, he admoniſhes phyſicians not to think it below them to

---

* Clio, cap. 197.

learn

learn from the vulgar, the hiftory of any cure which could be of ufe to them; and adds, "I am perfwaded that the whole art "was firft acquired in this manner.*" Strabo † alfo fays, that the fame cuftom of carrying their diftempered people into the ftreets for advice, prevailed among the Egyptians and Portuguefe.

THIS law of the Babylonians and Egyptians produced another cuftom which likewife became a large fource of medicinal knowledge. When a remarkable cure was performed on any perfon of diftinction, this perfon (perhaps from gratitude or benevolence) was fometimes at the expence of erecting a pillar, or fixing a table in one of the temples of Æfculapius, on which the means of his cure was written in legible characters, for the benefit of the public: And Strabo ‡

* Οὕτω γαρ᾽ δοκέω πάσαν τὴν τέχνην ἀναδειχθῆναι.

† Geograph. lib. 14. pag. 972. edit. Wolters.

‡ Narrant Hippocratem e dedicatis ibi curationibus exercuiffe ea quæ ad victus rationem fpectant. Ejufd. verf. pag. ead.

says, it was pretended that Hippocrates drew a great deal of his knowledge from those consecrated tables, which were put up at Cos in the famous temple of Æsculapius. The same sort of tables were hung up in the temple of Isis, to which Tibullus * seems to allude, where he says,

> Nunc Dea, nunc succurre mihi, nam posse mederi
> Picta docet templis multa tabella tuis.

And Mercurialis † informs us, that there is one of those tables in marble, taken out of the temple of Æsculapius in the Isle of Tiber, still to be seen at Rome in the Massæan palace.

As to that branch of physic which regards the conservation of health, there was no considerable progress made in it, which has come to our knowledge, any more than in curing distempers, until very near the time of Hippocrates. It is true, Diodorus Sicu-

* Lib. eleg. 3.
† De arte gymnast. lib. 1. cap. 1.

lus ‡ feems, at firſt fight, to give us a favourable idea of the antient Egyptian phyſic in general, when he informs us that the phyſicians of Egypt were maintained at the public charge, and obliged by the laws to conform their practice to rules invented and fettled by men of great judgment and experience in former times, which were recorded in certain venerable books, for the benefit of poſterity; and from thoſe rules the modern phyſicians durſt not depart, but at the peril of their lives, in cafe any patient ſhould happen to die under the new regimen; whereas their perſons and reputation were quite fecure by adhering to the old. But when we come to examine the ſpecimens, with regard to the conſervation of health, which our hiſtorian has preſerved, we comfort ourſelves under the loſs of thoſe facred regiſters. " To pre-
" vent diſtempers, (fays he) they preſcribed
" glyſters, purging potions, vomiting or faſt-
" ing every fecond, third, or fourth day:"

‡ Bibl. hiſt. lib. 1. p. 92. ed. Weſtling.

And

And he subjoins their reason for this smart discipline, because, according to those antient physicians, "the greatest part of the
" aliment we take in, is superfluous*, which
" superfluity is the cause of our distempers."

HERODOTUS mentions the same sort of discipline among the Egyptians, tho' not practised quite so frequently: " The Egyp-
" tians (says he) vomit and purge themselves
" thrice every month, with a view to pre-
" serve their health, which in their opinion
" is chiefly injured by their aliment ‡.

To form any clear or connected judgment from those short and scattered hints, which may be gleaned among authors of remote antiquity, concerning the preservation of health, it will be necessary to distinguish four periods of human life, to each of which a peculiar care is due with regard to health, namely, childhood, youth, manhood and

---

* Bibl. hist. lib. 1. pag. 29. ‡ Euterpe, sect. 77.

old

old age. It is true, that parents, in antient times, took the same care of their infants as they did of themselves, but their care extended no farther than to provide for their subsistence from day to day, either by the breasts, or such coarse aliment as they could afford; which cannot properly belong to the art of preserving health. Of these four periods, the Gerocomice, or care of old age, is the only one (so far as I know) taken notice of before Pythagoras.

The earliest * instance we meet with of the Gerocomice, is the care which king David's servants took of him, when he was old ‡, and stricken in years, by getting a healthy young virgin to lie in his bosom, which was a very proper means to warm and

---

* We have indeed, long before David's time, in the 27th chapter of Genesis, an account of savoury meat, bread, and wine, prepared for Isaac when he was very old; but that seems to have been rather an occasional repast to raise his spirits, and support his strength for a short while, than any thing done with regard to the preservation or restoration of health.

‡ 1 Kings i. 1.

cherish

cherish him; and which (when kept within the bounds of innocence and decency) is justified by the opinions of Galen*, Paulus Ægineta †, lord Verulam ‡, and Boerhaave §.

HOMER, whom Pliny ¶ justly calls "the source of sublime ideas," and who, in several places of his poems, does great honour to physicians, comes next, and seems to have been acquainted with the γεροκομικη, by the proper care of old age, which Ulysses recom-

---

* "Nothing contributes so much to a good digestion as a sound healthy human body touching the stomach." Meth. med. lib. 7. cap. 7. & De simpl. med. facult. lib. 5. cap. 6.

† "It is very difficult to relieve a person who is cold and dry at the same time; and a plump healthy boy to lie in his bosom, is one of the best remedies he can use." Lib. 1. cap. 72.

‡ Verulam recommends fomentations of living animals, from history. Hist. vit. et mort. 8vo. pag. 300.

§ Boerhaave frequently told his pupils, that an old German prince, in a very infirm state of health, being advised to lie between two young virtuous virgins, grew so healthy and strong, that his physicians found it necessary to remove his companions.

¶ Ingeniorum fons Homerus. Hist. nat. lib. 17. cap. 5. And again, Homerus quidem doctrinarum et antiquitatis parens, lib. 25. cap. 2.

mends

mends to his father Laertes, in the laſt book of the Odyſſey, line 258.

——— ἐπεὶ λούσαιτο φάγοι τε,
Εὐδέμεναι μαλακῶς· ἡ γὰρ δίκη ἐςὶ γερόντων.

Warm baths, good food, ſoft ſleep, and generous wine, Theſe are the rights of age, and ſhould be thine.

POPE.

On this paſſage Galen remarks that " the " poet's rule was excellent, which directed " an old man after bathing and refreſhing " himſelf with food, to take ſome reſt; for " old age being naturally cold and dry, " thoſe things which moiſten and warm, as " bathing, eating,' and ſleeping, are the " moſt proper for it."

BUT with reſpect to the preſervation of health in all periods of life indiſcriminately, tho' Moſes * ſtigmatiſes gluttony and drunkenneſs as immoralities, which deſerve the ſevereſt puniſhment; and Solomon ‡ ſays that intemperance biteth like a ſerpent; and tho'

* Deut. xxi. 20.   ‡ Prov. xxiii. 32.

Homer

Homer * declares againſt drinking wine to exceſs; yet Pythagoras †, the Samian, ſeems to have been the firſt who recommended univerſal moderation and temperance as conducive to health. He calls drunkenneſs an enemy to the whole man; and maintains, that no man, who values his health, ought to treſpaſs on the bounds of moderation, either in labour, diet, or concubinage. To this account, which Laertius gives, Jamblichus ‡ adds, that the ſcholars of Pythagoras uſed unction and bathing, and were trained up to ſuch exerciſes as ſeemed moſt proper to increaſe their bodily ſtrength; but I greatly ſuſpect that, in this place, he confounds Pythagoras the philoſopher with Pythagoras the

---

* Οἶνός σε τράει μελιηδὴς, ὅςτε κỳ ἄλλες
Βλάπτει, ὅς ἄν μιν χανδὸν ἕλῃ, μηδ' αἴσιμα πίνῃ. Od. lib. 21. l. 293.
  To copious wine this inſolence we owe,
  And much thy betters wine does overthrow.
         Pope.

† Diog. Laërt. in vit. Pythag. edit. Menag. Segm. 9. In this paſſage, the ſenſe will oblige every phyſician (if I miſtake not) to adopt the correction of Mer. Caſaubon, and to retain πόνων, contrary to the alteration made by Iſ. Caſaub. and to inſert the addition made by Hen. Stephens.

‡ De vita Pythag. cap. 21.

exercitator

exercitator mentioned by Pliny*, who trained up his champions for the combat, without the leaft regard to their health, and firft taught them to eat flefh.

After Pythagoras, Iccus †, a phyfician of Tarentum, thought it neceffary to recommend temperance, together with exercife for the prefervation of health; and his own fobriety was fo remarkable, that *the repaft of Iccus* became a proverbial phrafe for a plain and temperate meal.

Herodicus, neverthelefs, one of the preceptors of Hippocrates, has been generally celebrated as the inventor of this art of preferving health, and of teaching the infirm to regulate their exercife and diet in fuch a manner as to prolong their lives for many years; and is cenfured by Plato ‡ for

* Hift. nat. lib. 23. cap. 7.
† Steph. Byzant. de urbib. in voce Taras.
‡ De republ. lib. 3.

thus keeping people of crazy conftitutions alive to old age; whereas, in his opinion, if a tender perfon did not foon recover ftrength, he had better die out of the way. " He was mafter of an academy, (continues " Plato) where youth were taught their ex- " ercifes, and being himfelf valetudinary, " he contrived to blend exercife with fuch " other medicinal rules, as preferved his " own infirm conftitution from finking un- " der his complaints; thus he dragged on " a dying life to old age, and did the fame " injury to feveral other valetudinarians." Plato was of opinion, that an infirm confti- tution is an obftacle to the practice of vir- tue, becaufe it makes people imagine them- felves to be always ill, and mind nothing but their own wretched carcaffes; for which reafon, continues he, " Æfculapius would " not undertake to patch up perfons habi- " tually complaining, left they fhould be- " get children as ufelefs as themfelves, be- " ing perfwaded that it was an injury both " to the community, and to the infirm per-
" fon

"son himself, that he should continue in
"the world, even tho' he were richer than
"Midas *."

IF this tenet of Plato is rational or humane, let us never blame the Hottentots ‡ for carrying their parents into the woods to die there, when they become so decrepid with age as to be unable to help themselves. Nor ought we to find fault with the Padæan Indians, of whom Herodotus † relates, that "when any man fell sick among them, his "next neighbours killed him directly, lest "he should lose his flesh, and eat him up. "For which reason, as soon as any of that "nation found himself indisposed, he with- "drew privately into some desart place, "where he had no manner of care taken of "him dead or alive," unless he happened luckily to recover, and return home of himself.

* ὀδὲ θεραπευτέον αὐτȣς. ὀδὲ ὶι Μίδȣ πλουσιώτεροι ἦὲν. De Republ. 3.

‡ See Kolben's history of the Cape of Good Hope.

† Thalia, sect. vel cap 99.

IT

It is a misfortune, indeed, to have an infirm conſtitution. But are all infirm perſons uſeleſs? Are not their underſtandings frequently clear, and of great ſervice to the community, when their bodies are unfit for labour? And what muſt become of the pleaſure and reward of beneficence, if all objects of compaſſion were permitted to periſh for want of aſſiſtance? Beſides, how many recoveries from various ailments does every age and every country produce! And how many perſons, after ſuch recoveries, have become a benefit and an ornament to their country!

When we conſider, therefore, that Plato, who, next to Socrates, was the glory of the heathen world, could not, with all his ſcrutiny, and uprightneſs of intention, avoid falling into this and other vile and groſs abſurdities *; ſhould not our hearts glow with gratitude

---

* I mean, among other immoralities, the ſhameful licence of promiſcuous concubinage, which he gives to men and women at a certain age. I ſhall cite his own words from the latin tranſlation

gratitude and praise to the blessed author of the christian system, which has made the path of virtue so clear and plain, that no man is in danger of losing his way, but he who shuts his eyes?

But to return: The Gymnastic art, to season * youth for the fatigues of war, and

translation of Serranus, to shew that I do not charge him wrongfully: " Quando igitur jam mulieres et viri ætatem generationi aptam egressi fuerint, licere viris dicemus cuicunque voluerint, præterquam filiæ, et matri, et filiarum filiabus, commisceri; licere et mulieribus cum quolibet copulari, præterquam filio atque patre, ac superioribus, et inferioribus eorundem." De republ. lib. 5. pag. 461. tom. 2. interpret. Serrani.

The Stoics also allowed the same scandalous indecencies: " Placet item illis uxores quoque communes esse inter sapientes, ut quilibet illi congrediatur quæ sibi occurrit." Laërt. vit. Zen. sect. 131.——They likewise banish pity (which Zeno ranks with envy and grief) from their wise man. *This is our celebrated Portic Philosophy.*

* Homer represents the Grecian soldiers as highly entertained with their warlike exercise.

———— λαοὶ δὲ παρὰ ῥηγμῖνι θαλάσσης
Δίσκοισιν τέρποντο —
      Iliad 2. lin. 280.

———— on the sandy shore
The troops in air their sportive jav'lins throw,
Or whirl the disk, or bend the stubborn bow.
         POPE.

harden

harden champions * for the combat, was, indeed, practifed long before the time of Herodicus, but he is generally reputed the firft who introduced the *medicinal* gymnaftic. He was of Selymbria a town in Thrace, or, as others conjecture, of Lentini in Sicily. Plutarch fays of him, that labouring under a decay, which he knew could not be perfectly cured, he was the firft that blended the gymnaftic art with phyfic, in fuch a manner as protracted to old age his own life, and the lives of others afflicted with the fame diftemper.

It is the opinion of the learned and judicious Daniel Le Clerc †, that the three books on diet, afcribed commonly to Hippocrates, and publifhed with his works, might have been compofed by Herodicus; but in this I beg leave to differ from him, for three reafons: *Firft*, Becaufe Hippocrates, in a

* We are told by Pliny, lib. 7. cap. 56. that the inftitution of the Olympic games was as old as Hercules.
† Le Clerc. hift. de la medic. par. 1. liv. 3. ch. 13.

book † allowed by all the world to be his own, obferving, " that the antients wrote nothing concerning diet worth taking notice of," could not decently have omitted to do honour or juftice to his preceptor, had he been the author of thofe excellent tracts. *Secondly*, Becaufe in the paffage *, on which this accurate hiftorian feems to build his conjecture, Galen does not afcribe three books on diet to Euriphon, Phaon, Philiftion or Arifton, but the fingle book concerning *wholefome diet* on which Galen himfelf has written a commentary, where he afcribes that performance to Polybus, as we fhall fee hereafter. And *thirdly*, Becaufe thefe books difcover fuch a thorough knowledge of the nature and effects of aliment, according to the theory of thofe times, and accommodate diet fo judicioufly to the preventing and removing various complaints,

---

‡ De rat. vict. in acut. fub principio, he fays, ἀτάρ ἐδὲ περὶ τῆς διαίτης οἱ ἀρχαῖοι ξυνέγραψάν ἐδὲν ἄξιον λόγυ.

* Compare Le Clerc, in the place laft cited, with Galen in libros Hippoc. de rat. vict. in acut. comment. 1. num. 18.

that

that it is not likely a master of an academy should be capable of composing them, nor indeed any man but an accomplished physician, which Herodicus was not; of whom Hippocrates complains that he killed ‡ several persons, by obliging them to use exercise in a fever.

CHAP. VI.

Of Hippocrates.——His general and particular precepts relating to the preservation of health.

WE come now to a period of time much more enlightened than the former, by the genius and industry of Hippocrates, justly called *the father of physic* *, who has

---

‡ Herodicus febricitantes tum multis obambulationibus, tum multâ luctâ et fomentis conficiebat, idque malè. Febris enim fami, luctæ, obambulationibus, cursibus, frictioni, iis utique omnibus est inimica. De morb. vulg. lib. 6. sect. 3. aphor. 23.

* Primus Hippocrates medicinæ præcepta clarissimè condidit. Plin. nat. hist. lib. 26. cap. 2.

It is necessary to acquaint those who may be disposed to compare the citations from Hippocrates with the original, that they must look into the edition of Fœsius, printed at Geneva, an. 1657. in two vols. fol.

done

done more towards the advancement of that science, than any other man ever did. He was born in Cos, an island in the Archipelago, about 450 years before the Christian æra, of a noble family, being lineally descended by his father from Æsculapius, and by his mother from Hercules, and (which is most to his honour) was a man of strict virtue and piety. Among other parts of physic he treats on the preservation of health, with greater extent and accuracy than one would imagine, considering the time * in which he lived, and the little help he had from his predecessors.

THAT we may have a full and clear apprehension of his directions on this subject, I shall endeavour, *first*, to range in order all his precepts and remarks on the *Six articles necessary to life*, vulgarly called the NON-NATURALS. *Secondly*, I shall take notice

* Hippocrates, according to dean Prideaux, lived about the time of the Peloponnesian war, i. e. as the reverend Mr. Shuckford thinks, A. M. 3570.

of some general rules which he has laid down with regard to health, and of his observations upon them.

The six articles indispensably necessary to the life of man are, air, aliment, exercise and rest, sleep and wakefulness, repletion and evacuation, together with the passions and affections of the mind.

Of AIR.

Those cities* which are situated towards the west, and are so covered from the east, that the salutary winds from that point, have no access to blow away their noxious vapours, must of necessity be unhealthy †, and

* De aër. loc. et aq. pag. 283. lin. 12. edit. Fœsii.

† This, and some other aphorisms concerning the winds, relate chiefly to the climate and situation of Greece, and the adjacent countries, where Hippocrates made his observations, and where the east and north winds blow over immense tracts of land, divided here and there by narrow seas; but are not so applicable to the countries where these winds blow directly from the ocean. With regard also to the heat and cold of the seasons, the more northern climates do not require so cooling a diet in summer as that where our author lived.

their

their inhabitants subject to many and bad distempers.

THE air has an extraordinary influence on the human body in reference to health and sickness, since we see that a man may live two or three days without aliment, but can scarce subsist a moment without air*, so necessary it is to the life of every animal. When therefore we find a distemper prevail † universally, and seize on persons of all ages and conditions, how different soever their diet or manner of living may be; it is evident that such a distemper cannot arise from what people eat or drink, because they differ widely in that respect, but from the air which surrounds them, and which they all breathe in common; and it would be needless, in such a case, to alter the method of life that has always agreed with them; nay, it would be hurtful, because sudden changes, in all

* De flatib. pag. 296. lin. 50.
† De nat. hom. pag. 228. lin. 50. et seq.

cases,

cafes are dangerous. The only courfe to be taken under fuch a calamity, is to alter the nature and qualities of the air, (if that be practicable) or to remove from it to an air which is untainted.

WE ought to attend to the qualities of the air, whether it be hot* or cold, grofs or fine, moift or dry, and how it varies with regard to thefe qualities; and we muft by experience learn the different effects of thofe variations upon our health: And he who would attain to any ufeful knowledge † in the art of healing, muft obferve the feafons of the year, for they differ extremely one from the other, and great are the changes which happen in them; and he fhould efpecially obferve thofe winds which are moft familiar to the country where he lives.

* De morb. vulg. lib. 6. fect. 8. aph. 18. pag. 1199.
† De aër. loc. et aq. in princip. pag. 280.

THE

The North * wind blowing long, renders the body compact, strong, nimble, and of a good colour, for it purges the air from grofs vapours, makes it pure and bright, and therefore is of all winds, generally fpeaking, the moft healthful: But ftill it is attended with fome inconveniencies, becaufe to perfons unaccuftomed to it, and to tender conftitutions, it gives coughs †, fore throats, pain of the breaft, coftivenefs, chillnefs, and ftrangury.

The fouth wind ‡, on the contrary, moiftens the brain too much, weakens and relaxes the body, and occafions defluxions.

A very dry § feafon is, upon the whole, more healthful than a very wet one.

---

* De morb. facr. pag. 308. lin. 5. et. feq. Vid. infuper, fect. 3. aphor. 17. pag. 1247.

† Sect. 3. aphor. 5. pag. 1247.

‡ De morb. facr. pag. 308. lin. 26. et fect 3. aphor. 17.

§ Sect. 3. aphor. 15.

It is known by experience, that we can eat more *, and digeſt better, in winter and ſpring, than in ſummer and autumn; and indeed the former, eſpecially the winter, require a more plentiful nouriſhment than the latter.

In winter †, to reſiſt the cold, let your aliment be dry and warming. In ſpring ‡, when the weather grows mild, the diet ſhould be accommodated to the ſeaſon, and ſomewhat cooler and lighter. In ſummer, when the ſeaſon becomes hot and dry, the food ſhould be cooling, and the drink diluting. But after the autumnal æquinox §, your aliment ſhould again be of a warming nature, and your cloaths ¶ thicker, by degrees, as you approach the winter.

THE

---

* Sect. 1. aphor. 15. et. 18. pag. 1243.
† De vict. rat. lib. 3. pag. 366. lin. 40.
‡ Ibid. pag. 367. lin. 37. et. ſeq.
§ Ibid. lib. 3. pag. 368. lin. 34. et. ſeq.
¶ It is very remarkable, that tho' Hippocrates admoniſhes people to accuſtom themſelves gradually to a cooler diet, as
the

THE fpring*, generally fpeaking, is the moft fafe and healthy, but the autumn the moft dangerous and fickly of all the feafons. And, particularly, the fpring and beginning of fummer agree beft with children, and very young perfons; fummer and the beginning of autumn, with old men; and the latter end of autumn, together with the winter, are healthieft for the middle aged.

THE fpring breeds blood †, the fummer bile, and the other feafons fuch humours as

the fpring grows warm, yet he never advifes them to lay afide any of their winter garments at that time; whereas, in autumn, he exprefly orders them to guard againft the approaching cold, ἐσθῆτι παχείη, *by thick cloathing*. And if he was fo cautious in the warm climate of Greece, furely we who live in this ifland, where the weather often varies from hot to cold three or four times in a day, fhould never lay afide any of our winter cloathing before the month of May, nor even then, unlefs the weather fhould be uniformly warm.

Our judicious Sydenham obferves, that the giddy practice of throwing afide our winter garments too early in the fpring, and of expofing our bodies, when overheated, to fudden colds, has deftroyed more than famine, peftilence and fword. De feb. intercurrent. fect. 4.

* Sect. 3. aphor. 9. pag. 1247.
† De humor. pag. 50. lin. 53.

correfpond

correspond with their respective natures. The spring * also is the best season of the year to lose blood, or take physic, if either of them should be proper, and can be conveniently deferred to that time. When the temperature † of the air corresponds with the nature of the respective seasons, the year is healthful, and distempers slight; but when the weather is unnatural with respect to the seasons, distempers are stubborn. Sudden transitions ‡, from great heat to extreme cold, are dangerous, and always produce bad distempers; and when these changes happen in the same day for any considerable time, we may expect stubborn autumnal diseases.

We find that not only the form and constitution of men's bodies, but their manners also, have a great affinity with the nature of

* Sect. 6. aphor. 47. pag. 1258.
† Sect. 3. aphor. 8. pag. 1247.
‡ Sect. 3. aphor. 1. et 4.

the climate which they inhabit. In Asia[*], where the seasons are mild, and vary but little with regard to heat or cold, the productions of the earth are larger, and more beautiful than in Europe, and the men more humane and benevolent, but at the same time more indolent and slothful; for it is the extreme changes of the seasons from heat to cold that rouse the passions of the Europeans, and excite them to illustrious atchievements. It is true, that the nature of the Asiatic government [†] contributes to make the men of that country still more inactive than otherwise they would be; for as they live under arbitrary and despotic princes, without liberty or property, it is not worth their while to undergo dangers in performing gallant actions, where the whole fruit of their labour is reaped by an insolent tyrant, and the brave adventurers have nothing but wounds and death for their portion. Under such an absolute and lawless government, it is the interest of a valiant man to be reputed a coward.

[*] De aër. loc. et aq. pag. 288. lin. 50. et seq.
[†] Ibid. pag. 290. lin. 35. et. seq.

Of ALIMENT.

He who would thoroughly underſtand this ſubject, muſt not only know * what qualities every ſort of food is endowed with from nature, but alſo what new qualities it receives from art, in the various ways of dreſſing it. Flour of wheat, for inſtance, mixt with the bran, is opening, and of ſmall nouriſhment; but when pure and unmixt, nouriſhes much, and is not at all opening. And it is of great moment † to a man's health, whether his common bread be white or brown, well or ill baked.

Every phyſician ‡ ſhould endeavour to underſtand the nature and conſtitution of different perſons, with reſpect to what they eat and drink, and ſhould not only make himſelf acquainted with the various complaints which ariſe from various ſorts of aliment, but ſhould alſo know why they happen to

---

* De vict. rat. lib 2. pag. 355. lin. 4, 25.
† De priſc. medic. pag. 13. lin. 17.
‡ Ibid. pag. 16. lin. 47. et ſeq.

ſome,

some, and not to others. Cheese *, for example, is hurtful to some, but agrees perfectly well with others; the cause of such a difference, therefore, should be found out, and the nature of those humours known to which cheese is an enemy, that so they may be corrected, or cheese avoided.

THE human body contains four humours ‡, very different with respect to heat, cold, moisture and dryness, viz. Blood, phlegm, yellow bile, and black bile, which several humours we see frequently brought up by vomiting, and discharged by stool. Health consists in a due mixture of these four, and whatever produces a redundancy in any of them, does hurt.

IT is very injurious to health to take in more food † than the constitution will bear, when, at the same time, one uses no exercise to carry off this excess. On the other hand §,

* De prisc. med. pag. 17. lin. 7.
‡ De natur. homin. pag. 225. lin. 41. et seq.
† De flatib. pag. 297. lin. 36.
§ De prisc. med. pag. 11. lin. 17. et seq.

it

it is equally pernicious to take in lefs nourifhment than the conftitution requires; for abftinence has great power over our nature, either to procure health, or to caufe weaknefs and death. Many and various are the evils which arife from fulnefs, but thofe which proceed from emptinefs are no lefs grievous; and it requires diligent obfervation to diftinguifh them, fince we have no rule by which we can exactly know them, but only what we feel within ourfelves. It is therefore a difficult task to point out the beginning of any trefpafs either on the fide of fulnefs or emptinefs; and he who falls into the feweft errors is much to be commended.

A variety * of aliments, difcordant in their nature, fhould not be indulged at one meal, becaufe they make a difturbance, and create flatulencies in the bowels.

Tho' larger † meals than nature requires, will certainly breed diftempers, if perfifted in;

* De flatib. p. 297. lin. 38. † Sect. 2. aph. 17. p. 1245.

yet,

yet, upon the whole, it is to be obferved, that a very fpare and abftemious diet is more dangerous ‡ than one fomewhat free and full; and a man fuffers more from a fmall trefpafs on habitual abftemioufnefs, than from a confiderable diminution of a full diet. A precife cuftom of living, therefore, is not fafe.

Whatever we eat which the ftomach * can fubdue, turns to good nourifhment; but what we cannot digeft has a contrary effect, and contributes to wafte the body. Some †, from the ftrength of cuftom and conftitution, can eat three plentiful meals every day. Thofe who have ufed themfelves to make two meals in a day, if they fhould happen to lofe one of them, grow weak and faint, have no inclination to work, and complain of pain at their heart. They feel alfo their bowels hollow, their eyes heavy, their

‡ Sect. 1. aph. 5. pag. 1243.
* De loc. in hom. pag. 422. lin. 19.
† De rat. vict. in acut. pag. 388. lin. 38. et feq.

mouth bitter, and their extremities cold. Nevertheless, when they have, by any accident, loſt one of their meals, (ſuppoſe their dinner) they ought not to eat a plentiful ſupper to make up their loſs; for, if they do, it will lie heavy on their ſtomach, and they will have a more reſtleſs night after it, than if they had both dined and ſupped heartily. He, therefore, who has been accuſtomed to two meals in a day, and has miſſed his dinner, and faſted beyond his uſual time, and finds himſelf empty and faint, ſhould avoid cold, heat, and labour for that day, and ſhould make a lighter ſupper * than uſual of ſome harmleſs ſpoon meat, rather than of any ſtrong ſolid food.

On the other hand †, if they who have been accuſtomed to one meal in a day, ſhould

---

* I have often experienced the benefit of this precept, when, in the hurry of country practice, I chanced, at any time, to loſe my dinner; for if I eat a hearty ſupper of fleſh meat, I was ſure to be ſick, but if I ſupped on a diſh of chocolate, or a meſs of water gruel, or toaſt and negus, I reſted perfectly well.

† De priſc. med. pag. 12. lin. 1.

chance

chance to eat two, they soon grow dull, heavy and thirsty; and this single trespass has been the source of great distempers to many.

He who has taken a larger * quantity of food than usual, and feels it heavy and troublesome in his stomach, his wisest course will be to vomit it up directly †.

That sort of aliment is justly reckoned the lightest ‡, which being taken in a moderate quantity, or to some little excess, causes neither fulness, nor griping, nor wind, but is quickly digested, and, after a proper time, easily discharged. That sort, on the contrary, is heaviest, which being taken in a moderate, or even in a small quantity, cannot be subdued by the stomach, but occasions a fulness and uneasiness.

* De affect. pag. 530. lin. 15.

† The wise son of Sirach confirms this precept, and says, Eccluf. xxxi. 21. " If thou hast been forced to eat, arise, " go forth, vomit and thou shalt have rest." And most certain it is, that hundreds have lost their lives, and thousands have suffered sickness and pain, from their ignorance or neglect of this rule.

‡ De affect. pag. 527. lin. 34.

Excess* in drinking is not quite fo bad as in eating.

Growing † perfons have much innate heat, and therefore require a pretty large fupply of nourifhment, otherwife their bodies will wafte away; whereas old people having but a fmall degree of heat, require only a fmall quantity of aliment; for too large a quantity would quite extinguifh the little heat they have remaining.

The forts ‡ of meat and drink moft agreeable to the human body, and moft conducive to good nourifhment, health, and ftrength, are bread, flefh, fifh, and wine; and yet, if thefe are taken to excefs, they bring on diftempers and death fooner than aliments of a weaker, and lefs nourifhing nature.

* Sect. 2. aph. 11. pag. 1244.
† Sect. 1. aph. 14. pag. 1243.
‡ De affect. pag. 528. lin. 17.

Prepare* for persons of a weak and delicate constitution such food as shall not excite any flatulency, acid eructations, or griping; and give them such as shall be neither too opening nor too binding.

When ‡ a person recovering from a distemper, eats his meat heartily, and yet receives no strength, it shews that he eats more than he can digest; but if he eats very moderately, and receives no strength, it appears that there are bad humours in the body which should be evacuated.

When † the body is impure or loaded with bad humours, the more you nourish it, the more you hurt it.

Of particular sorts of FOOD and DRINK in common use.

Coarse § or brown bread keeps the body open, but does not nourish much: White

---
* De affect. pag. 527. lin. 27.
‡ Sect. 2. aphor. 8. pag. 1244.
† Ibid. aphor. 10.
§ De vict. rat. lib. 2. pag. 356. lin. 2. & seq.

bread, pure, and separated from the bran, nourishes more, but opens less: Leavened or fermented bread is light in digestion, and passes easily through the body; but unfermented bread does not go off so easily, tho' it nourishes more, where the stomach can conquer it.

BREAD * baked to day, (provided it be not eat hot from the oven) is, generally, preferable to that baked yesterday, and old flour makes but bad bread.

THE flesh ‡ of wild animals is drier than that of tame, and of stall fed, than that fed by pasture. The flesh of animals, in the vigour of their age, and of such as are castrated, is best, and that of animals not used to any hard labour, is tenderest. The flesh † of granivorous birds is not so moist or oily as that of ducks, and others which frequent the waters.

* De vict. rat. lib. 2. pag. 356. lin. 35.
‡ De vict. rat. lib. 2. pag. 358. lin. 16. et seq
† Ibid. pag. 357. lin. 42.

MUTTON

MUTTON * is good both for the delicate and the robuft; but beef is heavy; and pork is proper only for the robuft ‡ who ufe exercife, but is too ftrong for the weak and fedentary.

FISH §, that lives in ftagnated waters, or that is very fat, is hard to digeft; but fuch as lives near the fea fhore is light. Boiled fifh alfo is lighter than roafted. Bitter † things bind and dry the body; acid things make people thin, and gripe the ftomach;

---

* De affect. pag. 528. lin. 51. et feq.

‡ Galen declares, that of all food, pork is the beft and moft nourifhing to people of robuft conftitutions who ufe a great deal of exercife; and this he confirms from the experience of the athletæ, or champions trained up for the olympic games: " Suppofe two champions (fays he) of the fame " ftrength, to ufe the fame exercife, and feed on pork; if " either of them fhall change his diet, and live on an equal " quantity of any other fort of meat for but one day, he will " immediately find himfelf weaker; and if feveral days, he " will not only grow feeble, but meagre alfo, for want of " his proper fuftenance." Claf. 2. de aliment. facult. lib. 3. cap. 2.

§ De affect. pag. 529. lin. 19.
† Ibid. lin 32.

falt

salt things promote stools and urine; fat and sweet things breed moisture and phlegm.

Milk * is hurtful to those who are feverish, or afflicted with a headach; to those whose bowels are subject to flatulency or grumbling; and to those who complain of thirst. It is bad also for such as void bile, or a considerable quantity of blood by stool; but good for the consumptive and emaciated, provided they have not a pretty sharp fever, or any of the above mentioned complaints, at the same time.

Onions ‡, leeks, radishes, are hot and acrimonious. Mustard and cresses will occasion a dysury. Celery is diuretic. Such herbs as are aromatick and odorous, are heating. The colwort species resolves the bile. Lettuce is cooling and relaxing. Cucumbers are cold, crude, and hard to digest. Ripe pears open the belly, but unripe bind it. Apples, of the acid kind, are more easily di-

* Sect. 5. aphor, 64. pag. 1255.
‡ De vict. rat. lib. 2. pag. 359, 360.

gested

gested than the sweet and luscious. All sorts of pulse* are windy, dress them which way you will.

Honey †, taken alone, promotes urine, purges too much, and rather weakens than strengthens; but mixt with other things, nourishes well, and gives a good colour.

Of WINE.

Pure ‡ unmixt wine, drank too freely, weakens a man, which is plain to be seen by his actions.

Sweet § wines hurt the head less, and promote stools more than strong or dry wines, but they excite a flatulency in the intestines, and swell the bowels; nor do they agree with bilious habits of body, because they increase thirst. They also promote expectoration more, and urine less, than

---

* De vict. rat. in acut. pag. 404. lin. 28.

† De affect. pag. 529. lin. 50.

‡ De prisc. med. pag. 17. lin. 4.

§ De rat. vict. in acut. pag. 392. lin. 23. et seq.

dry white wines. These are useful observations to which our ancestors were strangers. Tawny, or austere black wines, may be drank, with benefit, when the body is loose, provided there be no disorder in the head, and no impediment in spitting, or making water. It is likewise observable, that wine, diluted with water, is more friendly to the head, breast, and urinary passages; but wine alone, or mixt with very little water, agrees best with the stomach and bowels.

Hunger * is abated by a glass of wine.

Of WATER.

These waters † are best which spring from high places, and rising grounds; and it will recommend them still more, if their aspect be towards the rising sun; for such are generally limpid, light, and of a good flavour.

Rain water ‡, collected in clean vessels, is light, sweet, and limpid; for that part of

* Sect. 2. aphor. 21. pag. 1245.
† De aër. loc. et aq. pag. 284. lin. 20.
‡ Ibid. pag. 285. lin. 6.

the water attracted by the sun, which produces rain, is the finest and lightest of the whole. But this water is apt to grow putrid, by having a great many foreign particles mingled with it, to prevent which it will be proper to boil and strain it for use.

All waters are bad which are produced from ice* or snow † dissolved, for the lightest and most subtile parts of the water fly off in freezing, leaving the grossest and heaviest behind. I cannot therefore approve of such water for any use. As turbid water from ice and snow is bad in winter, so standing

---

* De aër. loc. et aq. pag. 285. lin. 44.

† Boerhaave, in his elem. chem. tom. 1. pag. 601. speaking of snow-water, seems at first sight to contradict Hippocrates, and to affirm that snow-water is pure and wholsome. But when we consider that Boerhaave speaks of such snow-water as can never come into common use; and supposes (for chymical experiments only) his snow to have fallen in a desart, far removed from any inhabitants; and the surface of that snow to have been carefully collected; and concludes, that such snow-water would be pure, light, and good; whereas Hippocrates speaks of common snow-water impregnated with all the dirt and salts of the earth which it has washed: When we consider this wide difference, I say, we shall find no contrariety in their sentiments.

water

water ‡ is ill coloured, ſtinking and unwholſome in ſummer, and occaſions various diſtempers.

The healthy † and ſtrong may drink ſuch water as comes in their way indiſcriminately; but they who drink water for recovery of health, muſt be careful in the choice they make. The lighteſt, pureſt, and ſofteſt waters are moſt fit for them who are apt to be coſtive, whereas the hardeſt waters do moſt ſervice to thoſe whoſe bowels are too moiſt and phlegmatic.

Hot * temperaments receive benefit from drinking water. Water drinkers ┼ have generally keen appetites.

Of Mineral WATERS.

Hippocrates juſt mentions hot § ſprings, chalybeate ſprings, nitrous ¶ ſprings, and o-

‡ De aër. loc. et aq. pag. 283. lin. 34.
† Ibid. pag. 284. lin. 38.
* De morb. vulg. lib. 6. ſect. 4. aph. 13. 18. pag. 1180.
┼ Ibid. aphor. 18.
§ De aër. loc. et aq. pag. 284. lin. 15. et ſeq.
¶ ἢ νίτρον.

ther

their mineral waters; but having had little experience of their virtues, he gives them no great character.

Of BATHING.

Every phyſician * ought to know what hurt may be done by unſeaſonable bathing.

A bath † of freſh water gives moiſture and coolneſs to the body, but that of ſalt water heats and dries it. A hot bath waſtes and chills a perſon who uſes it faſting, but warms and moiſtens after meals. A cold bath, on the contrary, warms a man who goes in faſting, but chills and dries after meals. Tepid bathing ‡ is beneficial in many diſtempers: It gives eaſe in pains of the ſide, breaſt, and back, helps the breath, promotes ſpitting, and urine, relieves a weight in the head, and removes laſſitude. But it requires nice management to fit up and uſe a bath properly.

* De priſc. medic. pag. 17. lin. 29.
† De vict. rat. lib. 2. pag. 361. lin. 46.
‡ De rat. vict. in morb. acut. pag. 395. lin. 6. et ſeq.

The passage to it should be short, and the steps in and out very easy. The patient should be composed and silent while in it, and should be washed and rubbed by the assistants. The misfortune is, few houses have the proper conveniencies for bathing, and where these are wanting, a bath does more harm than good. Bathing, in general, is improper for those who bleed at the nose, or are very weak or sick at the stomach; or too loose, or too costive, unless these last are previously purged.

Of Cold WATER for common drink.

I can ascribe no great virtues to cold water, says our Author *, but only that it is sometimes useful in acute distempers, for it neither † eases a cough, nor promotes expe-

---

* De rat. vict. in morb. acut. pag. 394. lin. 30. et seq.

† Hippocrates seems in this place to describe the effects of cold water upon distempered bodies only, for there is no doubt that cold water is the best and most wholesome common drink in nature to strong healthy children, to vigorous youth, and to others of a good constitution who have been habituated to it, and with whom it has been generally found to agree.

&ctoration

ctoration in inflammations of the lungs, but causes an irksome weight and fluctuation in the stomach. Neither does it quench thirst, but rather increase it. It is found also, in some constitutions, to increase the bile, to impair the strength, and to distend the bowels. As it is cold and crude, it passes off slowly, and promotes neither stool nor urine. And even in fevers, if you give it when the feet are cold, you do mischief. Nevertheless, in complaints of a great weight in the head, or when the understanding is disordered, we must either give water alone, or a small white wine, and some water after it; for by that mixture the wine will do less hurt to the head and understanding.

Of SLEEP and WAKEFULNESS.

EACH * of these carried beyond its proper bounds, is injurious to health. Excessive § watching prevents the aliment from being digested, and generates crude humours.

* Sect. 7. aph. 73. pag. 1261.
§ De rat. vict. in acut. pag. 392. lin 17.

But the contrary extreme of too much sleep relaxes the body, oppresses the head, and makes a man look as if he was parboiled.

Nature * directs us to accustom ourselves to wake † in the day and sleep in the night; and he who acts contrary to this order, will suffer for such folly.

The body, when one is asleep, should always be well covered ‡ with cloaths; but the bed chamber should be large and airy.

When a man's dreams at night correspond with the actions of the day, and represent only such things as are natural and proper to be done, they denote a good state of health, and shew that there is neither ple-

---

* Galen observes upon this maxim, that in the time of Hippocrates custom did not differ from nature; "but now (says he) the rich invert the order of nature, and turn night into day." De san. tuend. lib. 6. cap. 5.

† Prænot. pag. 39. lin. 40.

‡ De morb. vulg. lib 6. sect. 4. aph. 14. cum interpretatione Galeni.

nitude which requires evacuation, nor emptiness which requires a supply, nor any other beginning distemper. But those dreams which are contrary to the actions of the day, denote a bodily disorder †, which is great or small, as those dreams depart more or less from a man's natural actions or habits. I advise therefore, that in such cases, the disorder may be removed, and distempers prevented. If, for instance, we dream of evacuations, it shews that the body is too full, and wants proper discharges by vomiting, abstinence, or exercise. On * the other hand, a man, who dreams that he eats common food with an appetite, is too empty, and requires nourishment. Frightful dreams also discover a *stoppage of the blood* ‡, and ought to be removed by proper means. And he who minds these rules will always enjoy good health.

† De insomn. pag. 376. lin. 13.
* Ibid. pag. 380. lin. 5.
‡ ἐπίςασιν τῦ αἵματος σημαίνει.

Of REPLETION and EVACUATION.

To preserve * a good state of health, a man should void by stool every day, the dregs of what he has digested the day before.

THOSE § who eat and drink little, and yet go through a great deal of fatigue, are commonly costive, and do not go to stool, sometimes, in three or four days; from which they are in danger of falling into a fever, or a looseness. But those who feed plentifully, and also undergo much fatigue, have soft and figured stools in proportion to their food and exercise. And it is observable, that when several persons, who are all temperate and healthy, eat the same quantity, but differ in their exercise, those who labour the least have the greatest number of stools, and those who labour most have the fewest.

* De morb. pag. 511. lin. 23.
§ Prædict. lib. 2. pag. 87.

THE

The complaints which proceed from repletion* are cured by proper evacuations; and those which arise from too large evacuations, are removed by a gradual repletion.

It is best ‡ for young people to have their bodies moderately open, and for old people to be somewhat bound.

Those † who discharge much by urine, have but few stools.

When § it becomes necessary to cleanse the body, those who are thin and bear vomiting well, ought to take a puke; but those who are fleshy and hard to vomit should be purged downward. And it is in general to be observed, that a puke, where it agrees, is best in summer, and a purge in winter.

---

* De natur. homin. pag. 228. lin. 17.
‡ Sect. 2. aph. 53. pag. 1246.
† Sect. 4. aph. 82. pag. 1252.
§ Sect. 4. aph. 4, 6, 7.

Those who are in a good state § of health, are hurt by purging phyfick.

Moderate * commerce with the fex is of fervice to fuch as are loaded with phlegm. But commonly it binds the belly.

Of MOTION and REST.

The complaints † which arife from immoderate labour are cured by reft; and thofe which proceed from floth are removed by exercife.

If the whole body ‡ fhould reft a great deal longer than ufual, it will not become ftronger for that reft; and the fame obfervation holds good with refpect to every member of the body. And if, on the other hand, after a long habit of idlenefs, a man

§ Sect. 2. aphor. 36, 37.
* De morb. vulg. lib. 6. fect. 5. aph. 22, 26.
† De natur. hom. p. 228. lin. 18.
‡ De vict. rat. in morb. acut. pag. 391. lin. 29.

enters directly upon hard labour, he will be sure to do himself hurt. The feet, by a long state of rest are disqualified for much walking, and the other limbs, by long inaction, lose in a great measure their use. And a soft bed is as irksome to a person unaccustomed to such ease, as a hard bed is to him who lies at home on down.

He*, who from constant fatigue falls into an inactive state, must live abstemiously, otherwise his body will be soon tortured with pain, and oppressed with a load of humours.

Those † who seldom use any motion, are wearied by the smallest exercise; but such as are accustomed to labour, can bear a great deal without fatigue.

Friction ‡, or chafing, makes the body warm, firm, and fleshy.

* De vict. rat. in morb. acut. pag. 392. lin. 5.
† Ibid. pag. 364. lin. 33.
‡ Ibid. lin. 7.

Reading * aloud, and singing, warm and dry the body: And of all exercises walking seems the most natural to men in good health.

Universally speaking, moderate † exercise gives strength to the body, and vigour to the senses.

Exercise ‡ is wholesomest and best before meals.

Of the Passions and Affections of the MIND.

Violent § anger contracts the heart and lungs, and fills the head with hot humours; but tranquillity of mind unbends the heart.

Fear ¶ and grief, if they continue long, portend melancholy.

* De vict. rat. in morb. acut. pag. 363. lin. 5.
† Ibid. pag. 362. lin. 46.
‡ De morb. vulg. lib. 6. sect. 4. aph. 28. pag. 1181.
§ Ibid. sect. 5. aph. 8. pag. 1184.
¶ Ibid. sect. 6. aphor. 23. pag. 1257.

Terrour,

TERROUR[*], shame, joy, and anger have a great influence on the body, and determine it to actions correspondent to their respective natures; thus the sudden sight of a serpent will make the countenance pale; and to walk upon the edge of a pit will make the legs tremble.

CARE[†] and meditation are the exercise of the mind.

Having thus given a detail of all that I could find in the writings of Hippocrates, relating to the six articles necessary to human life, I shall, in the next place, proceed to his other general rules with regard to the preservation of health.

The first general RULE.

EVERY[‡] excess is an enemy to nature. And this he confirms by another Aphorism[§], which informs us, that in la-

---
[*] De humor. pag. 49. lin. 35.
[†] De morb. vulg. lib. 6. sect. 5. aphor. 10. pag. 1184.
[‡] Sect. 2. aphor 51. pag. 1246.
[§] De morb. vulg. lib. 6. sect. 6. aph. 5. pag. 1190.

bour, meat, drink, sleep, and commerce with the sex, a just mediocrity and moderation should be observed: And by a third, which declares, that evacuations *, pursued to excess, are dangerous, and plenitude carried to an extremity is equally pernicious.

The Second General RULE.

It is dangerous † to change suddenly a long habit which a person has contracted; or to run from one extreme into another. He says also in another § place, that people must have a particular regard to what they have been accustomed to in food, raiment, exercise, sleep, concubinage, and the passions of the mind. And he is so positive with respect to the truth of this rule, as to declare, that even a bad diet ‡, which has been long persisted in, whether by eating or drinking, is less injurious to health, than a sudden transition to a better diet. This he also il-

---
* Sect. 1. aph. 4. pag. 1243.
† De rat. vict. in morb. acut. pag. 389. lin. 20.
§ De morb. vulg. lib. 6. sect. 8. aph. 43. pag. 1201.
‡ De vict. rat. in. morb. acut. pag. 388. lin. 20.

lustrates

lustrates farther, by shewing that he who has been habituated to drink wine*, and comes of a sudden to water, will feel the inconveniencies of the change, from the weight and flatulency produced by the water; while, on the other hand, a quick transition from water, or from wine and water, to wine alone, occasions thirst, palpitations, and disorders of the head.

The Third General RULE.

The great preservatives † of health, are *Temperance* and *Exercise*. Or, as he expresses himself more distinctly in another place, if an exact proportion ‡ could be adjusted between the quantity of aliment taken in to nourish every individual, and the measure of exercise sufficient to carry off that quantity, so that the one should not exceed, or fall short of the other; such adjustment would fix the true standard of health, and

---

* De rat. vict. in morb. acut. pag. 389. lin. 46.
† De morb. vulg. lib. 6. sect. 4. aph. 20. pag. 1180.
‡ De vict. rat. lib. 1. pag. 341. lin. 23.

distempers

distempers might with certainty be avoided. For as *aliment* fills §, and *exercise* empties the body, the result of an exact equipoise between them must be, to leave the body in the same state they found it, that is, in perfect health. And tho' he allows that such a balance between diet and exercise cannot be precisely settled *, because ages, constitutions, and seasons differ widely, and require a different treatment, yet he thinks it possible to observe the smallest excess on either side, as soon as it happens, and so prevent it from going farther and increasing into a distemper; for most distempers, says he, do not seize people suddenly, but grow † by degrees. And he values ‡ himself not a little on being the first who found out this *preventive care*, and wonders that none of the antients thought of it, since nothing could be more worthy of their attention.

§ De rat. vict. lib. 1. pag. 341. line. 7.
* Ibid. lib. 3. pag. 366. lin. 5. et seq.
† Ibid. lib. 1. pag. 341. lin. 37.
‡ Ibid. lib. 3. pag. 369. lin. 1.

I have discovered * those symptoms, says he, by which every excess, either of food above exercise, or of exercise above food, may be known in its beginning, and prevented from breaking out into a distemper; which will prove nearly of the same benefit to mankind, as if a just æquilibrium between diet and exercise could be found out.

It is difficult to reduce the many symptoms enumerated by Hippocrates, in his third book of diet, belonging to this excess either of aliment or exercise, to distinct classes; I shall endeavour, however, to do it with all the plainness and concifeness I can, consistently with the spirit and meaning of the author; and, to that effect, shall range them in the following order. First then, he treats of those symptoms which arise from the excess of food above exercise. And secondly, of those which arise from the excess

* De rat. vict. lib. 3. pag. 366. lin. 18.

of exercise above food. The former may be reduced to six assemblages or classes.

First, Some feel a stuffing § and fulness in their nostrils, after supper, without any apparent cause, but cannot discharge any mucus, until they have used some exercise next morning; their eye-lids, in a little while, grow heavy, and, by degrees, they lose their appetite and colour; which is at last followed by a defluxion or fever, when any accident has put their load of humours in motion. These are marks of a gradual repletion, tho' people are ready to blame some particular inadvertency they were guilty of; which, however, could, by no means, produce such complaints: But we must not wait until this repletion is accumulated; on the contrary, as soon as we have observed the first mentioned symptoms, we must diminish the quantity of our food, and increase our exercise, until all those marks of repletion are removed.

§ De rat. vict. lib. 3. pag. 369. lin. 10. et seq.

Secondly,

Secondly, Others*, when their diet bears too great a proportion to their exercise, not only sleep well in the night, but are likewise drowsy in the day; the repletion still increases, and their nights begin to grow restless; their sleep afterwards becomes disturbed with frightful dreams of battles. When this happens, there is danger lest the accumulated humours should fall upon some part and overwhelm it. But that danger must be prevented by substracting from the aliment, and adding to the exercise.

A *third* sort† of complaints, arising from repletion, is a pain, or lassitude, sometimes in one part and sometimes in another, and sometimes all over the body. People think to relieve themselves from this lassitude by laziness and indulgence, until they increase their complaints into a fever, which should have been prevented by a contrary course of abstinence and exercise.

* De rat. vict. lib. 3. pag. 369. lin. 45.
† Ibid. pag. 370. lin. 9.

A *fourth* assemblage * of symptoms is indigestion and flatulence, which daily increasing, occasion a disturbance in the intestines; and the food is thrown out, at first, liquid and corrupted, without pain; but afterwards, the bowels being eroded by the acrimony of the humours, a discharge of blood or a dysentery succeeds, which is a dangerous distemper, and ought to have been prevented by taking less food, and using more exercise, when the flatulency and bad digestion began to grow troublesome.

Fifthly, Some † from repletion are apt to grow pale, and to be troubled with acid eructations, but they may prevent danger by taking a vomit, and by using a smaller quantity of food, and more exercise for some days.

Lastly, Some ‡ persons, from repletion, especially such as are gross, sweat profusely

* De vict. rat. lib. 3. pag. 371. lin. 3. et seq.
† Ibid. lin. 45.
‡ De rat. vict. lib. 3. pag. 372. lin. 17. et seq.

in their sleep, which gives them no great uneasiness in the beginning; tho', in process of time, it becomes the cause of pain and distempers. And it is observable, that they are most apt to fall into this disorder, who, from a long habit of idleness, come, of a sudden, to use exercise. But those bad consequences may be prevented by a substraction of food, and a gradual increase of exercise.

Having thus given a distinct view of the various kinds of complaints produced by an excess of food above exercise, he comes next to shew the inconveniencies which proceed from the contrary excess of exercise above food, and these may be reduced to three sorts.

First, Some from too much exercise*, in proportion to their diet, complain, after a little time, of a heat in their bellies, and then of pain; they loath their food also, and their bowels become ulcerated, which brings on a looseness very difficult to stop. But a

* De rat. vict. lib. 3. pag. 373. lin. 40. et seq.

prudent

prudent forefight will obviate thefe growing evils, by fubftracting one half of the exercife, and by ufing a cool dry diet for some days, one third lefs than in a ftate of health; and then proceed gradually to take more fuftenance, and ufe lefs exercife than before.

Secondly, Others*, from excefs in exercife, are afflicted with an extreme coftivenefs, a drynefs and bitternefs of the mouth, and, after a while, with a fuppreffion of urine and ftool. Whatever they eat or drink is then thrown up, and at laft the fæces are vomited, which commonly terminates in death. But whenever one perceives a heat and drynefs predominant, it will be eafy, by removing them, to prevent further mifchief, and that is done by warm bathing, quiet fleep, a cooling, moiftening, and nourifhing diet, gradually increafed; and by withdrawing one half of the former exercife.

A *third* fort †, from a diminifhed proportion of food with refpect to their labour, fall

---

* De vict. rat. lib. 3. pag. 374. lin. 17. et feq.
† Ibid. pag. 375. lin. 10.

into

into shiverings after walking or any other exercise, so that sometimes their teeth chatter with cold; they afterwards grow drowsy, and when they awake, yawn and stretch; and are at last seized with a malignant fever. To prevent which, they must lessen their exercise one half, and use at first some cool, soft, food, and drink diluted wine, and rise by degrees to such a proportion of diet as will better support them under their labour.

And here the good old man adds, that those whose labour [*] exceeds their sustenance, and who have impaired their strength by fatigue, may take a chearful glass once or twice, *but not to excess.*

Some have pretended that Hippocrates, in this place, advises people to get drunk on certain occasions. Others have gone farther, and recommended the getting drunk once or twice every month as conducive to health;

[*] De vict. rat. lib. 3. pag. 375. lin. 26. et seq.

and have quoted Hippocrates to juftify their intemperance. But fuch opinions have no fort of foundation in this paffage. The word ufed by Hippocrates is μεθυσθῆναι, *to drink a chearful glafs*, which, in this place, is precifely equivalent to the expreffion πίνοντα θερμαίνεσθαι, *to be warmed with wine*, frequently met with among the Greek writers. Plutarch, in his fympofiacs, or *table converfations*, compares μέθυειν to ἐρᾶν, or *wine* to *love*, as each equally renders men warm, chearful, and unreferved. And hence, fays he, it is commonly reported that Æfchylus compofed his tragedies when he was warmed with wine. I have cited his words * at the bottom of the page. He makes in the fame place this obfervation of his grandfather Lamprias, that he difputed beft, and unravelled the difficulties of philofophy with moft fuccefs, when he was at fupper, and well warmed with wine. *The cups*

---

* Ἐλέχθη δὲ καὶ ὅτι τῷ μέθυειν τὸ ἐρᾶν ὅμοιόν ἐστι. Ποιεῖ γὰρ θερμοὺς καὶ ἱλαροὺς καὶ διακεχυμένους.—Καὶ τὸν Αἰσχύλον φασὶ τὰς τραγῳδίας πίνοντα ποιεῖν καὶ διαθερμαινόμενον. Plutarch Sympof. lib. 1. quæft. 5.

went round with the debates, says Dryden in his life of Plutarch, *and men were merry and wife together.* The fame word μέθυω, is used also in the gofpel of St. John ii. 10. and from the circumftances there defcribed is judicioufly tranflated, *when men have well drunk,* or *have drank to be chearful.* The meaning of Hippocrates is precifely the fame in this precept, which is evident from the reftriction annexed, πλὴν ἀλλὰ μὴ ἐς ὑπερβολήν. *Sed non fupra modum.*

LET not therefore the patrons of drunkennefs fcreen themfelves under the authority of Hippocrates, who was a man of the greateft temperance and probity, and whofe precept is fupported by the obfervation of Homer that lived three hundred years before him, and fays,

Ἀνδρὶ δὲ κεκμηῶτι μένος μέγα οἶνος ἀέξει *.

The weary find new ftrength in generous wine.

POPE.

* Iliad, lib. 6. lin. 262. edit. Glafguenf.

CHAP.

CHAP. VII.

Of Polybus, Diocles Caryſtius, Cornelius Celſus, and Plutarch, concerning health.

Of POLYBUS.

WE have, among the works [*] aſcribed commonly to Hippocrates, a ſhort tract, *concerning wholſome diet,* which Galen, in his commentary upon it, ſuppoſes to have been written by Polybus the diſciple and ſon-in-law of Hippocrates.

THIS Polybus, after the death of his maſter, taught [†] his ſchool with great reputation. He lived about 410 years before Chriſt.

IN this tract the author adviſes thoſe, who are in circumſtances to live as they pleaſe, to eat heartily, in winter, of bread and roaſted

---

[*] De ſalub. vict. rat. pag. 337. lin. 1. et ſeq.
[†] See Le Clerc's hiſt. de la med. part 1. liv. 4. chap. 1.

fleſh,

flesh, but to drink sparingly; and let their wine be unmixt and good, in order to keep themselves warm, and free from a load of bad humours in that cold and damp season.

In summer, for contrary reasons, he recommends a cool diet, consisting chiefly of vegetables and boiled meat, and orders people to drink plentifully of small diluting liquors.

In spring and autumn he directs a middle regimen between those two extremes, approaching in the spring, as the weather grows milder, to the cool diet of summer, and receding from it gradually in autumn, not only toward the warm aliment, but also toward the warm cloathing * of winter.

A regard must also be had to different ages and temperaments; the young, the dry,

---

* De salubr. vict. rat. pag. 338. lin. 13. See on this place the notes of Galen, who thinks, that by *vestes puras*, the author may mean warm cloathing, tho' he does not approve of the phrase.

thin, and black, requiring a cool moist diet; and old people a warm moist diet throughout the whole year; whereas persons of a gross relaxed habit of body, the flabby, and red-haired, ought always to use a drying diet.

Such as are fat *, and desire to be lean, should use exercise fasting; should drink small liquors a little warm; should eat only once in the day, and no more than will just satisfy their hunger; and should ly on hard beds: Whereas those that are lean, and want to be plump, should pursue a contrary course.

Of DIOCLES CARYSTIUS.

The next who has touched upon this subject of the preservation of health, was Diocles of Carystos in Euboea, an island of the Archipelago near the coast of Greece. He was a physician of great merit, and had the honour of being called the second Hippocrates. We have still his letter † to Antigonus,

---

* De salub. vict. rat. pag. 338. lin. 14. et seq.

† This letter is commonly printed with Paul Ægin. lib. 1, cap. 100.

one

one of the succeffors of Alexander the great, which shews the time in which he lived.

In this letter he tells the king, (whom he compliments with the titles of mufician, mathematician, and philofopher) that as no tempeft arifes in the heavens without previous figns, which failors, and other skilful perfons know, fo no diftemper attacks the human body without firft giving notice of its approach. He divides the body into four principal parts, the *head*, the *breaft*, the *belly*, and the *bladder*.

The previous fymptoms of bad diftempers, likely to fall upon the *head*, are giddinefs, pain, and a weight over the eye-brows, finging in the ears, pulfation of the temples, dimnefs and fwelling of the eyes in a morning, lofs of fmell, or turgid gums. When any fuch fymptom therefore is felt, it fhould be removed by keeping the head warm, and purging it with muftard boiled in honey and water, or a gargle of a decoction of hyffop

and

and raisins. But if those previous signs are neglected, inflammations of the brain, quincies, or some other dangerous distemper may ensue.

DISTEMPERS of the *breast* are foreboded by sweating, chiefly over the thorax; a foul tongue; a salt or bitter taste in the mouth; pain under the ribs or shoulder blades; anxiety after sleep; coldness of the breast and arms; and a tremor of the hands. But these previous symptoms must be removed by gentle vomits, to prevent pleurisies and peripneumonies, which otherwise may follow.

DISTEMPERS of the *belly* are threatned to those who complain of gripings; bitter eructations; stiffness of the loins; flying pains all over the body without any apparent cause; numbness of the legs; or slight fevers. When one or more of these symptoms become troublesome, your diet should be such as you know by experience to be o-
pening,

pening, otherwife a dyfentery, hæmorrhoids, or gout may foon fucceed.

Lastly, The forerunners of bad diftempers about the *bladder* are a fenfe of fulnefs when you have eat but little; flatulency; dark coloured urine voided with difficulty; or a fwelling about the lower parts of the belly. When any of thefe fymptoms appear, you ought to make ufe of mild diuretics, fuch as the roots of fennel and celery infufed in white wine, of which you fhould drink a glafs or two every morning, upon an empty ftomach, mingled with fome fmall diuretic water. But if you neglect this precaution, a dropfy, ftone, or ftrangury may be the confequence.

Of CORNELIUS CELSUS.

Tho' many celebrated phyficians flourifhed in the fpace of three hundred years which interveened between Diocles, who lived under Alexander the great, and Celfus, who lived under Tiberius, yet it has unfortunately

tunately happened, that only a few shreds of their works have come down to us; and in these there is nothing of moment relating to our subject.

Celsus is much more methodical in his arrangement of those rules which he lays down for the preservation of health than Hippocrates; tho' he prudently borrows many of them from that great man. He observes the following perspicuous order.

First, He instructs strong hearty people how to preserve that good state of health which they enjoy.

Secondly, He admonishes the infirm and valetudinary to rectify the natural or acquired defects of their constitution.

And *thirdly*, He gives particular directions, accommodated to particular incidents, ages, seasons of the year, and infirmities. But in this abstract I shall not trouble the

reader

reader with such of his precepts as are now exploded, and of small importance; or have been mentioned already; or are calculated rather to cure some transient maladies, than to preserve health.

RULES for the Healthy and Robust.

A man who is sound and strong should ty himself down to no particular rule of diet, nor imagine that he stands in need of a physician; he ought frequently to diversify his manner of living; to be sometimes in town, sometimes in the country; he should refuse no manner of food that is commonly used; should, at different times, hunt, sail, sit still, but oftener use exercise; should sometimes indulge himself at feasts, and sometimes avoid them; sometimes eat and drink * more than

* Great disputes have arisen concerning this rule of Celsus, his words are, " modo plus justo, modo non amplius assu- " mere." Some approve of the full latitude he gives, others highly blame it. Verulam thinks that excess in eating and drinking should now and then be indulged: " Epulæ profusæ " et perpotationes non omnino inhibendæ sunt." Hist. vit. et. mort. pag. 341. Melchior Sebizius, on the other hand, affirms

than is proper, and sometimes not exceed; should rather make two meals than one in a day, and always eat a great deal *, provided he is able to digest it.

firms, that by this advice Celsus gives full scope to intemperance, and sets himself up for a patron of gluttons and drunkards: " Quibus verbis comedonum, bibonum, helluonum, patronum " agere videtur ; et latam quod aiunt, fenestram, asotiæ et " confusioni aperire : nam si quod dicit verum est, videntur " sanè regulæ Hygieines inverti, quæ opportunum tempus, de- " centem quantitatem, et debitam qualitatem requirunt. Natura " enim ordinem requirit, suntque motus illius definiti, et ordina- " ti." De aliment. facult. lib. 5. probl. 72.

And Sanctorius says, that it is not safe for all healthy persons to observe this rule : " Celsi sententia non est omnibus tuta." Sect. 3. aph. 42.

The truth is, a healthy man should not bind himself down to an over strict and arid abstemious diet, as Hippocrates has observed ; nor to a regular uniformity in his way of living, because, in case any necessity should oblige him (which frequently happens) to alter the habit he has contracted, a quick transition to a new method might prove dangerous. It is the wisest course therefore, for persons in health, to vary their way of living often, that so, no new change may happen which can hurt them. This diversity, nevertheless, ought to be kept within the bounds of temperance ; and Celsus gives too great a latitude, which seems to encourage excess, directly contrary to the first general rule of Hippocrates.

* This rule is liable to be mistaken, for a man should never overload his stomach, but ought to rise from meals with some appetite.

COMMERCE

Commerce with the fair sex is neither too wantonly to be indulged, nor too timorously to be shunned. When moderate, it renders the body lively, but too frequently used, wastes and enervates. This frequency, nevertheless, is to be estimated by a man's age and strength, for that commerce is harmless which is not succeeded by pain or low spirits.

He concludes his directions to the sound and robust, with this admirable precept, *viz.* " Be * careful in time of health not to destroy, by excesses of any kind, that vigour of constitution which should support you under sickness."

RULES for the Delicate and Infirm.

People of tender constitutions (among whom may be reckoned the greatest part of our citizens, and almost all men of letters)

* Cavendum ne in secunda valetudine adversæ præsidia consumantur. lib. 1. cap. 1.

must be regular in their way of living, and correct, by care, those disorders which arise from a weak frame of body, from a bad air, or much study.

A tender person should dwell in a well lighted, chearful house, which is airy in summer, and enjoys the sun in winter; and should avoid mid-day heats, morning and evening colds, and damps of all kinds. Let the bookish and contemplative man take care not to study too soon after meals. And let even the man of business and the statesman spare a few hours for the purpose of health, and be sure to use some convenient exercise every day before meals, such as reading aloud, walking or playing at* ball
of

---

* The Greeks played with four sorts of balls, the *little ball;* the *great ball;* the σφαῖρα κένη, or *empty ball;* i. e. blown up with air like our foot ball; and the κώρυκον, which was a *huge leathern ball,* hung from the ceiling, and stuffed with bran or sand, as those who tossed it were robust or delicate.

The Romans had also four sorts, first the *follis,* which was a pretty large sort of hand ball, made of skin blown up with
air,

of some sort, which exercise he should persist in, until he finds himself either in a gentle sweat, or a little tired, but no longer.

air, in which, according to Suetonius, Augustus Cæsar took great delight; and was, as we learn from Martial, a proper exercise for young and old.

Folle decet pueros ludere, folle senes.
Lib. 14. epigr. 43.

2. The *trigonalis*, of which Celsus says that it exercises the upper parts of the body, and which the learned Mercurialis conjectures to have been nearly the same with *tennis:* " eo " prope modo quo nostrates supra funiculum ludunt."

3. The *paganica*, or common village ball, made of leather stuffed with feathers, larger than the *trigonalis*, and harder than the *follis*.

4. The *harpastum*, which was a small ball tossed, rebounded, and catched from the ground, not unlike, it should seem, to the play at *fives* in England. Mer. de re gymn. lib. 2. cap. 5.

All I shall remark upon the whole, is, that the high encomium justly bestowed by Galen upon the play at *little ball*, as the best of all exercises to preserve health, is equally applicable to *tennis*, and to the play called *golf* in Scotland, and that it is pity such manly and healthful exercises should be so much disused.

Golf is a safe and moderate exercise, performed on a bare smooth common, by driving two small hard balls with proper *bats*, always forward to very distant holes in the ground, about a foot deep, and nine inches over; and the party whose ball is driven into the hole with the fewest blows, (which are carefully numbered on both sides) obtains the victory.

LARGE

LARGE * meals are ever hurtful to a tender constitution. Confections and delicacies are bad on two accounts, first, because they tempt people to eat more than enough; and secondly, because they are hard of digestion.

Of UNEXPECTED INCIDENTS.

IF a man must necessarily remove his habitation into a worse air, he had best do it in the beginning of winter.

IT is imprudent to contract a habit of idleness at any time, because a man may chance to be under a necessity to work.

To a person sweating with labour, there is nothing more pernicious than to drink cold water; nor is it proper for such as are wearied with a journey, tho' their sweat be gone off.

FATIGUE is often eased by change of labour, and he who is tired with any unusual

---

* Ubi ad cibum ventum est, nunquam utilis est nimia satietas.

sort of work, is refreshed by that to which he has been accustomed.

Those who are much fatigued should, if possible, sleep in their own* beds, for a strange bed does not refresh them near so much.

Of Constitutions and Ages.

It is expedient, before all things, to understand a man's particular nature and habit of body. Some are too meagre, others too fat; some hot, others cold; some moist, others dry; some too costive, others too lax. Now, all those extremes should be rectified as much as possible, and every constitutional complaint, which endangers health, gently and gradually removed.

The meagre † should be plumped up by very gentle exercise, and long intervals of rest,

---

* This is generally true, but not universally.

† " I reduced a huge fat fellow to a moderate size in a " short time, (says Galen) by making him run every morning, " until

rest, a soft bed, long sleep, tranquility of mind, fat * meat, frequent meals and as plentiful as he can well digest, and by keeping the belly gently bound.

Fat persons should be made thinner by warm bathing †, strong exercise, hard beds, little sleep, proper evacuations, acids, and one meal in a day.

"until he fell into a profuse sweat; I then had him rubbed hard, and put into a warm bath; after which I ordered him a small breakfast, and sent him to the warm bath a second time. Some hours after, I permitted him to eat freely of food, which afforded but little nourishment; and lastly, set him to some work which he was accustomed to, for the remaining part of the day."

"On the other hand, a man that is too lean, may be made plump, 1. By such food as will produce sweet juices and good nourishment. 2. By gentle exercise, which gives a firmness to that nourishment. And 3. By avoiding heat, fatigue, and every violence that can dissipate the nourishment he has received." Galen de sanit. tuend. lib. 6. cap. 8.

* Fat meat, if a man can digest it well, will help to plump him up, otherwise it will do him no service.

† For a short and clear account of the magnificence, variety, use, and abuse of baths among the antients, see Mercurial. de re gymnast. lib. 1. cap. 10. and Petri Dunetii dictionar. antiq. Rom. et Græc. sub voce Balneæ. And among the moderns, especially on cold bathing, see doctors Baynard, Floyer, Wainwright, and Lucas.

Hot

Hot constitutions are cooled by drinking water, and acid liquors. And the cold are warmed by the use of the flesh brush, by salt meat, and good wine.

The dry are rendered moist by less exercise, and a fuller diet, especially by drinking more than usual; by cold bathing, and by resting sometime after their morning exercise before they eat.

The lax are made firmer by increasing the usual exercise; by making but one meal in a day instead of the two they made before; by drinking little, and deferring that until they have done eating; and by sitting still for some time after meals.

The costive, on the contrary, are relaxed by increasing the quantity of food, by drinking large draughts at meals, and by using exercise soon after eating.

Old

Old people have greater reason to be cautious not to trespass upon the rules of health, than young persons, who have more strength.

Of the SEASONS of the Year.

In summer it is best to make smaller meals than in winter, but more frequent.---- The cold bath is also proper at that season.

In autumn, when the days begin to grow cold, we should be careful not to go abroad in too light cloaths, or too thin shoes.

Of the habitual INFIRMITIES of different Parts of the Body.

Those whose heads are infirm, should pour cold water upon them every morning; should eat moderately of food easy to digest; should make wine and water their common drink; that, in case the head, at any time, grows worse than usual, they may have recourse to, and relief from water alone.

Nor will a weak head bear writing, reading, vehement speaking, or intense thinking at any time, but especially soon after meals.

Cold water is also good to wash blear eyes, and to gargle sore throats.

Those who are subject to an habitual looseness should play at tennis, and accustom themselves to such sorts of exercise as shake the trunk of the body. They should also avoid a variety of dishes at one meal, and should deal very little in broths, greens, or small sweet wines; and should sit quiet for a considerable time after meals.

People subject to colics, should forbear to eat or drink any thing cold; and whatever they know by experience to be flatulent.

The symptoms of a weak stomach are paleness, meagerness, loathing, frequent vomiting, and a head-ach, sometimes when the ftomach is empty: And fuch perfons fhould always eat things of eafy digeftion, and drink the rougher forts of wine, if they can bear them, cold; and ufe alfo fuch exercife as fhakes the trunk of the body.

Those who are afflicted with the gout in their feet or hands, ought, between the fits, to give all the exercife they can bear, to the parts affected, in order to render them firm and hardy; but in the fits reft is neceffary. Concubinage is a great enemy to gouty complaints.

Under every conftitutional infirmity it is proper to promote a good digeftion; but to gouty people it is indifpenfably neceffary.

PLUTARCH.

Plutarch flourifhed in the time of Trajan, and, tho' himfelf no phyfician, has compofed an elegant dialogue on the prefervation of health; and has given us feveral ufeful obfervations upon that fubject

He

He thinks it unbecoming a philosopher, who is at great pains to make himself master of music and geometry, to be at the same time, totally ignorant of what belongs to his own body.

At some of the high festivals in Athens, says he, besides the entertainment exhibited to the public, there was also money distributed among the spectators, which made the pleasure double. In like manner, physick*, which is quite as elegant, copious, and delightful as any of the liberal arts, has this advantage above them all, that it bestows good health on those who understand it, and will be directed by its precepts.

It is an observation of some importance to health, (tho' now and then disregarded

---

* Plutarch happpily reaped the benefit of his regard and application to this science; for we are told by Dryden, in his life of this Philosopher, that " it was his prudence so to ma-
" nage his health by moderation of diet and bodily exercise,
" as to preserve his parts, without decay, to a great old age;
" to be lively and vigorous to the last; and to preserve him-
" self to his own enjoyments, and to the profit of mankind."

by

by phyſicians) that a coldneſs, in the extreme parts of the body, which drives the natural heat inwards, ſhews a tendency to a feveriſh diſpoſition; and that we ought therefore to guard our limbs* well from cold at ſuch times, as we uſe no motion to throw the heat outwards.

Another obſervation is, that perſons in health ought ſometimes to taſte that ſimple and inſipid food, which alone is proper in time of ſickneſs; that ſo they may not be diſguſted at the ſight of it, nor, like froward children, ſet themſelves againſt it, when it becomes neceſſary: And for the ſame reaſon we ought to drink water ſometimes, tho' we have wine at hand; becauſe in ſome illneſſes

* If this obſervation of Plutarch was found uſeful in Greece and Italy, how much more in our colder climate. And I will venture to affirm, that perſons, whoſe legs and feet are for the moſt part cold, cannot enjoy a good ſtate of health. And I will ſay farther, that woollen under ſtockings, worn by people of tender conſtitutions, to keep up by their warmth, an equable circulation in the extreme parts, would prevent many a fit of pain, ſickneſs, and low ſpirits, which they muſt feel without ſuch a precaution.

it

it will be proper to drink water only. In short, we should discipline our minds so as to make them value that alone which is proper and conducive to health; and not think ourselves undone when a simple or coarse meal is set before us. It was wisely said by one of the antients; " chuse that manner of " living which is most reasonable, and cu- " stom will reconcile you to it."

A third observation is, that thin people are generally the most healthy; we should not therefore indulge our appetites with delicacies or high living, (tho' we had it in our power) for fear of growing corpulent[*]. We may be sometimes invited to the entertaiments of great men, where custom obliges us to do as others do; and where it is hardly possible to avoid excess: Let us therefore be prepared for such incidents, by having our bodies pure and healthy, lest we should add load to

---

[*] Corpulency is not always the consequence of high living, for in some constitutions it excites feverish disorders, and various other complaints.

load,

load, or fewel to the fire; but even at such entertainments, if we should be pressed to drink unreasonably, we must refuse to comply, tho' our refusal should give offence; and say with Creon:

> Better to forfeit your esteem to day,
> Than grieve you with my groans, or death to-morrow.

It was the advice of Socrates, " that we " should beware of such food as may tempt " us to eat when we are not hungry, and of " such liquors as may entice us to drink " when we are not thirsty." Such, it is true, may be used when they become necessary to our nourishment, or health; but we must take great care never to let those delicacies prevail with us to overcharge our stomach. The folly of those is very great, who out of mere vanity load themselves with dainties at great men's tables, that they may boast, among their friends, of those high priced rarities with which they were feasted; whereas it would be much more to their honour, if they could say that they had such a command of themselves as to abstain from them.

Among all the destructive follies of voluptuousness, there is none more ridiculously extravagant than that of those who pay high prices to celebrated whores, a Phryne or a Lais, while they neglect their wives at home, who have many more valuable charms than these mercenary wretches. How discreetly does the poet Menander introduce a pimp, leading in a train of beautiful prostitutes, to ensnare a company of well disciplined young men; " at whose approach the youths hung " down their heads, eating the repast which " was set before them, nor would any of " them once look up at these bewitching " destroyers."

Those who have a true taste for pleasure, should, for the sake of that pleasure, live temperately; because, without temperance, there can be no health, and without health we can relish no enjoyment. What avail the greatest delicacies to a sick stomach? Is not a good appetite the most exquisite sauce?

It

It is reported of Alexander the great, when, upon a march, he turned away his cooks, that he should say, " he carried much bet- " ter cooks along with him than those he " turned off, *viz.* a long morning's journey " to whet his appetite to his dinner, and a " frugal dinner to make his supper relish " well."

I am sensible, continues our author, that great fatigue, heat and cold, sometimes raise fevers; but we may also observe that those external causes rarely bring distempers upon such as are temperate, and free from any redundancy of humours. It is this redundancy that throws the body into stubborn diseases, just as stinking mud, agitated by external causes, taints the air, and every thing that comes near it. Hippocrates says, " that a " spontaneous weight and lassitude of the " limbs forebode a distemper approaching." And whence proceeds this weight, but from a plenitude which compresses the nerves? Unreasonable, therefore, is the practice of
them

them who think to remove this fort of weariness, by eating and drinking plentifully, whereas abstinence and exercise are the true cure of it.

Tho' I cry down voluptuousness, as a destroyer of true pleasure, yet I do not recommend an over scrupulous and rigid abstinence, which exposes the body to many dangers, sinks the spirits, and disqualifies us for labour or pleasure, by making us timorous, and perpetually suspicious of some bad design against us, and never permits us to perform any action with true courage or magnanimity. We must keep a medium between these two extremes, and like skilful mariners, neither shorten our sails too much in fair weather, nor spread them too wide in a storm.

And as we must observe a moderation in diet, exercise and pleasure, so likewise our sleep must neither be too long nor too short; and even our dreams should be natural and easy; for when we find them absurd and frightful, we have reason to suspect a fulness, or some bad disposition of the humours of our body. In the same manner, when any sudden causeless fear, or grief, or fretfulness seizes us, it is more than probable that some malignant vapour from our distempered bodies mingles with our spirits and disorders them.

It would be of great moment towards the preservation of our health, if, when we visit our friends under any illness, we should, without an air of curiosity, or affectation of physical learning, kindly inquire what had done them hurt, whether fatigue, abstinence, or any surfeit, had occasioned their illness; that so we ourselves may learn the necessity of temperance from the experience of others, and take care to avoid those excesses which were the cause of their misfortunes.

Three things, says Plutarch, appear to me to be chiefly conducive to health, *viz.* exercise, temperance, and a thorough acquaintance with one's own constitution *.

---

* Tho' Plutarch borrows these rules from Hippocrates, yet as he recommends each of them in a very entertaining manner, what he says may become more useful by being better remembred.

As to the exercife of men of letters, (whom he feems principally to regard) it is furprizing to think what benefit they receive from reading aloud every day; we ought therefore to make that exercife familiar to us. What riding in any eafy chariot is, compared with other exercifes, the fame is reading aloud, compared with dialogue or converfation. The voice moves gently upon the thoughts of another, and glides fmoothly along without that vehemence which generally attends difputations. But tho' reading aloud is a very healthful exercife, violent vociferation may prove pernicious, as it has been frequently the caufe of burfting fome blood veffel.

Socrates did not diflike dancing when it was only for health, but faid "it was fo
" far inconvenient as it took up too much
" room, whereas to a man who ufed the ex-
" ercife of finging, or reading aloud, a
" chamber large enough to fit in, was fuffi-
" cient." It is carefully to be obferved, that this exercife of reading aloud, or any
other,

other, muſt not be uſed immediately after repletion or fatigue, for ſuch an error has proved hurtful to many. Idleneſs and ſloth have always been looked upon as a plentiful ſource of diſtempers, and the man who thinks to procure himſelf health by indolence, is like him who, by continuing always ſilent, hopes to mend his voice. Beſides, the very end and aim of health, which is action, is deſtroyed by ſloth; what is his health good for, who never does any thing to help himſelf or his friends?

Some have recommended walking after ſupper; others, imagining that motion diſturbed digeſtion, thought reſt preferable. The rational views of both may be obtained, by giving reſt indeed to our bodies, but by entertaining our minds with chearful converſation, which will neither fatigue the ſpirits through cloſe attention, nor occaſion inconveniencies of any kind; ſuch as thoſe agreeable and amuſing queſtions in natural philoſophy, hiſtory, or poetry, which ſome call

the

the *defert* at the entertainments of men of letters. And thus we fhall conform ourfelves to the advice of the phyficians, who defire that fome fpace of time may intervene between fupper and bed, to prevent crudities.

The fecond thing highly conducive to health is temperance in eating and drinking, and in all other gratifications of our fenfes. For my part, I think it were better to accuftom ourfelves, from our youth, to fuch temperance, as not to require any flefh meat at all: Does not the earth yield abundance, not only for nourifhment, but for luxury? Some of which may be eat as nature has produced them, and fome drefled and made palatable a thoufand ways. But fince cuftom has made it almoft natural to us now to eat flefh, we may eat it indeed, but moderately, and not gorge ourfelves with it like lions and wolves.

The moft noble of all liquors is wine; the moft ufeful drink; the moft palatable medicine; and, of all delicacies, the moft

grateful

grateful to the ftomach. But if we fhould happen to be fcorched by heat; fatigued with bufinefs; exhaufted with intenfe thinking; or feized with any feverifh diforder; a glafs of warm water only, or mixed with but little wine, will refrefh us more than wine alone, which having a natural activity and heat, is apt to exafperate our diforder, whereas it is our bufinefs to mitigate fuch complaints, by the foftnefs and coolnefs of the water.

The third thing neceffary to health, is to be fo well acquainted with our own conftitution as to know perfectly what agrees or difagrees with us. It is reported of the emperour Tiberius, that he faid "it was fhame-"ful for any man paft threefcore, to reach "his hand to a phyfician to feel his pulfe." This was a peevifh expreffion; but ftill I think it reafonable, that a man fhould have fome knowledge of his own pulfe, becaufe there is fuch a variety in pulfes; and fhould be acquainted with his own temper of body, with refpect to heat or cold; and fhould obferve from experience what agrees with him,

and

and what does not; for that foul, in my opinion, muſt be careleſs which has dwelt ſo long in a body, and yet is obliged to ask a phyſician, whether that body is healthieſt in ſummer or in winter? Whether moiſt or dry food is beſt for it? And whether the pulſation in the wriſt be quick or ſlow? People have learned to give directions to their cooks how they ſhould prepare their food, but do not trouble themſelves to know whether that food be wholeſome or not; and provided their taſte be gratified, health is quite out of the queſtion. Theſe are not the dictates of reaſon, eſpecially when we conſider the importance of health; and that this acquaintance with our own conſtitution is eaſily acquired by a little attention and care.

Three errors which are very common among men I heartily wiſh reformed: One is that of taking ſtrong purges or vomits to carry off the redundancy of their ſhameful intemperance, and the complaints which it brings upon them. He who takes a rough purge to relieve his body from too great a

load

load of food or humours, behaves himself like an inhabitant of Athens, who, finding the multitude of citizens troublesome to him, should contrive to drive them out, by filling the city with Scythians and wild Arabs. Instead of these violent drugs therefore, which corrupt the body, he should, without any preparation, directly puke up his load; or live abstemiously for a few days.

Another error is committed when people bind themselves down to certain stated rules of abstinence, or think it expedient to fast on certain periodical days; imagining, without reason, that such a formal restraint will contribute to their health. These punish themselves, without any necessity, by adhering to useless rules, which make their whole lives uncomfortable. A man under such bondage lives altogether for himself, and rather resembles a shell fish, which remains fixt to its rock, than a rational creature who has any commerce with the world, or would be useful to mankind.

A

A third error which studious men are apt to fall into, is not less dangerous; they read and meditate incessantly, without allowing proper relaxation or refreshment to the body; and think that a frail machine can bear fatigue, as well as an immortal spirit. This puts me in mind of what happened to the camel in the fable, which refusing, tho' often premonished, to ease the ox, in due time, of a part of his load, was forced at last to carry, not only the ox's whole load, but the ox himself also, when he died under his burthen. Thus it happens to the mind which has no compassion on the body, and will not listen to its complaints, nor give it any rest, until some bad distemper compells the mind to lay study and contemplation aside; and to lie down, with the afflicted body, upon the bed of languishing and pain. Most reasonably, therefore, does Plato admonish us to take the same care of our bodies as of our minds; that like a well matched pair of horses to a chariot, each may draw his equal fhare of weight. And when the mind is moft bufy in the contemplation of virtue, the body fhould then be cherifhed with the greateft care, that fo it may give no obftruction in fuch a noble purfuit.

Of AGATHINUS.

AGATHINUS was contemporary with Plutarch: He practifed phyfic at Rome, and is mentioned in feveral places by Galen*. We have his thoughts concerning the cold bath among the collections of Oribafius †; and as this author is full and clear with regard to the practical part of cold bathing, which when ufed with the neceffary precautions, may be very fubfervient to the prefervation of health, it will be proper to know the fentiments of this ancient phyfician upon fo interefting a fubject; efpecially as his directions will fuperfede the trouble of confulting others upon the fame article.

* In lib. 1. Hipp. de morb. vulg. comment. 2. fect. 25. Et de different. pulf. lib. 4. cap. 10. et 11.

† Medicin. collect. lib. 10. cap 7.

" THOSE

"Those who defire to pafs through this tranfitory life with health, (fays he) fhould bathe themfelves frequently in cold water. I can fcarce find words to exprefs the benefit which people receive from this practice; and even in extreme old age, cold bathing, to fuch as have been habituated to it, will render the body firm, and the countenance lively; will ftrengthen the appetite, affift concoction, preferve the fenfes entire; and, in a word, will give vigour to the whole animal oeconomy."

I have been told, continues our author, that it is a common cuftom among the barbarous nations, to dip their infants daily in cold water; but we parboil our children with warm ablutions, perfuaded thereto by our nurfes, becaufe, forfooth, the infants go to fleep foon after the fatigue of being wafhed in warm water, and reft pretty well in the night; but the confequence is, that children, fodden in this manner, frequently fall into convulfions and epilepfies, very difficult to be removed.

Our aliment should be thoroughly digested and distributed, or, in other words, the stomach should be empty, and the body light when we go into the cold bath. We should also walk a while, or use some other gentle exercise, to give us a moderate warmth and alacrity of spirit, immediately before we enter; but we must by no means heat or fatigue ourselves at that time. The ears should be closely stopped to prevent the cold water from getting into them. When we are ready, we ought to plunge instantly in the water, or have it poured upon us, but the former is best. Such as have strength and resolution to bear it, may dip their whole bodies over-head, a second or third time under water; but whether they dip once or oftner, they should be always exceedingly well dried and rubbed when they come out. The water should neither be of an icy coldness nor of too remiss a degree, but ought to be always pure and bright. Sea water is best, especially for the first trials.

Some think that those who are not accuſtomed to the uſe of the cold bath, ought not to begin it before the middle of ſummer; " but I have ſeen many begin with
" great ſafety at all times of the year; it
" is nevertheleſs my own opinion, ſays our
" author, that the ſpring is preferable to
" any other ſeaſon for the commencement
" of this practice."

✟✟✟✟✟✟✟✟✟✟✟✟✟✟✟✟✟✟✟✟✟✟✟✟✟✟✟✟✟✟✟✟✟✟✟✟✟

CHAP. VIII.

Of Galen.——And ſuch of his rules as were but ſlightly touched upon before his time.

CLAUDIUS GALENUS was born at Pergamus a city in the leſſer Aſia, about the year of our Lord 131. He wrote ſix books concerning the preſervation of health, and ſeveral other tracts about the qualities and nature of aliments, and the difference of temperaments; from all which I ſhall extract the moſt material rules, that have not been recommended by others before

fore him, without entering into his fcholaftic difputes, or unneceffary digreffions too frequent in his writings. But let not the fafhionable pedantry of the times in which he lived, give us a mean opinion of this great man, whofe penetrating genius, extenfive knowledge, and juft conceptions both of the works, and author * of nature, have been the admiration of ages.

HE advifes his readers, for their own fake to perfift with fpirit and refolution in learning and practifing thofe rules which conduce to the prefervation of health, affuring them, for their encouragement, that by fo doing they may preferve their bodies to extreme old age, free from all forts of diftempers. " I was born (continues he) with an infirm " conftitution, and afflicted in my youth " with many and fevere illneffes; but fince

---

* Ufum partium demonftrando, " ego conditoris noftri " verum hymnum compono. Hoc autem omne inveniffe, quo " pacto omnia potiffimum adornarentur, fummæ fapientiæ eft: " effeciffe autem omnino quæ voluit, virtutis eft invictæ ac " infuperabilis. Quodque nihil fuis beneficiis privatum effe " voluerit, id perfectiffimæ bonitatis fpecimen effe ftatuo."
De ufu part. lib. 3. cap. 10. claf. 1. verfio vulg.

" I

"I arrived to the twenty eighth year of my age, and knew that there were sure rules for preserving health, I have observed them so carefully, that I have laboured under no distemper since that time, except now and then a fever* for one day, which my fatigue, in attending the sick, necessarily brought upon me. A man, whose body is clear from every noxious humour that can hurt it, is in no danger of contracting any illness, except from external violence, or infection. And why may not proper care be taken to keep the body clear from all such noxious humours?"

In order to adapt his rules to persons under all circumstances, Galen divides mankind into three general classes. In the first he reckons those who are naturally sound and strong, and at liberty, from their affluence, to bestow what time and care they please on their health. In the second, he

---

* De san. tuend. lib, 5. cap. 1.

places such as are of a delicate and infirm constitution. And his third class contains those, whose necessary occupations, in public, or private life, will not permit them to eat, sleep, or use exercise at regular hours.

As to the first, he says, that to preserve life and health, as long as is consistent with the lot of man, it is necessary that the original stamina should be good, for some are so crazy, " that Æsculapius* himself could " scarce prolong their lives to threescore." This class he divides into four periods, *viz.* Infancy, youth, manhood, and old age. Two of these periods, namely, infancy, and old age, had been touched upon but slightly before his time. But as to youth and manhood (whether of robust or tender constitutions) the general rules established by Hippocrates and others for preserving health, are, for the most part, the same which Ga-

* Sunt enim, qui ab ipso ortu adeo improspero corporis sunt statu, ut ne, si Æsculapium quidem ipsum iis præfeceris, vel sexagesimum annum videant. De san. tuend. lib. 1. cap. 12, Thoma Linacro, Anglo, interprete.

len

len alfo recommends, and therefore need not be repeated here.

To be brief, there are four articles, with regard to the prefervation of health, which Galen has confidered more attentively than any that went before him, *viz.* 1. Infancy. 2. Old age. 3. The difference of temperaments. And 4. The care neceffary to be taken by thofe whofe time is not in their own power. I fhall therefore endeavour to give a clear and fuccinct view of his precepts concerning thefe articles, in the order here fet down.

Article I. Of Infancy.

Children newly born fhould, if poffible, be fed with their mothers milk, which is much more natural to them than that of a ftranger. The nurfes fhould give them a good deal of exercife, both in the cradle and in their arms, and fhould be extremely diligent to find out what makes the infants uneafy when they cry, and, by their unufual agitation,

agitation, appear to be in pain, left these a-gonies should throw them into fits, or into a fever. " I attended a child (says our
" Author) who cried inceffantly; whom
" neither motion, mufic, nor the breafts,
" could pacify for one moment; and, upon
" ftrict fearch, found, that the bed in which
" he lay, his cloaths, and body were all
" nafty, but the inftant he was wafhed,
" and clean dreffed, he fell into a fweet
" fleep, which continued feveral hours."
Infants ought to be fed with milk only until they have cut their foreteeth, and then accuftomed by degrees to a more folid food, as bread and other light forts of aliment, with which nurfes are well acquainted. They should alfo be wafhed every morning with tepid water, and then well rubbed and dried; the nurfe obferving, for this purpofe, the time when the child's ftomach is empty after a long fleep; for they do hurt who wafh and rub infants upon a full ftomach. Galen finds great fault *, and feems quite out of humour

* De fanit. tuend. lib. 1. cap. 10.

with

with the northern cuſtom of plunging new born infants into cold water, and difdainfully ſays, "that he does not write for Germans or ſuch barbarians, any more than he would write for bears and lions;" and yet he recommends, to his polite Greeks and Romans, a more uncouth and painful practice of rubbing their tender infants all over with falt *, in order to render them healthy and hardy. But time and experience have every where aboliſhed the practice of ſalting, and, to the great benefit of infants, have, in many places and families eſtabliſhed the uſe of the cold bath under proper reſtrictions †, which may be ſeen at the bottom of the page.

---

* Ergo recens natus infantulus, cujus corporis conſtitutio omni nota vacat, primum quidem faſciis deligetur, ſed corpori prius toti ſale modice inſperſo, quo cutis ejus denſior ſolidiorque reddatur.—Ita vero qui ſecundum naturam ſunt infantes, vel ſolo ſale præparati munitique abunde fuerint: quando, qui ſiccorum myrti foliorum aut aliorum id genus inſperſione egent, iis plane vitioſus ſtatus ſit. De ſan. tuend. lib. 1. cap. 7.

† The cold bath, by ſtrengthening the ſolids, and promoting a free perſpiration, gives livelineſs, warmth, and vigour to infants, highly conducive to prevent rickets, broken bellies, ſcrophulous diſorders, and coughs, to which they are extremely obnoxious

page. In justice, however, to our author, I must take notice that he is rarely guilty of any mistake in practice; and tho' his theory has been much mended in after ages, yet his practical observations are to this day very va-

obnoxious in some countries. And nature seems to have pointed out this remedy, both to the ancient and new world. Virgil informs us, that it was a custom in Italy, long before the Roman times, to dip their new-born infants in the coldest streams:

<blockquote>
Durum a stirpe genus. Natos ad flumina primum
Deferimus, sævoque gelu duramus et undis.
Æn. lib. 9. lin. 603.
</blockquote>

And Sir William Pen, in his letter to doctor Bainard (hist. of cold bath, part 2. pag. 291.) has the following words: " I " am assured that the American Indians wash their young infants " in cold streams, as soon as born, in all seasons of the year."

With regard to infants of a strong constitution, there can be no objection to the use of cold bathing, especially if (to avoid a sudden transition from the warmth in which the fœtus was formed to an opposite extreme) parents would defer it to the next summer after the child is born. But to guard against any possibility of danger to the infant from this daily and quick immersion of the whole body, let the nurse observe whether he becomes warm and lively immediately upon his being taken out of the water, or soon after he is rubbed dry and dressed; if so, the cold water will undoubtedly prove of service to him; but if, on the contrary, the child become chilly and pale, and especially if any of his limbs should be contracted or benumbed with the cold, and continue so for some time after he is rubbed dry and dressed, the use of the bath must be intermitted for a few days, and tried again when the child is brisker; or in case the same symptoms should return, it must be quite laid aside.

luable

luable. He proceeds in his directions, and says, great care should be taken of the nurse's diet, exercise and sleep, that so her milk may be good. That milk is good which is perfectly sweet, white, and of a due consistence, neither too thick nor too thin; but bad milk is somewhat bitter or salt, of an improper consistence and colour, and of a disagreeable odour. The nurse must not go near her husband while she gives suck, and should immediately be dismissed if she is with child. Infants should not taste wine, because it heats the body, and hurts the head; besides, they do not want any, and therefore feel not the benefit, but only the hurt it does.

A pure air is also necessary for children, not such as is permitted to stagnate in a close room; nor such as is loaded with the steams of standing waters, the filth of great cities, with exhalations from dead animals, or rotten herbage. The same method of living may be observed in the second septennial period, as in the latter part of of the firſt; with this farther care, that the child be then taught to uſe moderate exerciſe, but not too violent, leſt it ſhould ſtint* his growth. *That* is alſo the proper ſeaſon to form his mind rightly, by teaching him the rudiments of uſeful knowledge, and by habituating him to that modeſty, and obedience, which will afterwards contribute greatly to the preſervation of his health.

Art. II. Of Old Age.

Old age, which may be called a natural diſtemper, or a middle ſtate between health and ſickneſs, is commonly dry and cold; for tho' the eyes, noſe and mouth, often run with water; and tho' a cough and ſpitting generally attend old people, yet theſe are all excrementitious humours, and not a nouriſhing uſeful moiſture. This coldneſs and dryneſs ſhould be relieved with a little wine, and ſuch food as is proper to moiſten and warm them. Chafing alſo, or rubbing with

* This opinion requires farther confirmation from experience.

the flesh brush, is good for them, as it increases the motion of the blood, excites a gentle heat, and thereby helps to distribute an equal nourishment to all parts of the body. After rubbing, it will be convenient for them to walk or ride in some vehicle, but not so far as to fatigue themselves with either; for too much exercise makes them meagre, whereas moderate exercise keeps up their flesh. It is a rule not to be neglected, that old persons should persist in the use of such exercises as they have been most accustomed to, for these are not only less fatiguing, but also more entertaining and agreeable to them. Nor is it safe for them, abruptly to substitute a new exercise in the place of an old one; for experience has taught us, that much walking has been hurtful to those who could bear riding * extremely well: And if any part of our body should happen to be more infirm than the rest, great care is to be taken, that our exercise do not over-

---

* He means riding in a chariot, and not on horseback.

fatigue the weak part; but let it be so contrived, that the stronger parts shall have motion enough, and the weaker part shall receive no damage. If, for instance, a man is subject to a giddiness, he ought not to use any exercise in which he must bend his head often, or turn round; but rather chuse to walk gently forward, or ride in some easy vehicle, without fatiguing himself. Or if a man's legs be weak, riding in a chariot will do him much more service than walking.

Old people should avoid every sort of food that produces thick and glewy juices, as unfermented bread, cheese, pork, beef, eels and oysters; and likewise every thing that is hard to digest. Their bread should be mixed with a due proportion of salt, and yest or leaven; should be well kneaded; and thoroughly baked; otherwise it will occasion obstructions in the liver, spleen and kidneys.

In case an old man should continue two whole days costive, he ought on the third to take some very gentle thing to open his body, dy, such as he knows by experience to answer that purpose; nor should he continue the same opening food or medicine always, but change it now and then for somewhat else, lest by becoming habitual, it should lose its effect.

He should also indulge himself in sleeping as long as will be sufficient to cherish and refresh him.

" Antiochus the physician, when he
" was above fourscore years old, walked
" from his house three* stadia to the fo-
" rum, where the principal citizens of
" Rome met every day; and in his road vi-
" sited such patients as lay near him. If he
" had farther to go, he took a chair † or
" some other vehicle. He had a small room
" in his house, warmed with a stove in win-
" ter, and temperate in summer, in which
" his body was well chafed and rubbed, af-
" ter going to stool every morning. In the

* Near half a mile. De sanit. tuend. lib. 5. cap. 4.
† Partim gestatus in sella, partim vehiculo vehebatur. Ibid.

"forum, about nine or ten o'clock, he eat
"some bread and boiled honey, and stayed
"there talking or reading to twelve. He
"then used some gentle exercise before din-
"ner, which was very moderate, beginning
"always with something that was opening.
"His supper was either some light spoon
"meat, or a fowl, with the broth in which
"it was boiled. And thus he lived with
"all his senses perfect, and all his limbs
"sound, to extreme old age.

Telephus the grammarian lived to al-
"most an hundred years, his breakfast was
"pure honey from the comb, mixed with
"gruel. He dined always on salad, or
"some fish, or fowl; and for supper he
"only eat a little bread with a glass of
"wine and water."

An old man's own experience must determine, whether a milk diet be proper for
him or not, since it is surprising to see what
different effects it has on different constitutions. " I knew a husbandman (says Ga-
"len)

" len) above an hundred years old, whose
" principal food was goats milk, with which
" he mixed sometimes bread, and sometimes
" honey; and now and then he eat it boiled
" with tops of thyme. A neighbour of his,
" imagining that milk was the cause of the
" old man's long life, would try it in imita-
" tion of him; but could never bear it in any
" form; for it lay heavy on his stomach,
" and soon raised a swelling in his left side.
" Another making the same experiment,
" found milk agree with him perfectly well,
" till after the seventh day of trial, when he
" felt a hard tumour in his left side, which
" occasioned a tension, with spasms, quite
" up to his throat. I have also known some,
" who, from a long use of milk, had con-
" tracted a stone in the kidneys, and some
" who lost their teeth, while others have
" lived upon it many years in good health."
The benefits which arise from milk to those
with whom it agrees, are, to keep the body
gently open; to produce sweet juices; and
good flesh; especially when the milk comes

from

from a pasture full of mild and wholesome herbs; for the milk cannot be good where the herbs are too acrid, too acid, or too astringent. The animal also, which gives the milk, should be quite healthy, and in the flower of her age. And I should advise people to drink asses milk, and goats milk alternately, because goats milk is the most nourishing; and asses milk, being thinner, is easiest of digestion.

That wine is best for old people which is strong and diuretic; it should be strong, in order to diffuse a proper heat over their cold limbs; and diuretic, to carry off any superfluous serosities, which, by remaining in the body, might become injurious to their health. They should therefore chuse their wine of a light thin body, because such is commonly diuretic: and of a pale or yellow colour, because such is the strongest; but they should abstain from thick, black or astringent wines, because they are apt to cause obstructions in the bowels. Nor indeed is sweet wine good for old men, unless they are very lean, and,

upon

upon that account, require rich wines to nourish them; but then they should be of the generous, pale, or yellow kind.

Art. III. *Of different* Temperaments, Complexions *and* Constitutions.

We may reckon nine different temperaments of the human body, of which four are simple, the hot, the cold, the moist, and the dry; four mixt, the hot and moist, the hot and dry, the cold and moist, the cold and dry; and one which keeps a medium between all extremes, and may therefore be called the good or healthy temperament. The simple temperaments are easily known by the sight and touch. Among the mixt or compound, those which deserve the greatest regard in practice, and are most easily distinguished by their respective marks, are, the hot and dry; and the cold and moist. These being directly opposite in their natures, require each a very different management.

The most common marks of a hot and dry temperament, are large, turgid veins;

a strong pulse; a broad breast and shoulders; a robust, muscular, well proportioned body and limbs; black, thick, curling hair; and a rough, brown, hairy skin.

On the contrary, a soft, white, smooth skin; fair hair; a narrow chest; small veins; a delicate body, generally plump; weak, ill-shaped limbs; and a feeble pulse, denote a cold and moist complexion.

As we daily observe men's temperaments differ so widely, that what does good to one, frequently does hurt to another, it is astonishing that any physician should attempt to prescribe rules for health, without taking notice of this difference; for as one shoe will not fit every foot, so neither will the same manner of living agree with all men. Nor can we pronounce universally of any aliment, that it is wholesome or unwholesome, because what agrees well with one, has been known to make another sick. "Two of my acquaintance (continues he) "had a warm dispute about honey; one
"maintained

" maintained that it was unwholefome, the
" other affirmed the contrary, and both
" pleaded experience, without confidering
" their refpective temperaments; the one
" being a phlegmatic old man, who lived
" a fedentary life, with whom honey muft
" agree, as it is of a warming penetrating
" nature; the other a young man about
" thirty, of a hot bilious temperament, to
" whom confequently honey muft be hurt-
" ful."

Some recommend exercife promifcuoufly for every perfon; others pretend that reft does as well. Some prefcribe wine, others water, but experience teaches us that the fame thing has often contrary effects on different perfons. " I knew fome men, who, if
" they abftained three days from labour, were
" fure to be ill; others I was acquainted with,
" who enjoyed a good ftate of health tho'
" they ufed little or no exercife. Primigenes
" of Mitylene was obliged to go into a warm
" bath every day, otherwife he was feized with
" a fever." Effects we learn from experience,
but

but the cause of those effects we learn from reason and reflection. Why did Primigenes require such frequent bathing? " I found
" by the burning heat of his body, by his
" studious life, and by his never sweating,
" that he wanted a free perspiration; but
" his skin being thick and hard, and stop-
" ping this perspiration, he required a warm
" bath to mollify his skin, and open his
" pores. I knew another whose tempera-
" ment was equally hot, but did not require
" bathing so frequently, because by his
" trade of walking much about the city to
" buy and sell several things, and by being
" of a quarrelsome disposition, and fighting
" frequently, he kept himself, for the most
" part, in a sweat, which prevented a fe-
" ver. A third person of a hot and dry
" constitution I was obliged to restrain
" from exercise, because he used it to ex-
" cess; and herein I followed the rule of
" Hippocrates, who says that hot tempe-
" raments should rather indulge rest than
" use too much exercise. On the other
" hand, I have restored health to seve-
" ral

" ral perfons of a cold temperament, by rou-
" fing them from a lazy life, and by per-
" fuading them to labour." It is plain therefore that different degrees of exercife and different forts of food are neceffary to different complexions. Thofe refpective differences are, indeed, to be inveftigated by the underftanding, but experience muft always confirm our reafoning.

It muft be farther obferved, that befides prefcribing a warm bath, and the moft gentle exercife to hot and dry temperaments, it is alfo neceffary that their food fhould produce fweet juices without any acrimony; that water fhould be their principal drink; that they fhould avoid anger; too much ftudy; and the fcorching heat of the fun. And as the heat of a temperament commonly proceeds from a redundancy of bile, we fhould diligently inquire whether this bile is apt to go off by ftool? If it does, we need not be very folicitous about the confequences of it, for nature will do her own work;

but if it returns upwards, it muſt be evacuated by a very gentle puke.

All the phyſicians and philoſophers who have treated on the elements of the body with any accuracy, have condemned the dry temperament, as being of itſelf a ſort of old age, and have praiſed the moiſt as the fitteſt to prolong life, and preſerve health and vigour to extreme old age. A moiſt temperament is indeed inconvenient in infancy, but afterward becomes the moſt healthful of all the temperaments that run into any exceſs. Thoſe therefore who preſide over health ſhould guard againſt ſuch things as dry and waſte the body too much, but ſtill without running into the contrary extreme; and this juſt medium is preſerved by a prudent uſe of exerciſe and bathing, by keeping the natural evacuations within their proper bounds; and eſpecially by ſuch food as will ſupply good juices, and by a moderate uſe of wine.

Art. IV.

ART. IV. *Of those whose* TIME *is not in their own power.*

To statesmen, and students, whose employments engross too much of their time, Galen prescribes the three following rules: First, that after any extraordinary attendance or meditation, they should live more abstemiously than usual; and affirms of himself, " that when at any time he was fatigued " and spent with business, he chose the most " simple food he could think of, which was " commonly bread alone:" And tho' he does not propose this rigorous abstinence as a model for others, yet he insists upon it, that after great fatigue, people's food should be light and of easy digestion. His second rule is, that their common diet should be plain and simple, and such as they can easily digest. And his third rule directs them to set apart some portion of their time for exercise every day, (whatever their engagements may be) or if that be impossible, to lose a little blood sometimes to prevent a

plethora,

plethora, and to take now and then fome gentle phyfic to purge their bowels from the corrupted humours accumulated there, by indigeftion, without which precautions, they muft of neceffity fall into bad diftempers. He alfo advifes fuch inferior fervants as are tied down to a fedentary inactive life, to take the opportunity of feftival days to relieve their bowels from corrupted humours by gentle purging. But alas, adds he, fo great is the intemperance of the vulgar, that inftead of employing thofe idle days in procuring health or any other good to themfelves, they, on the contrary, indulge their appetites to the utmoft, whenever they have any opportunity of fo doing, and thereby accumulate bad humours, which afterward break out in rheumatifm, gravel, or fome other diftemper, which afflicts them for the remaining part of their lives.

I fhall conclude Galen's precepts concerning health, with the following excellent advice which he gives to his readers: " I be-
" feech

" feech all persons, says he, who shall read
" this treatise, not to degrade themselves to
" a level with the brutes, or the rabble, by
" gratifying their sloth, or by eating and
" drinking promiscuously whatever pleases
" their palates; or by indulging their appe-
" tites of every kind. But whether they
" understand physic or not, let them con-
" sult their reason, and observe what agrees,
" and what disagrees with them, that, like
" wise men, they may adhere to the use of
" such things as conduce to their health,
" and forbear every thing which, by their
" own experience, they find to do them
" hurt; and let them be assured, that by a
" diligent observation and practice of this
" rule, they may enjoy a good share of
" health, and seldom stand in need of phy-
" sic or physicians."

CHAP.

CHAP. IX.

Of Porphyry, and those who condemn the use of animal food.

PORPHYRY of Tyre, who lived about the middle of the third century, and was a favourite disciple of Plotinus the Platonist, endeavours, in his celebrated book *concerning abstinence from animal food,* to revive the primeval simplicity of diet; and exclaims violently against the use of flesh meat.

He addresses his book to Firmus Castricius, who had relinquished the Pythagorean abstinence, and tells him, " you own"ed, when you lived among us, that a ve"getable diet was preferable to animal" food, both for preserving health, and for" facilitating the study of philosophy; and" now since you have eat flesh, your own" experience must convince you, that what" you then confessed was true." It was not from those who lived on vegetables, that

that robbers* or murtherers, fycophants or tyrants, have proceeded, but from flesh eaters. The neceffaries of life are few, fays he, and eafily acquired, without violating juftice, liberty, health, or peace of mind; whereas luxury obliges thofe vulgar fouls, who take delight in it, to covet riches, to give up their liberty, to fell juftice, to mifpend their time, to ruin their health, and to renounce the joy of an upright confcience. " In order to recover our health, and
" remove diftempers, do we not patiently
" fubmit to incifions, to caufticks, and to
" naufeous potions, befides rewarding thofe
" who prefcribe them; and fhall we give
" ourfelves no trouble to remove diftem-
" pers from our minds which are immor-
" tal?"

He takes great pains to perfuade men of the truth of the two following propofitions: *Firſt*, That a conqueft over the appetites and paffions will greatly contribute to pre-

* This is an affertion at random, without any proof; nor indeed is it poffible to prove it.

ferve

serve health, and to remove diftempers. *Secondly*, That a fimple vegetable food being eafily procured, and eafily digefted, is a mighty help toward obtaining this conqueft over ourfelves.

To prove the firft propofition, he appeals to experience, and afferts, that fome of his own companions, who had been tormented with the gout* in their feet and hands to fuch a degree, that they were under a neceffity of being carried about from place to place for eight years fucceffively, were perfectly cured by difengaging themfelves from the care of amaffing riches; and by turning their thoughts to fpiritual objects; fo that, together with their anxiety for wealth, their bodily diftempers foon left them. In confirmation of the fecond propofition he argues in the following manner: " Give me

* If his companions had brought the gout upon themfelves by high and riotous living, (which is very probable) a low, vegetable, milky diet, perfifted in, might be of fervice to them; which is no proof, that a total abftinence from animal food is either neceffary or expedient to prevent diftempers.

" a

"a man who confiders ferioufly, what he
"is, whence he came, and whither he muft
"go; and from thefe confiderations, re-
"folves not to be led aftray, or governed
"by his paffions: And let fuch a man tell
"me, whether a rich animal diet is more
"eafily procured, or incites lefs to irregular
"paffions and appetites, than a light vege-
"table diet? But if neither he, nor a phy-
"fician, nor, indeed any reafonable man
"whatfoever, dares to affirm this; why do
"we opprefs ourfelves with animal food?
"And why do we not, together with luxu-
"ry and flefh meat, throw off the incum-
"brances and fnares which attend them?"

Thus declaims the philofopher Porphyry, who might and ought to have informed himfelf better, by reading *Galen's treatife on the nature of aliments*, which would have eafily convinced him that a mixture of animal food with the vegetable kind, is more proper for the healthy, more ftrengthening for the infirm, and more eafily digefted, than a fim-

B b ple

ple diet of vegetables only. And, indeed, all that our philosopher has advanced on this head, favours more of the rant of an enthusiast, or the mortification of a hermit, than of physical knowledge, or just reasoning; and yet there have been multitudes of the same opinion with him.

The ridiculous notion of the transmigration of souls, and some other unaccountable fancies, have induced several sects of philosophers, and their admirers, to abstain from animal food, as far back as Pythagoras, and down* to this day.

The grave Plutarch has written two discourses in favour of this abstinence, tho' it is matter of fact, that he himself eat flesh, like other people. But as it would be of little

* " All the Pagans in the East Indies hold the transmigra-
" tion of souls. Tho' they all profess one religion, yet they
" are divided into eighty four sects or tribes, each of which
" has its peculiar rites. The first and principal tribe is that
" of the Brachmans, which is divided into ten several sects:
" The first five feed on herbs and grain, without ever eating
" any thing that has life; in which they are imitated by the
" whole tribe of the Banians." See doctor John Francis Gemelli's voyage.

use toward the preservation of health, to give a long historical detail of what has been advanced upon this head, I shall only take notice of our learned countryman doctor Cheyne, who in some measure adopted the same notions, and blended them with his rules of health. To understand the latter writings of this *ingenious* and *whimsical* author, we must carefully distinguish the MYSTIC from the PHYSICIAN. In his mystical character, he thus declaims: "I am*
"almost convinced, that the flesh of animals
"was not intended in the original design
"of the creator, for food to the human
"race, but only permitted as a curse or pu-
"nishment, to let them feel the natural ef-
"fects of their concupiscence, by painful
"distempers, which should give them a dis-
"like to the lust that produced these pains,
"and make them return to the love of vir-
"tue and of God.

* Discourse 2. pag. 54, 55. I shorten his declamation.

But when in his character of a physician he inquires into facts, and calmly considers the reasons alledged, for giving the preference to vegetable aliment in general, this consideration staggers him; and he is forced to acknowledge, that * " several sorts of ve-
" getables, and substances prepared from
" them, as onions, mustard, nuts, pickles,
" spices, aromatics, and especially ferment-
" ed liquors, are more inflaming and delete-
" rious, than some mild animal substances."

If, therefore, animals were not originally intended for human food, and yet there are some vegetables in common use more pampering and inflaming in their nature than several animal substances, how shall we moderate the difference between these opposite opinions, and reconcile the *Mystic* with the *Physician*?

The *experienced Physician* prevails at last over the *enthusiastic Philosopher* to abate of

* Discourse 2. pag. 75.

his rigour, and to accommodate differences, by the following friendly compromise: *viz.*
"That for bodily * strength, animal food, and fermented liquors are fittest, if moderately used; but for intellectual exercises, vegetable food, and unfermented liquors seem appropriated; and that consequently the best way to secure the golden mediocrity between bodily strength and spiritual vigour, is for the healthy to confine themselves to about a pound, or at least half a pound of animal food, and a pint, at least half a pint of fermented liquors daily; but for the valetudinary and studious to sink below this medium in both these, 'till by experience and observation they find what quantity of either they are easiest under; and to stick to that, should it be even to descend totally into vegetables, milk and unfermented liquors."

But notwithstanding the singularities of this learned writer, we find, among his apho-

* Discourse 2. pag. 88.

risms relating to health, some which deserve our attention, and have not hitherto been mentioned: Of these the four following are the principal.

1. He that would * be soon well must be long sick, that is, treat himself as a valetudinarian in most things. Aph. 8.

2. Riding on horseback is the best exercise to recover lost health; and walking, the best to preserve good health. Aph. 25.

3. Good hours will be always a most beneficial means to preserve health and spirits; to go to bed by ten, and rise by six. Aph. 30.

4. Vomits often and properly repeated, are the sole universal antidote and panacea of Britain; an ailing person cannot repeat them too often, (provided his constitution can bear them) and they will always prove beneficial and salutary †.

* Pract. essay on the regim. of diet, pag. 60. et seq.

† He means that gentle pukes, frequently repeated, are by experience found useful in curing hypochondriacal or nervous disorders produced by high living.

CHAP.

CHAP. X.

Of Oribasius, Aetius, and Paulus Ægineta on health.-----Of Actuarius and others, as Friar Bacon and Lord Verulam, who imagined that health might be preserved, and life prolonged by antidotes and panaceas.

ORIBASIUS, and the succeeding Greek physicians who wrote concerning health, have done little more than copy Galen; but I must observe to the honour of Oribasius, that he was the first of the Greek physicians* who can properly be said to have recommended

---

* Oribasius was indeed the first physician who expresly recommended riding on horseback for the sake of health; but it must be allowed that he took the hint from Galen, of whom it may be justly said, that as he learned a great deal from Hippocrates, so himself became a copious source of knowledge, to succeeding physicians. It was the opinion of Plato, that " exercise performed by one's own body, as walking, run- " ning or playing at ball, was preferable to passive exercise " in any vehicle, as riding in a chariot, or sailing." Galen having taken notice of these two sorts, says, (De sanit. tuend. lib. 2. cap. 11.) that " riding on horseback is a mixt kind " of exercise, partaking of each;" the horse performing the part of a vehicle, and the rider performing the active part of bodily exercise, by exerting himself in the management of his horse,

recommended the exercise of riding on horse-back toward the preservation or recovery of health; for he declares, in express terms, that " it strengthens* the stomach above " all other sorts of exercise, that it clears " the organs, and makes all the senses more " acute."

AETIUS wrote about the end of the fifth century. He is somewhat more particular than Galen in the care of infants †, and horse, and in keeping his seat. And when we consider, that in those days they knew not the use of stirrups, we must allow such bodily exercise to have been then rougher than now: This, I think, was hint sufficient to induce Oribasius, who copied Galen, to recommend riding on horseback.

But after all, there is nothing more certain than that riding on horseback was reckoned a healthful exercise many ages before Oribasius or Galen. For Xenophon in his oeconomics (lib. 2. sect. 3.) introduces Ischomachus telling Socrates, that " he rode on horseback to see his servants in the country " ploughing, sowing, and planting; adding farther, that he " rode over all sorts of roads, by way of exercise." Which conduct Socrates approves in the following words: Your " exercise, by Juno, pleases me much, which gives you, at " same time, τὴν ὑγείαν καὶ τὴν ῥώμην, both health and " strength of body.".

* Medic. collect. lib. 6. cap. 24
† Tetrabibl. 1. serm. 4.

choice

choice of nurses; but takes most of his other rules of health from him.

Paulus Ægineta, who, according to the learned and accurate doctor Freind, lived about the year 621, bestows his whole first book *de re medica* upon the subject of health, but has scarce said any thing new.

The last of the Greeks who has touched upon the preservation of health is Actuarius. He lived in the thirteenth century, and practised physic with a good deal of reputation at Constantinople. He treats of health in a cursory manner in the third book of his method of cure; but seems to depend more on the efficacy of particular antidotes to preserve health, than on any general rules. To give an instance of this with regard to the antidote which he calls *health*. He affirms[*], that any man who takes the quantity of a lentil of this medicine every day, will never be seized with any illness all his life; and

[*] Method. medend. lib. 5. cap. 6.

[202]

says that it will remove inflammations of all sorts, and will also *drive away witches and evil spirits.* Those who are feverish should take it in water, and those who are not feverish, in wine.

The ingredients of this wonderful composition are rue, pepper, myrrh, saffron, cinnamon, spikenard, euphorbium, mandrakes, poppies, and twenty simples more, all made up with honey.

It is true that this infatuation, of depending upon particular medicines to secure health, prevailed in the world many ages before Actuarius, and has continued down to our days; but he seems to be the first physician of any reputation whose credulity on this head was unbounded.

Homer mentions * the φάρμακον Νηπενθές, or " Egyptian cordial, which communi-
" cated the highest joy to those who took it,
" and banished every sort of melancholy.

* Νηπενθές τ' ἄλαχόν τε, κακῶν ἐπίληθον ἁπάντων. Odyss. lib. 1, lin 221.

Plny

Pliny describes a plant, " very like lettuce, called *Dodecatheon,* or *the twelve Gods,* which, infused in water, was said to cure all distempers*. And a sort of Piony, called *Panacea,* from its all-healing virtues."

In the time of Herophilus, some compositions had the pompous appellation of *the hands of the Gods* bestowed upon them; and Galen's remark upon them is good, *viz.* " Herophilus ‡ spoke truth, when he said that these compositions, considered in themselves, were of no value; or might do mischief, if he who prescribed them was ignorant; but when administred properly by a prudent and experienced physician, they might be called *the hands of the Gods,* from their utility."

This method of depending upon particular *nostrums,* was a shorter and easier road to

* Lib. 25. cap. 4.
‡ De comp. medicam. local. lib. 6. cap. 3.

health, than the rules of Hippocrates and Galen, which required *temperance* and *exercife;* and had it proved effectual, all the world would readily have gone into it; but it was found, after many trials, to be attended with perpetual difappointments. Such, however, is the weaknefs of the human mind, that among the moft ingenious men, which *this*, or *any nation* produced, fome were deceived into a belief of *univerfal Panaceas*, endowed with virtues fufficient to keep off diftempers to extreme old age; and others, extending their views ftill farther, propofed, by a proper ufe of a few chofen remedies, to protract the life of man beyond the common limits affigned to it by nature, which feem to have been nearly the fame from the days of the Pfalmift * down to ours.

From a multitude of Noftrum-mongers, that might be quoted here, I fhall felect Friar Bacon and lord Verulam, to fhew how fhort fighted man is; for who can be fecure

* Pfalm xc. 10.

from falling, if two such great geniuses could stumble?

FRIAR BACON, in his larger work, dedicated to Pope Clement IV. says, that the reason why the life of man is much shorter now than it was in the beginning of the world, is, " because people have neglected, " in all ages, to observe a proper regimen " for the preservation of health. This ne‑ " glect has been universal, the physicians " have been careless. In youth health is " never thought on. One perhaps among " three thousand, may think of it when he " grows old, hoping, too late, to stop " death from coming in, when he is just " at the door. But is there no way of re‑ " medying this evil which men's ignorance " and negligence have brought upon them? " Has nature no secret, which art may find " out, to procure health and long life? Yes. " There have been men, who by their re‑ " searches into the secrets of nature, have " discovered antidotes to ward off old age.

And

And the " good experiment-maker*, in his
" book concerning the proper regimen† of
" old people, gives an enigmatical de-
" fcription of a certain compofition, which
" when rightly underftood, retards, for ma-
" ny years, the advances of old age:" *viz.*
You muft take that which is temperate in
the fourth degree. That which fwims in
the fea. That which vegetates in the air.
That which is caft out by the fea. That
which is found in the bowels of a long lived
animal. A plant of India: And two creeping things which are the food of Tyrians
and Egyptians. And let them all be properly prepared. This *riddle* Bacon explains
in the following manner: That which is
temperate in the fourth degree is *gold*, chy-
mically prepared. What fwims in the fea
is *pearl*. The flower of *rofemary* grows by
virtue of the air. *Sperma-ceti* is thrown

* Peter de Maharn-court a Picard, whom Bacon calls do-
minus experimentorum.
† This book I could find no where.

out

out by the fea. The *bone* found in a ftag's heart is taken out of the bowels of a long lived animal. The Indian plant is *lignum aloes*. And the creeping things are *ferpents*, of which the flefh muft be properly prepared. This antidote, fays Bacon, " prevents " the corruption of any conftitution, and " the infirmities of age for many years."

But alas! In fpite of this antidote, his friend pope Clement died foon after, and left him to the mercy of his old enemy, Jerom de Afcoli, general of the Francifcans, afterwards Pope Nicolas IV. who condemned his doctrine, and committed him to prifon, where he was confined ten years. And poor Bacon, who deferved a better fate, after a great deal of bad ufage from an ignorant and fuperftitious world, died at Oxford in the feventy-eighth year of his age, A. D. 1294. leaving us a convincing proof of the vanity of fecrets to prolong life, even in the beft hands.

The great lord Verulam, after ridiculing * the complaint of Hippocrates, that " life was fhort, and the healing art long

* Pag. 1

" and

" and tedious." And after juftly ftigmatiz-
ing † the vain and extravagant encomiums
beftowed upon chymical fecrets, and celebrated antidotes, which at firft flatter, and
at laft deceive, he himfelf propofes a method *to prolong life,* which, upon a fair trial,
will be found equally fallacious with the
boafted preparations of the chymifts.

The two great caufes * of death, fays he,
are firft, " the internal fpirit, which like
" a gentle flame, waftes the body: And fe-
" condly, the external air that dries and ex-
" haufts it; which two caufes confpiring to-
" gether, deftroy our organs, and render
" them unfit to carry on the functions of
" life:" But this wafte and depredation committed by the *internal Spirit,* may be repaired, firft, by making the fubftance of it more
denfe, through a regular courfe of *opiates* taken in fmall dofes, and at certain times;
and fecondly, by moderating its heat, which

† Pag. 194. et feq. hift. vit. et mort.

* Caufa periodi eft, quod fpiritus inftar flammæ levis perpe-
tuo depredatorius; et cum hoc confpirans aër, qui etiam corpora
fugit, et arefacit officinam corporis; et organa perdat, et inha-
bilia reddat ad munus reparationis.

may be done, says he, by a proper use of nitre.

He owns, indeed, with a generous frankness, that " his manner * of life did not " permit him to make the necessary expe- " riments upon these medicaments," which is much to be lamented, for without repeated experiments it will be utterly impossible to establish opinions of this nature; and he who considers that *opium* is found by experience to weaken the nerves, and that *nitre* cools to a great degree, will scarce think these drugs proper for old age, when warmth and vigour are wanted.

Our author treating also of *air*, which he reckons the other great cause of premature death, recommends *chalybeate baths*, and *greasy unctions*, to exclude it; but being sensible that this would stop the perspiration, and occasion distempers, he orders glysters

* Difertè profitemur nonnulla ex iis quæ proponimus experimento nobis non esse probata; neque enim hoc patitur nostrum vitæ genus. Hist. vit. et mort. pag. 203.

and purges, as a fuccedaneum, to carry off the redundant humours; which method would not anfwer very well in practice.

Upon the whole, our noble author difcourfes here not fo much like a phyfician, as a profound philofopher, whofe univerfal knowledge and fublime genius prompted him to controul the common appearances of nature, and to ftretch, if poffible, the human life beyond its ufual period. But it is remarkable, that tho' this great man took three grains of his favourite *nitre* every morning for the laft thirty years of his life, he died neverthelefs in the fixty-fixth year of his age.

His general precepts concerning long life are much more valuable; *viz.* Firft, that a frequent remembrance of the entertainments of youth chears and enlivens old people to a great degree. And here he obferves, that the emperor Vefpafian could not be prevailed upon, to alter his father's dwelling-houfe, tho'

very

very incommodious, left he should forget how he had passed his youth there; and that on festivals he drank out of his grand-mother's wooden cup edged with silver.

In his second precept he advises men to spend their youth and manhood in such a prudent manner as will enable them to retire from the fatigue of business when they grow old, and employ their time in such contemplations, amusements and rural recreations of building and planting, as will give entertainment to their minds, and vigour to their bodies.

His third rule directs to take particular care that the stomach, *the father of the family*, be always kept in good order; to which nothing contributes more than, now and then, to take a little something that will open the body gently, without giving it any disturbance.

His fourth rule is, that once every two years, those who begin to grow old, should
alter

alter their whole juices *, and make themselves very lean, by a courfe of diet-drinks and abſtinence, in order to ſweeten their blood and renew their youth.

✢✢✢✢✢✢✢✢✢✢✢✢✢✢✢✢✢✢✢✢✢✢✢✢✢✢✢✢✢✢✢✢✢✢✢

C H A P. XI.

Of the Arabian phyſic.----Its commencement.----Of Rhaſes and Avicenna concerning health.----Return of phyſic from Arabia to Europe.----Of the Tacuin or Elluchaſem Elimithar.

THE ſcience of phyſic having paſſed from the Greeks to the Arabians and Perſians, we muſt follow it thither, and enquire what improvements they have made in our ſubject of the preſervation of health.

Two accidents principally contributed to carry the Grecian phyſic into the eaſtern

---

* Boerhaave, in a great meaſure, adopts this rule, and ſays, "mutationes fere radicales humorum per reſolventia, horum dein excretiones ſuccedentes.——ſæpe diſponunt corpus ——ad vitam longam." Vid. inſtit. med. ſect. 1059. 1062. But more of this hereafter.

parts of Afia. One was the marriage of Sapores * king of Perfia to the daughter of the emperor Aurelian, who, in compliment to her, fent thither feveral Greek phyficians, by whom the Hippocratical medicine was propagated in that country, probably at Nifabur the capital of Chorafan, built by the fame Sapores, A. D. 272. and hence it was (as the learned doctor Freind conjectures) that moft of the celebrated profeffors in phyfick, Rhafes, Hally-Abbas, and Avicenna, were educated in thofe parts.

THE fecond accident was the taking of Alexandria by the Saracens, A. D. 642. For tho' the famous library there was deftroyed, it is probable that the writings of the old Greek phyficians might be fpared, merely (as our ingenious hiftorian † obferves) becaufe they treated of phyfick; the defire of health being as ftrong in the Arabians as in other people.

* Freind's hift. of phyfick, part 2. pag. 19.
† Hift. of phyfick, part 2. pag. 4.

RHASES

RHASES was the first Arabian I know of, who has given general rules of health. He was born in Persia, and was called to Bagdat when he was thirty years old, where he was afterwards chosen, out of a hundred eminent physicians, to take care of the celebrated hospital in that city. And there he died at the age of fourscore, A. D. 932. He was also physician to Almanzor lord of Chorasan, to whom he dedicated several of his writings; and, among the rest, *a treatise on the preservation of health.*

IN this treatise he has exhibited a plain and useful summary of several important rules of health, which (tho' mostly borrowed from the Greeks) deserve to be set, in one view, before the reader, as follows:

1. HEALTH is preserved by a just measure of exercise and the other *Non-naturals;* and also by the cleanliness of the place in which we live; and by a perseverance in the use of such things as we have been long accustomed

customed to, unless our customs have been bad, in which case we ought to depart from them, not abruptly, but by slow and regular degrees.

2. Exercise should be used when a man's stomach is empty; and should be left off at the moment he finds it begin to grow tiresome and uneasy.

3. A man ought not to postpone his meal when a sound and natural appetite prompts him to eat; but should never eat so much as to overload his stomach, or straiten his breath.

4. He who loaths his food, should fast for some time, or take a gentle dose of physic.

5. No liquor is equal to good wine.

6. A man who eats much, and uses little exercise, should frequently take some easy purge.

7. If a man finds any uncommon change in himself for some days, that is, if he sleeps, sweats,

sweats, or otherwise discharges more or less than usual, he should inquire into the cause of that alteration, and remove it before it can produce any bad effect.

8. CHEARFULNESS adds to one's strength and spirits, but grief impairs both.

9. A meagre man should avoid frequent concubinage, as he would an assassin. But it is one of the best cures for those who are desperately in love, and will often make them forget the beloved object.

10. GENTLE physick is better, generally speaking, for old people than bleeding; and good wine mixt with water, their best drink. Their exercise should be such as is pleasant to them, and proportioned to their strength; their food should be of easy digestion; and their sleep long.

AVICENNA was born at Bochara in Persia, A. D. 964. and died in the fifty-eighth year of his age. The fame of his work called

led the *Canon* prevailed so much, not only in Asia, but also in Europe, that there was scarce any other doctrine taught in the schools of physic before the restoration of learning, about the close of the fifteenth century. I have read with care all that he says concerning the preservation of health, both in his canon, and in his book * *of rectifying the errors committed in the use of the six things* necessary to man's life, and have found nothing in either that deserves the extravagant encomiums bestowed upon the author. He has principally copied Galen's rules of health, but has given them such a quaint conceited dress and air by his † refine-

* De removendis nocumentis quæ accidunt in regimine sanitatis, ex errore usus rerum non-naturalium.

† Ars custodiendi vitam illa est, quæ corpus humanum perducit ad hanc ætatem quæ vocatur terminus vitæ naturalis, secundum observationem convenientium et necessariarum rerum, quæ sunt septem: Æqualitas complexionis. Electio eorum quæ comeduntur et bibuntur. Purgatio superfluitatum. Rectificatio ejus quod per nares attrahitur. Rectificatio indumentorum de summâ tangentium. Moderamen motionum corporearum et animalium, inter quas sunt somnus et vigilia. Ex libro canonis doctrin. 1. dictionis tertiæ.

ments and subtilties, that it is not easy to understand them. His own additions may be reduced to the few following, *viz.*

1. A man in a passion ought not to eat food that is of a heating nature; and one under terrour should not eat things too cooling.

2. ONE should be more abstemious on the days he takes physic than at other times.

3. No man should go to sleep immediately after bleeding.

4. AFTER fasting long at sea, or in times of famine at land, people should eat sparingly, and come to make full meals by slow degrees, otherwise they will destroy themselves, as it happened in the city of Bochara, where those who had lived on roots and herbs in time of the famine, when they came to have bread and flesh in abundance, filled themselves greedily, and died.

5. TENDER habits of body receive great benefit from bathing in chalybeate waters.

SOME

Some rules he recommends, which, among us, would be thought somewhat aukward and troublesome. I shall mention but two.

1. When a person is much fatigued after a long journey, let some milch animal be milked upon his head, and let him go to sleep.

2. When a man is obliged to travel into a far country, let him carry along with him some *earth* of his own country, to be mixt with the foreign water which he is to drink. This native earth well stirred in, and then standing to settle, will mend the noxious qualities of the foreign water, and prevent any bad effects from it. It should be observed, indeed, that the Arabians were the more obliged to be careful about their water, because their religion did not permit them to drink wine.

Having thus taken notice of the introduction of the Greek physick into Persia and Arabia,

Arabia, and having seen the rules of health recommended by two of their principal phyſicians; we muſt now purſue this art back again from Arabia into the weſtern parts of Europe, whither it was brought by means of the Croiſade, and by the Moors ſettled, during the eighth century, in Spain, where they eſtabliſhed hoſpitals at Seville and Corduba.

The truth is, phyſic was very low in Europe from this time to the cloſe of the fifteenth century, when, after the taking of Conſtantinople * by the Turks, many of the Greeks retired into Italy, and carried their ancient manuſcripts with them. Theſe ſtrangers, encouraged by ſome generous patrons of learning, eſpecially by the great Dukes of Tuſcany, ſet the faculty upon underſtanding and explaining the Greek phyſicians, and examining how far the Arabians had followed or deviated from them; which laudable reſearches opened the way (tho' ſlowly) to farther improvements.

* It was taken in May 1453

THE first performance concerning the preservation of health that appeared in this ignorant period, was the *Tacuin* or *tables of health*, composed by two Jew physicians, at the desire of Charles the great, and published under the name of *Eluchasem Elimithar*. This book is rarely to be met with, except in public libraries, which is no great loss, being but a mean, perplexed, whimsical performance*, and scarce worth taking notice of, but only because it happens to be sometimes quoted by the learned.

THESE tables, by their divisions and subdivisions, rather confound than edify the reader, as will appear by the words † of the author, cited at the bottom of the page.

CHAP.

---

* P. Daniel, in his history of France, says, that Charlemagne had a great aversion to all physical regimens, which we need not wonder at, when we are told, that the authors of the Tacuin were his physicians. His words are, " Il avoit une " horreur extreme de tous les regimes de médecine, qui alloit " presque jusqu' a ne pouvoir souffrir la presence d'un medi- " cin." Tom. 1. pag. 557. edit. Paris.

† Cum Dei auxilio compono tabulas continentes cibos et potus, et alias res necessarias circa ipsos, ad hoc quod sit compendiosum

CHAP. XII.

Of the Schola Salernitana and others, who wrote on the prefervation of health in verfe.

NEXT to the Tacuin comes the Schola Salernitana, written about the end of the eleventh century, for the ufe of Robert Duke of Normandy, fon to William the conqueror, who in his return from the holy war confulted the phyficians of Salerno about a wound he had received in his arm, which became fiftulous. This poem was probably intended to direct him in the care of his health when he fhould have no phyfician at hand to advife with, and continued

pendiofum regibus et dominis confpicere in ipfis; et dividam tabulas per domos. In prima domo ponam numerum; in 2da nomen; in 3tia naturam; in 4ta gradum; in 5ta melius illius fpeciei; in 6ta juvamentum; in 7ma nocumentum; in 8va remotionem nocumenti; in 9na humorem qui generatur ex ea, et confequenter, in aliis quatuor domibus, convenientias ejus fecundum complexiones, ætates, tempora anni, et naturas regionum. In domo 14ta opiniones hominum in ea. In 15ta electiones et proprietates. Deinde faciam canones univerfales in genere illius de quo loquimur: Et in rubrica primi marginis juxta quod dixerunt aftrologi de illo.

in high esteem* for a long time after, in so much, that about the fourteenth century Arnoldus de Villa Nova could not recommend himself more effectually to Frederic king of Sicily and Naples, and to his subjects, than by writing a commentary upon it. Nor can we wonder at their partiality in favour of this Gothic composition, when we consider the time in which it was produced. This book, in some editions †, bears the title of *The flower of physic.*

Of the six articles necessary to human life, the Schola Salerni dwells principally upon aliment, but touches also upon the rest in a cursory manner.

The advice ‡ to persons of a studious and sedentary life, that they should accustom themselves to light suppers, seems very ratio-

---

* Doctor Freind tells us that Benj. de Tudela a Jew, upon his return from his travels over the greatest part of the known world, A. D. 1165, commends Salernum for the best seminary of physic among the sons of Edom, i. e. the Christians.

† Hoc opus optatur quod flos medicinæ vocatur.

‡ Ex magna cœna stomacho fit maxima pœna,
Ut sis nocte levis, sit tibi cœna brevis. Cap. 5. lin. 1.

nal. And, perhaps, the moſt curious part of the whole poetical compoſition is the deſcription there given of the four complexions, *viz.* ſanguine, choleric, phlegmatic, and melancholic, and the marks by which the prevalence of each may be diſtinguiſhed. Perſons of a ſanguine complexion, ſays this author, are plump, ruddy, chearful, generous, brave and benevolent. The choleric are thin, dry, yellow, wrathful, bold and impetuous. The phlegmatic are pale, fat, ſlothful, feeble, and ſtupid. And the melancholic are ſallow, ſilent, wakeful, timorous, cunning and tenacious.

But upon the whole, if we read this poem without the notes and amendments of Villa Nova, and others who have honoured it with their explanations, we can hardly forbear aſſenting to the truth of the character given it by Lommius[*], of being *a rude and illiterate performance.*

[*] Minus placet quod fieri hodie a multis video, verſiculos aliquot inconditos, ſcholamque ſequentibus Salernitanam, quâ, vix ſcio, an quicquam in literis medicorum inelegantius ſit, aut indoctius. Lom. comment. in Celſi librum prim. de ſan. tuend. epiſt. nuncupatoria.

JOHN

John of Milan, Author of the *Schola Salernitana*, having been the firſt who preſcribed rules of health in verſe, it will be proper to ſubjoin here ſuch other phyſicians as have treated the ſame ſubject in a poetical manner, that we may place them in one view, tho' they lived in different ages; and indeed the trouble of comparing them will not be great, for they are but few.

The ſecond is Caſtor Durantes, who writes with much more elegance* and judgment

---

* He begins with a conciſe and lively deſcription of the air which a man ſhould chuſe to live in:

> Si cupis incolumen vitam producere, cœlum
> Effuge corruptum nebulis, nidore, lacunis;
> Quodque movit madidus morboſis Africus auris.
> Purum ama, et ad ſolem naſcentem, et lumine apricum,
> Purgatumque Euro, et Boreali frigore terſum.

But I muſt obſerve upon the whole, that it is dangerous to preſcribe rules in verſe on ſuch a delicate ſubject as health, becauſe the muſe may now and then raiſe the *Poet* above the reach of ſalutary precepts, and make him forget the *Phyſician*. To give an inſtance of this, Durantes enumerating, after Hippocrates, the qualities of good water, ſays,

> Sic aqua clara fluat, qualis nitidiſſimus aër,
>   Dulcis, et exigui ponderis, et gelida;

ment than his predecessor. He was a citizen of Rome, and physician to Pope Sixtus Quintus, to whom he dedicates his poem, upon which he himself, for the benefit of one of the court ladies, wrote a commentary in Italian, entitled *Il Tesoro della sanita*.

In this treasure of health, he gives, from Hippocrates and Galen, a clear and succinct account of the common rules to be observed with respect to the six things necessary to human life; and adds, here and there, a remark of his own, adapted to the place in which he lived. He recommends, for example, singing * of psalms, and reading of pious

> Et tenuis currat, nullo purissima limo,
> Sitque sapor nullus, sit procul omnis odor.
> Frigescat breviter, modico simul igne calefcat
> Utilis, et duris apta leguminibus.
> *Hanc mihi si quis aquam dederit, vinosa valete*
> *Pocula, nam vincit optima lympha merum.*

Thus the *Physician;* but the *Poet* recollecting, perhaps, that *nec vivere carmina possunt quæ scribuntur aquæ potoribus,* presently subjoins,

> Vina bibant homines, animalia cætera fontes:
> *Absit ab humano pectore potus aquæ.*

* Il cantare i salmi, et attendere all' istoriè theologichè, dilettando all' animo, lo pascono in modo, che tutte le virtù diventano piu forti a resistere all' infermita, et a superarle.

histories,

histories, to chear and elevate the mind, and enable it to refift and overcome the infirmities of the body. He is fufficiently prolix, in his poem, on the different forts of aliment in common ufe; where, among other things, he recommends rats †, frogs ‡, and hedgehogs §.

But of all the poetical performances on this fubject, that have come to my hands, doctor Armftrong's *Art of preferving health* is by far the beft. To quote every charming defcription, and beautiful paffage of this poem, one muft tranfcribe the whole. We cannot however expect new rules, where the principal defign was to roufe and warm the heart into a compliance with the folid precepts of the ancients, which he has enforced with great ftrength and elegance. And, up-

† Nil juvat umbrofi latitare cubilibus antri
  Glis tibi, vita et mors hic tibi fomnus erit. Pag. 216.

‡ Ranarum alba caro, fed femper durior efca. Pag. 282.

§ Utere Echino hilaris, ftomachum fovet, ilia mollit. Pag. 222. editionis Bonibell. Venet. an. 1596.

on the whole, he has convinced us by his own example, that we ought not to blame antiquity for acknowledging,

One power of phyſick, melody, and ſong.

CHAP. XIII.

Of Marſilius Ficinus and others, who joined aſtrology with phyſic, in order to preſerve health.-----Mention is alſo made of Platina Cremonenſis.

BUT to return to plain proſe: Some [*] learned Greeks were ſent for, and entertained by the illuſtrious family of the Medici and others, who taught their language and learning to ſeveral perſons in Florence and Venice, before the Turks took poſſeſſion of Conſtantinople in the 1453. But many more [†] retired after the taking of that city, and carried their Greek manuſcripts

---

[*] Particularly Joannes Argyropilus and Emanuel Chryſoloras.

[†] As Theodore Gaza, Laſcaris, &c.

with

with them into Italy, where they soon spread the Grecian literature among a people eager to receive and study it. Among other sciences that began to revive in the West from this calamity of the Greeks, physick raised her languid head, but could not, for a long time clear herself from the follies of astrology, superstition and witchcraft, with which she had been corrupted, since her departure from antient Greece.

MARSILIUS FICINUS, the translator of Plato's works, was the first physician, after the revival of learning in the western parts of Europe, who wrote concerning health. He was born in Florence, and educated in the family of the great Cosmo de Medicis, who appointed him preceptor to his sons, and bestowed a handsome estate upon him. Among his other voluminous works he published a treatise concerning health and long life: And in his dedication to Laurentius, grandson of Cosmus, he calls Galen the physician of the body, and Plato

the

the physician of the soul; and in his book mixes a great deal of the subtilties of Plato and Plotinus, with some useful rules copied mostly from Galen. To these, however, he adds several senseless and superstitious precepts of his own, that still shew the darkness of the age in which he lived.

1. He admonishes people, for instance, to consult a good astrologer * at every septennial period of their lives, and when they shall learn from him the dangers which hang over their heads, they may then go to the physician to prevent those dangers.

2. He recommends the internal use of gold ‡, frankincense, and myrrh, to old people, in imitation of the wise men who

* Tu igitur, si vitam producere cupis ad senectutem, quoties septimo cuilibet propinquas anno, consule diligenter astrologum: unde immineat tibi discrimen, ediscito; deinde vel adito medicum, vel prudentiam. De studiof. vit. producend. cap. 20.

‡ Sicut magi thus, aurum, et myrrham, tria dona, pro tribus planetarum dominis, Jove sciz. Sole, et Saturno, stellarum domino obtulerunt, ita senes accipiant eadem vitalia dona. De vit. stud. producend. cap. 11.

offered

offered thefe three to the creator of the ſtars, in order to obtain from him the benign influence of the three lords of the planets, *viz.* Sol, Jupiter, and Saturn.

In * the laſt place, he moſt abſurdly adviſes old men to copy the ſhocking practice of ſome withered witches (as fame had reported) to renew their youth and ſtrength.

To Ficinus, who flouriſhed before the year 1470, I ſhall here ſubjoin Martin Panſa, a celebrated German phyſician, tho' he lived about an hundred and fifty years later, to ſhew that, even then, aſtrology and ſuperſtition were not baniſhed from the faculty. But tho' a great many might be added, who were ſhamefully weak and credulous upon this article, as well as Panſa, I ſhall not trouble the reader with any more of their trumpery.

* Communis quædam eſt et vetus opinio, aniculas quaſdam ſagas, infantum ſugere ſanguinem; quo pro viribus juveneſcant. Cur non et noſtri ſenes ſanguinem moderatè miſſum e vena adoleſcentis ſani fugant. De vit. ſtudioſ. producend. cap. 19.

MARTIN

MARTIN dedicated to the senate of Leipsic, *anno* 1615, a treatise entitled *Aureus libellus de proroganda vita*. He was one of those who thought that the planets had a great influence on health, and that people should be careful to know which aspects and conjunctions of them might be favourable or hurtful to their respective constitutions, and that they should choose such habitations as their stars* directed. He informs us also, that we ought to be particularly mindful of our health every climacterical or seventh year, for which he gravely assigns the following reason, *viz.* because Saturn, a malignant planet, governs every seventh year of our lives; and as he is an enemy to our vital spirits, and ready to introduce some bad change into the animal oeconomy, it is our business, by prudence ‡ and

* Ut ad quamcunque regionem potissimum inhabitandam et excolendam tuum sidus te admonuerit, eandem tibi deligendam esse arbitreris. Part. 1. cap. 29.

‡ Si quæ vero ex infaustis aspectibus pericula impendent, tuum est arte et prudentia illa prævenire. Part. 1. cap. 29.

art

art to prevent the danger with which we are menaced.

Our author, however, in other places of his book, makes amends for amufing people with fuch fancies, by recommending cleanlinefs in their perfons, cloaths, houfes, and furniture; becaufe, fays he, " naftinefs ftops " the perfpiration, breeds vermin, and over- " fpreads the body with the itch, and other " cutaneous eruptions."

Another of his valuable rules, is, that men of letters fhould apply themfelves to clofe and ferious ftudy only in the morning, but to entertaining books in the afternoon; and that they fhould indulge their tafte for contemplation and reading more in winter than in a hot fummer, which waftes their fpirits.

He obferves in the third place, that thofe who gratify a fretful and cenforious humour, and are ever ready to find fault*, and think

* This difpofition to find fault difcovers alfo a poor and low genius, directly oppofite to that of Longinus, who declares exprefly, that he took no pleafure in the blemifhes of any author: αὐτὸς καὶ ἥκιϛα τοῖς πταίσμασιν ἀρισκομένος. Sect. 33.

to raife their own reputation by depreciating others, foon confume their vital balfam, and frequently meet with a premature death.

The next in order of time to Marfilius Ficinus is Antonius Gazius of Padua, whofe book *concerning health and long life*, was publifhed *an.* 1491, by the title of *Corona florida;* but, with the moft diligent fearch in feveral libraries, I could not find it.

Platina Cremonensis addreffed a fhort treatife on health to Cardinal Roverella, *an.* 1529. He was no phyfician, but copies principally from Celfus all that he recommends. I mention him here for being the firft (to the beft of my remembrance) who advifes tender people to chew * their food well, if they expect that the ftomach fhould digeft it; for how is it poffible, fays he, " that thofe who fwallow their meat whole, " fhould efcape crudities and eructations?"

* Thofe who have loft their teeth fhould be careful to have their meat cut very fmall, in order to facilitate their digeftion; and, for the fame reafon, old people fhould diminifh their folid, and increafe their liquid aliment.

C H A P.

CHAP. XIV.

Of Lewis Cornaro and some others, who were so very curious and nice in the care of their health as to weigh their aliment.

AFTER Platina came the celebrated Lewis Cornaro, a noble Venetian, who wrote an excellent treatise in praise of sobriety, from which I have made the following abstract.

The prevalence of custom, says he, is amazing, and frequently gets the better of our reason. Luxury has gained ground in Italy within my memory, and is now reputed honourable, tho' it has destroyed more people than either the sword or the pestilence.

How many, to my grief, have I seen of my friends, men of great capacities and noble dispositions, cut off in the flower of their age by intemperance; who, had they lived, would have been useful to their country, and an ornament to mankind! I myself pursued
the

the fame pernicious courfe, and would have perfifted in it, had not my tender conftitution, and weak ftomach, unable to bear excefs, thrown me into colics, pains of my fide, touches of the gout, a feverifhnefs and perpetual thirft, which hung about me from the thirty fifth year of my age to the fortieth, in defiance of the various remedies employed to remove them. My phyficians obferving that all their labour and skill was thrown away upon my infirm conftitution, told me frankly that there remained but one remedy more to fave my life, and that was a fober and regular diet, which might ftill reftore my health tho' reduced fo low; adding, that unlefs I entered upon it forthwith, I fhould in a few months put myfelf out of capacity to receive any benefit from it, and in a few months more I fhould be dead. Tho' they recommended the fame regularity to me fome time before to little purpofe, yet as I found my complaints increafing upon me, and as I had no inclination to die fo foon, I firmly refolved to follow their advice without

out lofs of time. A few days in this regular courfe convinced me that I had at laft found the right road, and a year put an end to all my former complaints, and reftored me to a perfect ftate of health.

To preferve this health, I not only continued my regular diet, which confifted in twelve ounces of folid food taken every day, including bread, yolks of eggs, flefh, fifh, &c. and fourteen ounces of liquids; but I was alfo careful to avoid heat, cold, fatigue, grief, watchings, and every other excefs that might hurt my health. It is true, I could not always efcape unlucky accidents, but I found by experience, that they had no very bad effect, where temperance in eating and drinking had been ftrictly obferved. The two following inftances confirm this truth: My brother, and fome more of my family, who did not lead the fame regular life I did, being greatly dejected at a law fuit carried on againft me, which, had I loft it, might have proved my ruin, fell a facrifice to their
melancholy

melancholy and intemperance; whereas I, who was principally concerned, enjoyed perfect health all the while, and lived to see my affairs brought to a happy conclusion. I was at another time overturned in a chariot, which was dragged by the horses a considerable way, and had my head and whole body much bruised, and one arm and one foot dislocated. My physicians advised bleeding and purging to prevent an inflammation; I told them, that if they would be pleased to reduce my foot and arm, I stood in no need of other helps, having no distempered humours to bring on defluxions. Thus I recovered without any other remedies, to the surprise of all my acquaintance.

Another truth of great moment I have also learned from experience, *viz.* that a regular method of living, long persisted in, cannot be altered without extream danger. It is now four years since my physicians and my family insisted upon my making some small addition to my food, alledging, that
as

as my age was advanced, and my strength impaired, I stood in need of more nourishment to support me. It was in vain to answer that, if my strength was impaired, my digestion by consequence must be weaker, and therefore my food should be rather diminished than increased. My remonstrance was not regarded, and I was forced to yield to their well meant importunities. Accordingly I increased my food to fourteen, and my drink to sixteen ounces; but I had not continued this addition above ten days, when, from being lively and chearful, I began to grow dull, low spirited, uneasy to myself, and troublesome to all about me; on the twelfth day I was seized with a pain in my side, which lasted twenty-two hours; then came on a fever, which continued thirty five days and nights, so that my life was despaired of. By God's mercy, however, and my old regimen, I recovered, and now at eighty three I enjoy a vigorous state of body and mind. I mount my horse from the level ground, I climb steep ascents with ease, eafe, and have lately wrote a comedy full of innocent mirth and raillery. When I return home, either from private bufinefs or from the fenate, I have eleven grand children, with whofe education, amufements, and fongs, I am greatly delighted; and I frequently fing with them, for my voice is clearer and ftronger now than ever it was in my youth. In fhort, I am in all refpects happy, and quite a ftranger to the doleful, morofe, dying life of lame, deaf, and blind old age, worn out with intemperance.

It remains only (fince a fober regular life is fo happy in its confequences) that I exhort and befeech all men of fenfe and refolution to poffefs themfelves of this fource of health, more valuable than all the riches of the univerfe.

Leonardus Lessius, a learned Jefuit of Louvaine, who lived about the end of the fixteenth century, was fo much pleafed with Cornaro's treatife on fobriety, that purely to recommend it, he has written a book
intitled

intitled *Hygiasticon*, or *The true method of preserving life and health to extreme old age.* In this book he praises a sober life as the principal means of health. By a sober life he understands, that we should neither eat or drink more than what is necessary for our respective constitutions, in order to perform the functions of the mind with ease. Or, to be more particular, he says, that the proper measure of meat and drink for every individual, is such a quantity as his stomach will be able to digest perfectly well, and will be sufficient to support him under the employment of body or mind that providence has appointed for him. But to prevent mistakes with regard to what the stomach may be perfectly able to digest, and to what may be thought sufficient to support men under their respective occupations, he recommends the following rules:

First, He who eats or drinks such a quantity as renders him unfit for any exertion of the mind to which his profession calls him, has certainly exceeded, and ought to retrench. And he, who in bodily labour or exercise was active and nimble before meals, if he becomes heavy and dull after meals, has certainly transgressed; for the true end of eating and drinking is to refresh, and not to oppress the body.

Second, Tho' there cannot be a certain and invariable measure prescribed to all persons, because of the difference of ages, constitutions, and occupations; yet, generally speaking, to those who are old, or of a tender constitution, and live a sedentary life, twelve, thirteen, or fourteen ounces of solid food, including bread, flesh, fish, and eggs, together with an equal * quantity of drink, will be sufficient. And this rule has been verified by the experience chiefly of those whose proper employment has been study and meditation,

* In this he is mistaken, for the quantity of drink should exceed that of the solid food, in almost all circumstances of life.

Third

Third rule, THE quality * of people's food and drink is little to be regarded, if it is but plain, and such as common use has recommended, and does not particularly disagree with him who uses it, provided the quantity be properly adjusted.

Fourth rule, To cure you of your fondness for high living, consider these delicacies you sit down to, not as they appear on the table, but as they will be quickly altered after you have eat them; for the richer their flavour and taste is now, the more corrupted and acrimonious they will become in your body, and the more hurtful will be their consequences.

OUR author, in the *last* place, proves the advantage of sobriety by the experience of such as made trial of it, some of whom lived in the deserts, on bread, dates, sallad and water, to an hundred years and upwards.

* This rule is calculated for persons of a strong constitution only, but not for the puny or delicate.

Paul,

Paul, the hermit, fays he, died at the age of 115 years; of which he fpent near an hundred in the defert, living for the firft forty on dates and water only, and for the remaining time on bread and water, as Jerom teftifies. St. Anthony lived to 105, of which he paffed more than eighty in the wildernefs on bread and water, with the addition, at laft, of a little fallad, according to Athanafius. Arfenius, the preceptor of the emperor Arcadius, lived to 120, of which he fpent the firft fixty-five in the focial world, and the other fifty-five in the defert with great abftemioufnefs. And Epiphanius lived with equal aufterity to almoft 115.

But the moft recent example, and the moft to his purpofe, was that of Lewis Cornaro, who died at Padua when he was above 100 years old, *anno* 1566.

CHAP. XV.

Of the physicians who wrote on health in the sixteenth century before Sanctorius, viz. Thomas Philologus of Ravenna; Vidus Vidius; Hieronimus Cardanus; Alexander Trajanus Petronius; Levinus Lemnius; Jason Pratensis; Joannes Valverdus de Hamusco; Gulielmus Gratarolus; Henricus Ranzovius; Æmilius Dusus; Ferdinandus Eustachius, and Oddi de Oddis.

THOMAS PHILOLOGUS of Ravenna addressed to Pope Julius III. a treatise, " De vita ultra annos 120 protrahen- " da," which he professes to have collected with great labour and assiduity from the writings of the learned. He complains that voluptuousness and avarice had shortened the lives of the noble Venetians to such a degree, that whereas formerly several senators, every one at least an hundred years old, used to appear on the streets together, venerable by

by their white locks and rich robes; there was not one to be seen in our author's time who had reached ninety: He therefore recommends temperance and purity of manners, as the principal means to promote longevity. He recommends likewise a pure air to those who desire length of days, and is the first physician I know of, who censures the pernicious custom of having public burying places in populous cities, which taint the atmosphere with cadaverous steams, and frequently occasion fatal distempers. " I am asto-
" nished, continues he, that the moderns
" should approve of a practice, which the
" wisest nations of antiquity prohibited by
" the most solemn laws."

About the middle of the sixteenth century, Vidus Vidius, a Florentine, published a large volume on the preservation of the health of the body in general*, and of every member in particular, cleared (as he pre-

* De tuenda valetudine generatim libri sex, membratim libri quatuordecim.

tends)

tends) from all the errors both of the Greeks and the Arabians. He had been invited to Paris by Francis I. and taught phyſic there, during the life of that auguſt and munificent patron of learning; and after his death was called home *anno* 1557, and highly encouraged by Coſmus duke of Tuſcany.

In this performance concerning health, Vidius has ſo cloſely adhered to the theory of Galen, " without one inſtance from his " practice to enliven it," and is ſo full of the endleſs diſtinctions and diviſions of Avicenna, that there is not one new or entertaining precept to be met with in his whole work, tho' he was undoubtedly a man of great literature.

The famous Hieronimus Cardanus is another of our voluminous writers on the ſubject of health, but has not added many rules of great importance to thoſe mentioned by former phyſicians. He was deſcended from a noble family in Milan, and born at Pavia (whither his mother fled from the plague)
anno

anno 1500. He is magnified by some for his extensive knowledge in the sciences, and was sent for from Italy, as far as Scotland, to cure the Archbishop of St. Andrews, which he did, of a dangerous illness: But others hold him in small esteem. His book on health and long life is reckoned one of his best performances; but he is a very unequal writer. He takes upon him to blame Hippocrates and Galen in things wherein all the world think them to be right, except himself. He exclaims, for example, against using any exercise that can fatigue a man in the smallest degree, or throw him into the most gentle sweat, or in the least accelerate his respiration; and gravely observes, that trees live longer than animals, because they never stir from their places: He maintains that Galen's treatise on health is full of mistakes; and as a proof of this, observes, that Galen himself died at seventy seven, which cannot properly be called old age. " Poor Cardan did not then foresee that this

" ob-

" objection (suppose it to have any weight)
" might one day be urged more justly a-
" gainst himself who died at seventy-five."

But to do him justice: He was the first who gave us marks or symptoms of longevity, which when they meet in the same person, are, for the most part, true indications of long life, *viz.* first to be descended from a long-lived family, at least by one of the parents. Secondly, to be of a chearful easy disposition, undisturbed by any irksome care or disquietude of mind: And, thirdly, to be naturally a long and sound sleeper.

The quantity of aliment which he recommends is very small, after the manner of Cornaro, whom he admires much: And though the abstemiousness which he enjoins would ill agree with persons of an active and laborious life, and soon exhaust their strength, and render them useless; yet to people of a delicate constitution, full of care and disquietudes, or confined to a sedentary life,

life, the meaſure of aliment which he allows, under the reſtrictions annexed to it, is perhaps the beſt rule of health in his book.

THE true meaſure of eating and drinking, ſays he, is, " that a man ſhall feel no ful-
" neſs or weight in his ſtomach, but ſhall
" be able to walk or write immediately af-
" ter meals, in caſe either ſhould be neceſ-
" ſary; that his ſleep ſhall not be diſturbed
" or ſhortened by his ſupper; that he ſhall
" have neither head-ach, nor bad taſte in
" his mouth next morning; and that he
" ſhall awake refreſhed and chearful after
" his night's reſt."

HIS fourth book on old age is the moſt entertaining part of the whole performance. Who can forbear being pleaſed with his chearful and ſocial diſpoſition at ſeventy-three, and with his lively hope which he ſtretches beyond the grave? For my part, ſays he, " I am more joyful now than ever
" I was in my youth. I ſhall die, 'tis true,
" and

" and leave my friends behind me, but I
" shall find others where I go, and I know
" that thofe who are left behind will quick-
" ly follow me."

Soon after the death of Carden, Alexander Trajanus Petronius publifhed his book concerning the aliment of the Romans, and the prefervation of their health, which he dedicates to Pope Gregory XIII. In it he treats of the fituation, air, winds, waters and healthy feafons of Rome; and alfo of the food, folemn fafts, and epidemical ailments of the Romans. This book is written with great judgment and accuracy, and is an excellent model for any phyfician who inclines to do the fame good office to the city in which he refides.

Several Authors, befides thofe already named, have written upon the confervation of health in the fixteenth century, before the celebrated Sanctorius. I fhall mention the moft eminent among them, for the fake of the curious, who may have a mind to confult

sult them, but shall not dwell long upon their works; and perhaps there have been but few improvements or variations in this branch of physic*, from the times of the Greeks and Arabians, down to Sanctorius, who flourished in the close of this century.

These authors stand in order of time, as follows:

Levinus Lemnius was born in Zeland *anno* 1505, and practised physic for several years with good success: But having had the misfortune to lose his wife, entered into holy orders; in consequence of which, his writings partake both of morality and physic. His exhortation to lead a virtuous life, in order to secure the health both of body and mind, sets forth, that " health is preserved " by temperance in eating and drinking, " wherein excess is indecent, as well as per-

---

* Les regles pour la confervation de la fanté, et ce qu'il y a à dire fur les qualitez et le choix des alimens, etant un fujet où il y a le moins de variations depuis les tems les plus anciens jufqu' au nôtre. Le Clerc, Plan de l'hiftoire de la medicine, pag. 3.

" nicious;

"nicious; and by a moderation in all the
"other articles which Galen* calls the
"preservatives of health, but moderns call
"the *Six Non-naturals*, not that they are
"by any means *unnatural*, but because they
"are not within the body like our blood
"and humours, though they have influence
"enough to hurt or destroy it, when a bad
"use is made of them."

JASON PRATENSIS a Zelander, likewise wrote a treatise *De tuenda sanitate*, anno 1538. He regrets that his many avocations, and a nine months illness did not permit him to write up to the idea which he had of his subject. He is, nevertheless, a lively writer, and a good classical scholar, which makes his book very entertaining, tho' it has little or nothing new with respect to health.

ANTONIUS FUMANELLUS VERONENSIS wrote *De senum regimine*, anno 1540; where-

* Lemnius did not advert, that Galen was himself the person who introduced the appellation *Non-natural*.

in he declares, "that he follows the sen-
"timents of Hippocrates and Galen."

JOANNES VALVERDUS de HAMUSCO, a Spaniard, published his treatise *De animi et corporis sanitate ad Hieronimum Verallum Cardinalem*, anno 1552. It is short, but written with a great deal of good sense; and as the author had an opportunity of travelling into distant countries, his observations enabled him to add this new rule to the old ones, *viz.* That it is necessary to diversify our method of living, according to the nature of the climate in which we may chance to reside. "When I was in Scotland * (says he) I could not forbear eating more frequently than I used to do in my own country."

GUILIELMUS GRATAROLUS a Piedmontese, published his book *De literatorum, et*

* Cum ego, qui meridionalem magis incolo regionem, apud Scotos agerem, non poteram me continere, quin pluribus vicibus cibum assumerem, quam antea essem consuetus.

eorum

eorum qui magistratum gerunt, conservanda valetudine, anno 1555. He inculcates a moderation in the five following articles; namely, eating, drinking, labour, sleep, and concubinage; and affirms, that those great fathers of physick, Hippocrates and Galen, have recommended the same moderation, as the principal means to secure health.

HENRICUS RANZOVIUS, a Danish nobleman, wrote *De conservanda valetudine, in privatum liberorum suorum usum, anno* 1573. The first and most valuable precept in his book, is, to worship and serve God, and to pray to him for health; " for (continues " he) tho' the stars have their influence, it " it will be always true, that

Astra valent aliquid, plus pia vota valent.

ÆMILIUS DUSUS composed his book *De tuenda valetudine ad Carolum Sabaudiæ Ducem, anno* 1582; but copies Galen in every thing that is material.

Lastly, FERDINANDUS EUSTACHIUS, son to the famous anatomist Bartholomæus Eustachius,

Euſtachius, wrote *De vitæ humanæ a facultate medica prorogatione*, dedicated to pope Sixtus V. *anno* 1589. This author has indeed refuted many arguments alledged to prove that the medical art is of no uſe in prolonging life; but is quite ſilent as to the means by which that end may be attained.

It would make this compilation too tedious to take notice here of all theſe authors that have advanced ſome fanciful ſpeculations on the different proportions of food at different meals, which they imagined to be of great importance to health; ſuch, for inſtance, as Oddi de Oddis, who, in his treatiſe *De cænæ et prandii portione*, publiſhed *anno* 1570, aſſerts, that people ſhould make ſupper their fulleſt, and dinner their lighteſt meal.

C H A P.

CHAP. XVI.

Of Sanctorius——His useful discovery of insensible perspiration, and observations upon it.——Of those physicians who adapted his method to their respective climates, as Dodart in France, Keil in Britain, De Gorter in Holland, Rogers and Robinson in Ireland, and Linen in Carolina.——Of their aphorisms.——Of the inhalation of moisture from the air, where mention is made of Doctor Jones.

SANCTORIUS SANCTORIUS was born in Istria, a territory in Italy belonging to the Venetians; and studied at Padua, where he afterwards became a celebrated professor. He was from thence invited to practise physick at Venice, for the benefit of the citizens; and tho' he left the university, yet the republic, as a mark of esteem, continued his salary to his death, which happened *anno* 1636, in the 75th year of his age.

HE opened a new scene in physick, to which physicians and philosophers were in a great

great measure strangers before his time; and, upon experiments, made with amazing diligence and assiduity for thirty years, has established several laws of *insensible perspiration*, or aphorisms, of which some are so useful toward the preservation of health, that it will be necessary to take notice of them; distinguishing, at the same time, and selecting such as are founded in nature and confirmed by experience, from those which were apparently suggested by the false theory of physick that still prevailed in his days. And it will be no incurious entertainment to compare his experiments made *by weighing the body*, with the observations of the ancients made on *temperance* and *exercise*, and to mark the harmony which subsists between them. Both have, by different means, established the same maxims for the conservation of health, so that his experiments and their observations mutually illustrate and confirm each other.

That Galen was acquainted with the insensible perspiration in general, is evident from

from his own words: "This excrementitious vapour*, says he, is expelled through small orifices, which the Greeks call pores, dispersed all over the body, and especially over the skin, partly by sweat, and partly by insensible perspiration, (ἄδηλος αἰσθήσι διαπνοὴ) which escapes the sight, and is known to few." And all the physicians from his time down to the close of the sixteenth century, had only a general and vague idea of transpiration, and may be said to have just known that there was such a discharge. But to Sanctorius was reserved the honour of calculating the true quantity of this perspiration by the balance; of shewing that it is larger than all the sensible evacuations taken together; and of settling rules by which it may be rendered highly subservient to health.

As the difference of climates makes a considerable difference in the quantity of perspi

---

* De sanit. tuend. lib. 2. cap. 12. sub. finem.

ration,

ration, phyficians of feveral countries have thought it worth while to repeat the ftatical experiments which Sanctorius made, in order to compare the fenfible and infenfible evacuations of the human body in their refpective climates with thofe in Italy.

The firft was doctor Dodart in France, a learned, inquifitive and confcientious phyfician, who began his experiments *anno* 1668, and continued them with little interruption for thirty-three * years.

The next was the ingenious Dr. James Keil in Great Britain, who, *anno* 1718, publifhed his tables of obfervations, made without any interruption for one whole year; together with feveral trials which he had made at different times, during the ten preceeding years.

After him came De Gorter in Holland, who printed the firft edition of his book,

* Hift. de l'acad. des fciences, *anno* 1707. Eloge de M. Dodart. Note, His medicina Stat. Gallic. is printed with Noguez's explanation of Sanctorius's aphorifms.

con-

concerning infensible perspiration, *anno* 1728, and his second edition *anno* 1736. From Keil and De Gorter, both men of a clear mathematical discernment, we learn to correct the calculations of Sanctorius, which otherwise might mislead the inhabitants of a colder region. And indeed De Gorter, (under the direction of Boerhaave) by his experiments and judicious reflections, has thrown a great deal of light upon this subject.

THEN came out the performance of a curious gentleman in Ireland, who having read Dr. Lister's Sanctorius; and having afterwards found that Keil, in his treatise on perspiration, made the insensible discharge in Britain much less than that in Italy, resolved to go himself through a course of statical experiments for one year; and in his letter to Dr. Rogers very modestly says, " some " irregular observations, from the 20th No- " vember 1720, to the 1st of May 1721, " I made, scarce worth mentioning; but af- " terwards I formed tables something more
" regular.

" regular. If I had thought that they
" fhould be made public, I had been more
" careful and correct."

In another paragraph he fays, " not hav-
" ing fufficient room in the fpace of a quar-
" ter of a fheet, I was obliged to leave
" out entirely thofe which treated of diet
" and exercife, and even thofe of ftools,
" except for two months."

This performance appeared firft with Dr. Rogers's ingenious " effay on epidemical " difeafes, *anno* 1734." And tho' the author of the experiments had fuch an humble opinion of his own performance: Yet in the doctor's hands it became a finifhed piece, which, as he fays, " brings the ftatical me-
" dicine to as great a certainty in Ireland,
" as it ever arrived to in Italy, under the
" laborious endeavours of the moft experi-
" enced Sanctorius." This is very wonderful, confidering that the Irifh *Country Gentleman* employed fewer months in making his experiments, than the *Italian phyfician* did years.

years. But be that as it will, the learned gentleman's experiments and notes, and the subsequent aphoristical rules (from whatever source they were drawn) are both ingenious and useful.

We have, in the ninth * volume of the philosophical transactions, Dr. John Linen's statical experiments, made at Charlestoun in South Carolina for one whole year, from March 1740 to March 1741, with the laudable view of finding out the cause of the *epidemic distempers,* which return regularly in that country at *stated seasons.* But general tables, made in a very different climate, without any aphorisms drawn from them, cannot contribute much to the preservation of health in this country.

The last performance relating to statical experiments, that has come to my hands, is doctor Bryan Robinson's dissertation on *the food and discharges of the human body,* published *anno* 1748: But his numerous calculations, and refined manner of reasoning, are

---

* The origin. transact. and not the abridgments.

above

above the comprehenſion of common readers, and conſequently do not correſpond well with my preſent purpoſe. To give a ſpecimen of the latter; in page 77, he expreſſes himſelf in the following words, "anger and joy increaſe, and fear and ſadneſs leſſen, both perſpiration and urine. The ſoul which has great power over the body, by virtue of the æther, when it is made uneaſy by the paſſion of anger, raiſes a ſtrong vibrating motion in the æther, within its ſenſorium, which motion is propagated thro' the nerves to all parts of the body."

But to return to Sanctorius. This phyſician has divided his book of aphoriſms into ſeven ſections. In the firſt he makes ſome general obſervations on weighing the inſenſible perſpiration: In the ſecond he treats of air and water: In the third, of meat and drink: In the fourth, of ſleep and wakefulneſs: In the fifth, of exerciſe and reſt: In the ſixth, of concubinage; and in the ſeventh, of the paſſions and affections of the mind.

I

I shall transcribe promiscuously from Sanctorius, and the other authors on statical experiments above mentioned, such maxims as conduce most to the preservation of health; and shall range them under their respective sections, according to the method of Sanctorius.

SECTION I. Of weighing the insensible Perspiration.

1. INSENSIBLE perspiration, by the pores of the skin, and by the breath, is greater than all the sensible evacuations joined together; for, if a strong healthy man, who uses moderate exercise, in good weather, eats and drinks eight pound weight in a day, he will discharge five of them by insensible perspiration; and we are more relieved by a free insensible perspiration, than by all the sensible evacuations united.

2. HEALTH continues firm as long as the body returns daily to the same weight by insensible perspiration; it begins to decline

cline when the body is reduced to the fame weight by a larger difcharge of ftool or urine than ufual; but if the body does not recover the fame weight in fome days, either by infenfible perfpiration, or by fome fenfible evacuation, the approach of a fever, or fome bad ftate of health, is to be apprehended.

3. THE purer our perfpiration is, or the lefs mingled with any fenfible moifture, the more wholefome it is.

4. To feel the body heavy, when it is actually light on the balance, fhews a worfe ftate of health, than to feel it weighty when it is really fo. On the other hand, to feel it light, when it is really heavy on the balance, fhews an excellent ftate of health.

5. PAIN of the head, or of any other part of the body, diminifhes the perfpiration.

6. IT is a fure fign of good health when a perfon can climb up an afcent with pleafure.

7. LENIENT

7. Lenient gentle purges do not lessen the perspiration, but only discharge an useless load; whereas strong purges hinder it, and are hurtful in many respects.

8. The bodies of young healthy men, who live moderately, grow weightier every month, by two or three pounds, and sometimes, towards the end of the month, they feel a weight in their heads, or a weariness; but soon return to their usual standard again, by a discharge of turbid urine, or some other evacuation.

9. The principal causes which stop perspiration are, a cold damp air; hard viscid food; disuse of exercise; fasting; terror; restless nights; and an increase of any sensible evacuation.

10. There is a great deal more perspired in youth than in old age; and the quantity of perspiration differs according to different constitutions, ways of living, climates and seasons.

11. A

11. A very material question follows, *viz.* How shall a man fix upon the precise quantity of perspiration, which will secure to him a permanent state of good health to old age? Sanctorius says, that he may secure it by the following experiment:

Let him, after a plentiful supper, compute how much he has discharged by insensible perspiration in the space of twelve hours: Suppose, for example, that he has lost fifty ounces; let him again weigh himself some morning, after having taken no supper at all, nor committed any excess in his preceeding dinner; and then calculate how much he has thrown off by insensible perspiration; suppose twenty ounces. This being known, let him chuse such a diet, and use such exercise, and such a moderation in the other *Non-naturals*, as will bring his insensible perspiration to a medium between fifty and twenty ounces, *i. e.* to thirty five ounces every day, and by this method he may

preserve

serve his health to an hundred years. *But this is a tedious method, which no man will submit to, and it is plain the author himself did not; for he died in the 75th year of his age.*

Keil says that the true rule of diet to every man, is his natural undepraved appetite. By this monitor he is directed, without the trouble of weighing himself, to the exact quantity of meat and drink which he ought to take in; for nature never craves more, nor is easy with less, than what is proper for her.

De Gorter, in answer to this question, says, " I have found, by repeated trials with
" the balance, that if a healthy man eats and
" drinks as much as is sufficient to satisfy
" his hunger and thirst; and rises from ta-
" ble without quite filling his stomach, or,
" with some remaining appetite; his daily
" discharges will be equal to what he has
" taken in; or, in other words, he will en-
" joy a good state of health; because health
" principally depends upon such an equali-
" ty."

" In

"In order therefore to secure a constant state of good health, continues he, a man should be careful to use such exercise, and such a moderation in the other means of life, as will excite this natural appetite of hunger and thirst every day; and then should satisfy it with plain wholesome meat and drink in the temperate method above recommended."

This is the proper answer to the question of Sanctorius, which every man's own experience may verify with little trouble.

Sect. II. Of Air and Water.

1. In a cold, pure, healthy air, the perspiration is indeed obstructed; but the fibres are strengthened, and the matter retained is neither dangerous nor painful; whereas, in a damp impure air, the perspiration is stopped, the fibres relaxed but not strengthened, and the matter retained is both bad and troublesome.

2. The perspiration is obstructed by any air which is too cold, too moist, or very tempestuous.

3. The air of a city is generally worse than that of the country, being grosser, from the steams of the inhabitants; and more apt to pall the appetite.

4. Cold air, and a cold bath, warm robust bodies, and make them feel lighter to themselves; but infirm bodies feel themselves colder and heavier from them; and the more suddenly the cold comes, the more it hurts.

5. A cool and pleasant gale does more hurt to bodies overheated, than either air, or water extremely cold; for the former obstructs and relaxes, which makes the body heavy; whereas the latter, tho' it obstructs for a while, yet strengthens at the same time, and soon makes the body feel lighter.

6. Swimming in cold water, after violent exercise, is pleasant but pernicious.

7. Fanning

7. Fanning stops the perspiration, and makes the head hot and heavy.

8. Continual rain is more unwholesome than continued dry weather, because it makes the body heavier.

9. A man is more apt to complain of weariness in summer than in winter, not from any greater weight of his body, (which by the balance is about three pound lighter) but because his fibres are relaxed, and weaker in a warm air.

10. Strong people perspire most in the summer days, and in the winter nights; and an obstructed perspiration which disposes the body to a malignant fever in summer, does little harm in winter, because the perspirable matter is more acrid in hot weather than in cold.

11. Of all the seasons, the autumn is the most unhealthy, because the perspirable fluid is both obstructed, and apt to grow putrid; but

but it cannot hurt him whom the coldnefs of that feafon fhall find well cloathed; who ufes a proper diet; and whofe body confequently continues nearly of the fame weight as before.

12. Those who lay afide their winter garments too early in the fpring; and put them on too late in autumn; will often have fevers in fummer, aud defluxions in winter.

13. The perfpiration is as large from a good fire in winter, as from the fun in fummer.

Sect. III.   Of Meat and Drink.

1. The body perfpires little, while the ftomach is too full, or quite empty.

2. A full diet is hurtful to thofe who ufe very little exercife, but indifpenfably neceffary to fuch as ufe a great deal of exercife which is not violent.

3. If you know what quantity * of food you ought to take daily, and can adjust your exercise to it, you know how to preserve your health to old age.

4. That sort of food, of which the weight is not felt in the stomach, nourishes best, and perspires most freely. And that quantity is most wholesome, which, after meals, leaves the body as nimble and active as if one had eat nothing.

5. He who being hungry, goes to bed without any supper, will perspire but little. And if he does so frequently, will be apt to fall into a fever.

6. The flesh of young animals; and good mutton; and wheat bread properly leavened, or mixt with a due quantity of barm and salt, and well baked; are excellent sorts of food, light and easy of digestion.

7. The body feels heavier after four ounces of any strong food that nourishes

* This aphorism, and several more, are borrowed from Hippocrates.

much, such as pork, eel, or any fat flesh or fish, than after six of food that affords but little nourishment, as tender fresh fish, chickens, and small birds; for where the digestion is difficult, the perspiration is slow.

8. Unusual fasting renders the body too light, and frequently repeated brings on a bad state of health.

9. The body becomes more heavy and uneasy after six pounds taken in at one meal, than after eight taken at three meals; and he destroys himself by degrees who makes but one meal in the day, let him eat much or little.

10. He who eats more than he can digest, is nourished less than he ought to be, and consequently emaciated.

11. To eat immediately after any immoderate exercise of body or mind is bad; for a body fatigued perspires little.

12. Every

12. Every body has its particular latitude, that is, its vessels may be stretched to a certain degree, and yet restore themselves. Four pounds of meat and drink is as much, or more than some constitutions can well bear; whereas others can take in eight pounds without any inconvenience.

13. A man's common diluting drink at meals should be double the quantity of the solid food he eats.

14. Good wine, moderately drank, assists digestion, and increases the perspiration.

Sect. IV. Of Sleep and Wakefulness.

1. Sanctorius asserts, that strong healthy persons often perspire fifty ounces in seven hours of sound sleep, and, generally, double the quantity of what they perspire in the same number of hours when awake. But by Keil's tables, and De Gorter's reiterated experiments, it is evident that our nocturnal perspiration rarely rises to sixteen ounces; and that in England and Holland men perspire more in the day than in the night. We find

find, however, notwithstanding this great difference in the quantity perspired in different climates, that sound sleep is equally refreshing in all countries, and that it not only promotes the nocturnal perspiration, which would be much less in a wakeful state, but likewise greatly increases our strength and spirits.

2. After a good night's sleep, the body feels lighter, both from the increase of strength which it receives, and from the quantity of matter which it throws off.

3. Those accidents which prevent sleep, are found also to obstruct the perspiration, which is much diminished by a restless night.

4. The perspiration is obstructed more by a cool southerly air when we are asleep, than by any intense cold when we are awake.

5. A change of bed commonly diminishes the perspiration; for things which we are

are not accustomed to, tho' perhaps better in their own nature, seldom agree with us.

6. STRETCHING and yawning after sleep increase the perspiration.

7. THE perspiration being copious in time of sleep, and hindered from flying off by the bed clothes, sick persons communicate their distempers to the healthy who ly with them; and even the healthy infect the healthy with any bad humours which they have about them.

8. We know that we have slept sufficiently, when in the morning we find our understanding clear, and our body active and lively.

9. BY too much sleep the body becomes cold, dull and heavy.

10. THE perspiration is obstructed more, and we catch cold much sooner, by throwing off our blankets in our sleep, than by throwing off our clothes when we are awake.

11. A

11. A moderate glafs of good wine induces fleep, and increafes the perfpiration, but drank to excefs, leffens both.

Sect. V. Of Exercife and Reft.

1. The body perfpires much more when it lyes quiet in bed, than when it toffes and tumbles there.

2. By moderate exercife the whole body becomes lighter and more lively; the mufcles and ligaments are cleanfed from every foulnefs, and the matter to be difcharged by perfpiration is prepared for it.

3. If after fupper one lyes ten hours in bed, he will perfpire freely the whole time; but if he lyes longer, both the fenfible evacuations and the infenfible perfpiration will immediately be diminifhed.

4. Violent exercife of body and mind perfifted in, brings on an early old age, and a premature death.

5. Exercise is then moſt wholeſome, when, after having digeſted our food twice in the day, our body returns nearly to its uſual weight before the next meals.

6. Riding on horſeback increaſes the perſpiration rather of the parts above, than below the waiſt; and an eaſy pace is much more wholeſome than a hard trot: But to ſuch conſumptive or infirm perſons as are fatigued more by riding on horſeback than in ſome eaſy carriage, the former cannot be ſo proper as the latter, becauſe their ſtrength ſhould be recruited, and not exhauſted by exerciſe.

7. To ride hard over a rough road, in an ill hung coach or chaiſe, is the moſt violent of all exerciſes, which not only precipitates the perſpiration, being yet crude, but alſo hurts the ſolid parts of the body, and particularly the kidneys. Leaping is in like manner an unhealthy exerciſe, on the ſame account.

8. To

8. To be carried a little way in a sedan chair, or horse litter, or barge, does not increase the perspiration so much as walking does; but such sorts of motion, if properly continued, are very healthful, and dispose the body to a free perspiration.

9. Moderate dancing promotes perspiration, and is a healthful exercise.

10. The principal and most useful sorts of exercise within doors are tennis, handball, dumb-bell, dancing, fencing, and shittle-cock*. The best without doors are walking, bowling, riding in wheel machines or on horseback †.

11. When the perspiration is defective, the remedy is exercise.

Sect. VI. *Of concubinage.*

1. Both extremes of excess and abstinence obstruct the perspiration; but much more excess.

---

* To which should be added (especially where a good digestion is wanted) a chamber-horse or tremoussoir.

† The golf also should be practised, where a proper field or bare common can be met with at a reasonable distance.

2. By excess the stomach is weakened, the natural heat diminished, and the perspiration obstructed; whence follow indigestion, flatulencies, palpitations at the heart, gravel in the kidneys, catarrhs, and loss of memory.

3. Excess is more pernicious in summer than in winter, because the digestion being weaker in that season, is more difficult to be recovered, and the perspiration being more free, any stoppage of it is sooner felt.

4. Next to the stomach, the eyes suffer most by this excess, which is very apt to bring a Gutta Serena.

5. One knows that concubinage has done no hurt, when after a subsequent sleep no languors or weariness are felt, but the breath is free and easy, the urine of a good colour and consistence, and the whole man brisk and lively.

5. Old men are destroyed by indulgences of this kind, which render them heavier, weaker, and colder.

Sect. VII.

Sect. VII. Of the Paffions.

1. Among the paffions, anger and joy increafe the perfpiration, but fear and grief diminifh it; and the other paffions have the fame effects in proportion as they partake of the oppofite natures of thofe mentioned.

2. Hence timorous and melancholic perfons are fubject to obftructions in the bowels, to hard tumours in feveral parts of the body, to hypochondriacal diforders, and to profufe cold fweats; for nothing makes the perfpiration more languid than fear and grief, and nothing makes it more free than chearfulnefs of fpirit.

3. The diftempers which arife from the affections of the mind, are not conquered by medicines, but by contrary affections; tho proper medicines, to promote or diminifh the perfpiration, may be of fome fervice at the fame time.

4. Moderate joy difcharges only what is fuperfluous by perfpiration; but immoderate,

rate, and sometimes sudden joy, discharges also what is useful; and, if it continues long, prevents sleep and dissipates the strength.

5. Food of easy digestion, which increases the perspiration, causes chearfulness; but that which is hard to digest and lessens perspiration, causes melancholy.

6. Those who perspire too much, and waste themselves through the violence of passion, do not recover their former healthy state so easily as those who perspire too much from strong exercise.

7. Those who are eager to win at play ought to play but seldom; for if they win frequently, their joy will not let them sleep, which impairs their health; and if they lose often, their grief will obstruct the perspiration.

8. A moderate victory conduces more to health than a glorious one; for every extreme is an enemy to nature.

9. Any

9. Any violent affection of the mind is more hurtful to health, than any violent motion of the body.

10. To vary our paffions, *i. e.* To be fometimes angry or chearful, and fometimes fearful or fad, produces, upon the whole, a more healthful fort of perfpiration, than to be always under the influence of the fame paffion, tho' ever fo agreeable.

11. Hence a man can purfue any ftudy better under a variety of different paffions, than under the continuance of one, or without any paffion at all. A man, for example, cannot purfue any bufinefs above one hour, if no paffion engages him in it; or, if he is engaged by one paffion only, he cannot attend to it clofely above four hours; but under a rotation of paffions, as at games of hazard, where joy for gain is interchanged with grief for lofs, a man may hold out many hours.

Having

Having thus seen that a large stream of subtile vapours perpetually flows from the human body, it will be proper, on the other hand, to know that there is a new supply of moisture constantly attracted from the air, which, if moderate, is of great use towards the preservation of health, by keeping all the parts of the body soft, pliant, and fit for motion. This attraction helps us to explain why the quantity of perspiration should, from the greater moisture of the air, be less in winter than in summer; in rainy weather than in dry; and in the night than in the day. From it also we learn the necessity of living in a clean house, and in a pure dry air, and of covering our bodies well in the night, in order to enjoy a comfortable state of health.

Our inhalation from the circumambient air is very considerable, as we see by Keil's observations on his fourth table, which shew that in one night, while he was asleep, his body had attracted eighteen ounces of moisture. It was likewise observed by Dr. Linen,

nen, upon a change of weather from clear and dry to moist and cloudy, that the inspiration exceeded the perspiration. And Dr. Robinson found, upon the like alteration of weather, that his body grew more weighty, tho' he had taken less aliment.

But the most valuable treatise I have seen upon this subject, is the inaugural dissertation of Dr. Jones on the resorbent veins that accompany and correspond with the numberless arteries through which the perspiration is discharged. This physician had his education in the university of Edinburgh, and his first essay plainly shews what extraordinary advances an ingenious young man may make there, as well in the curious as in the useful branches of physic. And indeed, considering the great endowments of the present professors, their assiduous attention to their respective departments, and the advantage of a magnificent infirmary, where, in the presence of the students, physic and surgery are practised with uncommon success, and the reason of that practice explained ed from the nature and construction of the human body; I may venture to say that, *for medical knowledge*, the university of Edinburgh is not inferior to any in Europe.

CHAP XVII.

Of foreign writers concerning health after Sanctorius, viz. Roder. a Fonseca, Aurel. Anselmus, Franc. Ranchinus, Rodolph. Goclenius, Joan. Johnstonus, Petrus Lotichius, and Bernardin Ramazzini.

THE human body, having been originally contrived with infinite wisdom, performed its functions perfectly * well at all times, by means of those materials and movements with which it was furnished by the hand of the creator, tho' man was ignorant of the mechanism by which his own actions were directed, and many ages had elapsed before physicians could give any rational account of the animal oeconomy.

* A nullo quidem edocta natura, citraque disciplinam ea quæ conveniunt, efficit. Hipp. de morb. vulg. lib. 6. sect 5. aphor. 2.

It

It is true that Hippocrates, Galen, and others among the ancients, by diligently observing the operations of nature, and following her steps, have given us excellent practical rules concerning health; but their knowledge of the animal machine was defective, and their reasoning obscure.

The nature and quantity of insensible perspiration, discovered by Sanctorius, opened to physicians a much clearer view into the reasons and grounds of the rules of health established by the ancients than they had before.

But after Harvey published his glorious discovery of the circulation of the blood about the year 1628, a flood of light (if I may use that expression) was poured upon the animal oeconomy, which at once dispelled the darkness wherein it was before involved, demonstrated the wonderful wisdom of God in the construction of our frame, and established a new and rational theory in physic, worthy of the human intellect. This discovery proved evidently from the mechanism of the body, that the rules of health, built upon the observation of the antients, and the experiments of Sanctorius, were rational and well founded; and every man that understood the structure of his own body, was convinced of the expediency of observing them.

Thus the theory of health was greatly improved by the knowledge of the circulation, but the practical rules for preserving health underwent few alterations, having been founded in nature, and confirmed by the experience of ages long before that discovery.

I shall touch very lightly on some of the foreign authors who have treated of health in the seventeenth and eighteenth centuries, and then take notice of the British writers upon the same subject.

And here it is necessary to remark that several authors, who make no extraordinary figure in a *history of health*, because they added ed few, or perhaps no new rules to thofe eftablifhed by their predeceffors, are neverthelefs very valuable, confidered fingly, and may be of great utility to thofe who read them, by exhibiting a plain and effectual method to fecure a found conftitution. For it is furely of fmall importance to fuch as value health, and are willing to obferve the precepts that lead to it, whether thefe precepts are old or new, provided they be clear and pertinent.

RODERICUS a FONSECA, a Portuguefe of Lifbon, principal profeffor of phyfic in the univerfity of Pifa, and afterwards of Padua, publifhed, *anno* 1602, a treatife *De tuenda valetudine et producenda vita, ad Ferdinandum Medicem magnum Hetruriæ ducem;* in which he propofes to conduct the infirm as well as the robuft to a healthy old age. He declares that he collected his rules from the Greeks and the Arabians, but more particularly from Galen's fix books of preferving health. The fix things neceffary to human life are by him called the *fix inftru-*

ments * by which health is maintained. He was undoubtedly a man of learning and good fenfe, and has made a judicious collection of ufeful precepts from the antients.

Aurelius Anselmus of Mantua publifhed his *Gerocomica, five de fenum regimine,* anno 1606. He was chief phyfician to the duke of Mantua, tho' but a young man, and declares that he writes concerning old age, becaufe it is the only period of life in which a man may be properly faid to live, as it excells all other periods in underftanding and prudence. Old people are much obliged to him for his good opinion of them; but it is obvious that his rules to direct them muft be grounded upon the experience of others. To him fhall be fubjoined,

Franciscus Ranchinus, profeffor at Montpelier, who alfo publifhed a *Gerocomice de fenum confervatione, et fenilium morbo-*

---

* Inftrumenta illa, cum quibus fervatur fanitas, diligenter explicanda funt : hæc vero funt numero fex, aër, cibus, potus, &c.

rum curatione, anno 1625. It is a very judicious performance, and shews the author to have been a man of erudition and good understanding.

RODOLPHUS GOCLENIUS, a German physician, dedicated a treatise *De vita proroganda* to Frederic count Palatine of the Rhine, and Otho Landgrave of Hesse, *anno* 1608. He collected his materials from several historians, philosophers and physicians, antient and modern; and has illustrated his medical precepts with historical facts, which renders them both useful and entertaining.

CLAUDIUS DEODATUS, physician to the bishop of Basil, published, *anno* 1628, his *Pantheon Hygiasticon Hippocraticum Hermeticum, de hominis vita ad centum et viginti annos salubriter producenda*. But notwithstanding the great expectation which he raises by his high title, his book (full of the vain boasts of the chymists) is calculated rather to obtrude particular *nostrums*, than to give prudent rules for the government of health.

JOANNES

JOANNES JOHNSTONUS, a Polish[*] physician of good reputation, addressed to a nobleman of that country a treatise called *Idea Hygieines recensita*, anno 1661. He discourses of the *six instruments* of health, and recites the common rules in a neat Roman stile.

SOME authors of this period have taken the trouble to write against particular sorts of food in common use. To give but one instance, Joannes Petrus Lotichius published a dissertation against cheese, anno 1643, entitled *Tractatus medicus philologicus novus de casei nequitia*, which seems to be rather ludicrous than serious or valuable.

I shall take notice of one foreign performance more, concerning health, because it is somewhat different from any that we have hitherto mentioned.

[*] I thought, by his name, that he was a Scotch man, but found my mistake in the following paragragh: " Non ingra- " tum tibi et reliquæ nobilitati futurum, si me patriis laribus " restituerem, reddita tandem, per Sueci regis mortem, pace."

[295]

In the year 1710, Bernardin Ramazzini, principal pofeffor of phyfick in the univerfity of Padua, publifhed a book, for the ufe of Raynald duke of Modena, entitled *De principum valetudine tuenda commentatio.* The health of a good prince, fays he, is the greateft bleffing imaginable to the public. And this he confirms by the example of the Romans, who fell into the utmoft grief and confternation upon hearing that Germanicus was dangeroufly ill at Antioch; and prefently, upon a fudden report that he grew better, ran with excefs of joy into the capitol, burfting the doors and crying out, *Rome is fafe, our country is happy, Germanicus lives!* But foon after, when they were affured that he was dead, gave way to their fury, broke down the temples of the Gods, overturned their altars, and threw the guardian Deities of Rome into the ftreets.

A prince who regards his health, continues he, fhould permit his phyfician to remind him of the following particulars:

1. He

1. He should be put in mind of the annual changes of the seasons, that his cloaths, palace, furniture, and method of living may be adapted to them.

2. He should be advertised when any epidemical distemper begins to spread, that he may remove into a more healthy air.

3. As the variety of delicacies, which cover the tables of princes, is a great temptation to excess, they should be exhorted to partake of a moderate quantity of such things only as they know by experience to agree with their constitution.

4. Princes should not be fatigued with business soon after dinner, nor with any business at all after supper, but should follow the example of Augustus Cæsar, who would neither read nor write letters after supper, lest they should disturb his sleep.

5. It is shameful in a prince to be a drunkard, and thereby become the jest of the

the mob; as Claudius Tiberius Nero was in derision called *Caldius Biberius Mero*. Let princes imitate Julius Cæsar, who, as Suetonius informs us, *vini parcissimus fuit;* and Augustus, who rarely drank above three glasses after supper.

6. Manly exercises, suitable to their high rank, according to the custom of the country, and especially riding on horseback, should be recommended to princes. They should also indulge themselves in other innocent and genteel recreations, and never fail to admit young people to partake of their diversions.

7. The constitution of the prince should be carefully studied, and well understood by his physician; and his diet, exercise, and evacuations ought to be regulated accordingly.

8. No man is ignorant of the bad effects which violent passions produce in the human body. Anger, fear, grief, and even excessive joy, have been the causes of death to many.

many. And princes are so far from having any right of exemption from these passions, that they are generally more exposed to them than any of their subjects. "Let a
" man read (says our author) the forty-fifth *
" chapter of the seventh book of Pliny's na-
" tural history, and when he has considered
" the many misfortunes, dangers, terrours,
" and real calamities which Augustus en-
" countered, let him honestly declare whe-
" ther or not he envies that exalted ruler of
" the world." It should therefore be the physician's study to know what passions his prince is most prone to, that, in the favourable moments of good humour, he may respectfully recommend a diet and regimen proper to subdue those enormities.

* Pliny there mentions the vexations Augustus met with from his worthless associates, Lepidus and Mark Antony. The necessity of concealing himself for three days in a ditch, after a defeat. Seditions and mutinies in the army. Hatred of banished citizens. Snares laid to take his life away. Treachery and wickedness of his own family and friends. Pestilence and famine in Italy. A fixed resolution to die, in consequence of which he fasted four days, whereby he was brought to death's door. And, at last, the mortification of leaving the son of his enemy, his heir, and successor to the empire.

CHAP.

CHAP. XVIII.

Of the British writers on health, viz. *Sir Thomas Elliot, Thomas Coghan, Edmund Hollyngs, William Vaughan, Thomas Venner, Andrew Boorde, Edward Maynwaring, Thomas Phayer, William Bulleyn, Francis Fuller, Dr. Wainwright, Dr. Welsted, Dr. Burton, Dr. Arbuthnot, Dr. Lynche, and Dr. Mead.*

IN the reign of Henry VIII. Sir Thomas Elliot, a learned knight, wrote a treatise, which he calls *The castle of health.* He was not bred a physician*, but was undoubtedly acquainted with some of their best books. He explains and recommends the precepts of Diocles to king Antigonus; and has judiciously collected several useful rules

---

* " Altho' I have never been at Montpelier, Padua, or " Salerno, says Sir Thomas, yet I have something in physic " whereby I have taken no little profit concerning mine own " health. If the physicians be angry that I have written phy- " sic in English, let them remember that the Greeks wrote in " Greek, the Romans in Latin, and the Arabians in Arabic. " Nor have I written for glory, reward, or promotion, God is " my judge."

of health from the ancients. He was so great an admirer of Galen, that (according to the taste of those times) he has followed him close through his perplexed distinction of things into *natural, non-natural,* and *contrary to nature;* and has illustrated every branch of that fantastical division. He has also interspersed some prudent remarks of his own. He observes, for instance, that moderation in sleep must be measured by health, sickness, age, constitution, fulness, and emptiness, since each of these requires a different proportion of rest. And speaking of the passions, he says, " if they be immo-
" derate, they do not only annoy the body
" and shorten life, but also impair, and
" sometimes utterly destroy a man's estima-
" tion."

Dr. WILLAM BULLEYN, who practised at Durham, in the time of Philip and Mary, was a famous botanist, and reputed a man of humour, good sense, and great humanity. In his *government of health*, he introduces John, who was a man of pleasure, disputing with Humphrey, who is an advocate,

cate for temperance; but there is nothing very useful or entertaining in their conversation.

THOMAS COGHAN, master of arts, and bachelor of physic, published his *Haven of health**, about the close of the sixteenth century. He had his education at Oxford, but it should seem, that he was not a regular practising † physician. His rules of health are taken for the most part from Hippocrates and Galen, especially from the latter. He treats of exercise particularly, in a concise and masterly manner, blending his own observations with the precepts of the ancients.

As " flowing water (says he) does not
" corrupt, but that which standeth still; e-

* When this performance came first into my hands, it wanted the title page, and was, by mistake, ascribed to Thomas Morgan in the former editions; but having met with the book complete since that time, it is now restored to its true author.

† Speaking of the black assizes at Oxford, which happened in July 1577. It is my opinion, (says he) that " this disease " (be it spoken without offence of the learned physicians) was " was a *febris ardens*.

" ven

" ven fo animal bodies exercifed are for the
" greateft part healthful; and fuch as be idle
" are fubject to ficknefs. Some exercifes are
" appropriated to different parts of the hu-
" man body; as running and walking for the
" legs and thighs; fhooting with bows and
" arrows for the arms; ftooping and rifing
" at bowls for the back and loins; finging,
" and reading aloud for the lungs. The
" mufcles are exercifed by all their refpec-
" tive motions, and fo are the veins and ar-
" teries which run through them. Gefta-
" tion is alfo excellent, efpecially for the
" tender. But tennis is preferable to every
" other exercife, becaufe it may be ufed by
" all, and at a fmall charge, and principally,
" becaufe it exercifes every part of the body,
" as head, eyes, neck, back, loins, arms,
" and legs, and at the fame time delights the
" mind; all which advantages can be found
" in no other exercife whatfoever. Where-
" fore the founders of colleges are highly
" to be praifed, who have erected tennis
" courts for the exercife of their fcholars.
" But let them follow the prudent rule of
" Hip-

"Hippocrates, by using exercise before
"meals; for it is hurtful immediately after
"a full meal, tho' that is the common pra-
"ctice in schools and colleges, which
"makes lads break out into boils and cuta-
"neous eruptions*."

The exercise of the mind is likewise necessary to health.

To watch and study at night is to strive against nature, and by contrary motions to impair the vigour both of body and mind. "Alfred (continues our author) who found-
"ed University College in Oxford, divided
"his time nobly, spending eight hours of
"the four and twenty in eating, drinking,
"and sleeping; eight in hearing and decid-
"ing causes; and eight in study." I shall mention but one more of his observations, *viz.* As suck is to infants, so is wine, moderately drank, to the aged, and is therefore called old men's milk.

---

* This observation he borrows from Hippoc. (who says) "Ulcera erumpunt, ubi quis non purgatus exercitatione uti-
"tur. De morb. vulg. lib. 6. sect. 5. aphor. 32. vers. Fœsii.

Our next treatife is, *Edmundi Hollyngi Eboraceni Angli, doctoris medici et profeʃʃoris Ingolftadiani, de falubri ftudioforum victu, hoc eft, de literatorum omnium valetudine confervanda, vitaque diutiſſime producenda, libellus,* publifhed *anno* 1602, and dedicated to Maximilian Count Palatine of the Rhine, and duke of both the Bavarias, to whom he was recommended by cardinal Alan*. He writes, in a concife and elegant manner, of air, aliment, exercife, *&c.* " thofe fix things †
" (as he calls them) indifpenfably neceſſary
" to every man's life, which promote
" health, or create diftempers according to
" the good or bad ufe that is made of them."

William Vaughan wrote his *Directions for health, anno* 1607. He makes an apology for intruding* into other men's bufinefs

---

* Illuftriſſimo olim Angliæ Cardinali Alano Serenitati veftræ commendatus, cujus gaudeo munificentiâ non vulgari.

† Præceptiones ad fex capita revocavi, prout fex funt res quæ in omni vita aut prodeſſe folent, aut obeſſe: nempe aër, cibus ac potus, fomnus et vigilia, motus et quies, excernenda ac retinenda, et animi accidentia.

* " For all that I am not a practitioner in this noble fcience,
" yet my chiefeft pleafure, ever fince my childhood, has been

finefs, as he was no profeffed phyfician. He treats his fubject by way of queftion and anfwer, and writes with a good deal of humour and fmartnefs. "How fhall tofs-pots "and fwill-bowls (fays he) be made to hate "wine?" He anfwers this queftion by asking another: "Look on the countenance of "a drunkard, and is it not disfigured? Does "not his nofe feem rotten, withered, or "worm eaten? Does not his breath ftink, "his tongue faulter? Is not his body cra"zy, and fubject to gouts and dropfies?"

IN another place he fays, that intemperance in eating, as well as in drinking, deftroys the faculties of the mind; "for how "is it poffible that the fmoaky vapours, "which breathe from a fat and full paunch, "fhould not interpofe a thick mift of dul"nefs between the body, and the body's "light!"

THOMAS VENNER, doctor of phyfic at Bath in the fpring and fall, and at other times near Bridgewater, publifhed his *Via*

"to read books of phyfic, in regard of my own health. Sir "Thomas Elliot, a learned knight in king Henry VIII's days, "was no practitioner, yet wrote on this very fubject."

recta

recta ad vitam longam, about the year 1620, which he addreſſed to Francis Lord Verulam. The principal aim of this performance was to recommend Bath, or the true uſe (as he ſays) of the baths of Bath, but he treats alſo of air, aliment, &c. He ſeems to have been an honeſt well meaning man, but very formal and prolix in expreſſing his mind when he writes in Engliſh; and a great admirer of Galen's diviſions and diſtinctions, which he diſplays on all occaſions; and tho' his book is for the moſt part written in his own language, he takes care to convey his favourite ſentiments* conciſely enough in Latin.

He informs us, that the Bath waters were not in his time preſcribed inwardly by any regular phyſician, becauſe from their bituminous and ſulphureous nature, they relax and

---

* Regulæ ad conſervationem vitæ ſaluberrimæ. 1. Aërem purum, ſuaveſque odores ſpirare. 2. Cibum adverſante ſtomacho non ingerere. 3. Cibos naturâ et coctione multum diſcrepantes non aſſumere. 4. Ad ſaturitatem nunquam edere et bibere. 5. Ventrem modicè laxum habere. 6. Veris initio corpus pharmaco conveniente purgare. 7. Veneris illecebras, ejuſque uſum immoderatum, tanquam peſtem, fugere. 8. Vitam probam et incorruptam degere.

weaken the stomach; but he owns that the meaner sort of people, by the persuasion of the Bath guides, used to drink a large draught of the water, with salt in it, to prepare them for the external use of the same water in bathing. He ranges different waters, according to their respective degrees of goodness, in the following order: *viz.* 1. Fountain water. 2. Rain water. 3. River water. 4. Well water. 5. Water conveyed through leaden pipes, which may be mended by boiling. 6. Standing water. 7. Water taken up near the sea shore, which is of a stinking smell and unpleasant savour.

Andrew Boorde, doctor of physick, published, *anno* 1643, his *Compendious regiment*, or *Dietary of health*, made in Montpelier, which he dedicated to *The armipotent and valiant lord, Thomas duke of Norfolk*. Besides the common cautions with regard to air, aliment, *&c.* he observes that tranquillity of mind is necessary to health; and that in order to preserve such a tranquillity, a man must be frugal. He therefore seriously recommends good oeconomy in the following words: " He that will spend
" more

"more in his house than the rents of his lands or his gains bring in, will come to poverty. He should therefore divide his rents or income into three parts: The first to provide for meat and drink; the second for apparel, servants wages, alms, and other deeds of mercy; and the third should be reserved for urgent cases in time of need, as sickness, repairs, and casual expences; otherwise he may fall in debt, and then his mind cannot be quiet; and the perturbation of the heart shortens a man's life."

Speaking of the different sorts of meat and drink in common use, he observes that they who put any thing to ale besides water, malt, barm, and godsgood, do sophisticate and spoil it; and that ale should be drank fresh and clear, and neither too old nor too new.

Dr. Edward Maynwaring published his *Tutela sanitatis*, or *Hygiastick precautions and rules*, anno 1663. The epistle to the reader is written in Latin, but the book in English.

"It is health (says he) that makes your bed easy, and your sleep refreshing; that
"renews

" renews your strength with the rising sun;
" that fills up the hollows, and uneven pla-
" ces of your carcafs, and makes you plump
" and comely, and adorns your face with
" her choicest colours; that makes your ex-
" ercife a sport; that increafes the natural
" endowments of your mind, and makes the
" soul to take delight in her manfion."

He has treated of Galen's *fix non-natu-rals* in a short and perspicuous manner, and has added a seventh to them, *viz.* Customs or habits voluntarily contracted by many, which prove useful or detrimental to health, according as they are good or bad, and which should therefore be indulged, or gradually corrected.

About this time, or rather earlier, Thomas Phayer wrote his *Regiment of life*, translated (as he owns) from the French, but amplified by himself.

He explains the different temperaments of people, namely, the sanguine, phlegmatic, choleric, and melancholic, pretty accurately; but I cannot say, that there is any thing extraordinary in his performance.

Soon

Soon after the commencement of the eighteenth century, Francis Fuller, M. A. publifhed his *Medicina Gymnaftica;* and tho' his aim was to recommend exercife as the principal remedy in a *confumption, dropfy,* and *hypochondriacal diforders,* yet there are fo many hints, conducive to the prefervation of health, fcattered through this valuable treatife, that, to them who ftudy what is falutary, the perufal of it will afford both inftruction and amufement.

He has from reafon and experience demonftrated the good effects of riding on horfeback, (which is quite as ufeful to preferve, as to recover health) and is perhaps the fulleft and beft author we have on that article.

Friction, or the flefh brufh, he has likewife treated of very accurately, which is of great ufe to preferve health. " It is very " ftrange (fays he) that this exercife of " chafing the skin, which was in fuch uni- " verfal requeft among the antients, and " which they put in practice almoft every " day, fhould be fo totally neglected and " flighted

" flighted by us, especially when we confi-
" der that their experience agrees so exactly
" with our modern discoveries in the oeco-
" nomy of nature."

In the year 1701 was published at Edinburgh doctor George* Sibbald's little book, entitled *Regulæ bene et salubriter vivendi.*

The few rules of health mentioned by this learned author are taken from Hippocrates and Celsus, to which he added one of his own, that shews him to have been a prudent man, and, at the same time, an agreeable companion.

" Go rarely to convival entertainments †, says he, but when you are there be chearful and keep company with your sober friends only, at seasonable hours, and when you have leisure.

---

* I met with this performance in the Bodleian library, but made no extract from it, imagining that as it was printed at Edinburgh, I might there find it easily; but I was mistaken, for, after the most diligent search, I could not find it till very lately, at an auction.

‡ Hilariter, sed raro et providè convivari, nec nisi cum amicis aut sodalibus, et horis feriatis.

Dr. Wainwright's *mechanical account of air and diet*, was published *anno* 1708; and tho' his chief design was to shew the necessity of mathematical knowledge to the rational practice of physic, yet by the way, he mentions some precepts relating to the preservation of health, under those two heads of *air* and *diet;* and we are much obliged to him for demonstrating the reasonableness and utility of his precepts by proper calculations and experiments. He proves that air too dense, or too much rarified, is hurtful to animals, and consequently that the highest hills, as well as the lowest vallies, are unhealthy. He demonstrates that a human body, of a middle size, supports a weight of near a tun and an half of air when the mercury rises to *thirty inches* in the barometer, more than it does when the mercury falls to *twenty-seven* inches; which must have a considerable effect on the motion of the blood and humours. He observes that an air too moist and filled with vapours, whereby its spring is weakened, relaxes the fibres of the body, and obstructs the pores; whence it happens that agues are so epidemical

mical in the fens of Cambridgeshire, and the hundreds of Essex.

With regard to *diet*, he shews that a healthy man has certainly exceeded in the quantity of his food, if he finds himself short breathed, or sleepy immediately after meals; because it is evident from those symptoms, that the stomach is too much distended, and presses upon the *diaphragm*, which straitens the *thorax;* and upon the superior trunk of the *vena cava*, which hinders the free return of the blood from the head.

He has also proved, by calculating the pressure of water upon the surface of the human body, and by shewing the necessary consequences of such a pressure, that " bathing is not to be practised rashly without good advice and proper precautions;" tho' it has been the ancient practice * of the Jews

---

* Bathing is also the modern practice of several nations, especially of the Egyptians, where the women use it, at a great expence, to make them plump and comely, and the men for coolness and health. See Prosp. Alp. de med. Ægyp. lib 3. cap. 15.

and Romans, not only as a cure of several distempers, but also for cleanliness and delight.

Dr. Welsted, in his elegant treatise *De ætate vergente*, published *anno* 1724, recommends the following excellent rules to be carefully observed by old people.

1. To be cautious how they change an old custom suddenly, tho' the change, at first sight, should appear commodious; for their strength is not, like that of youth, able to struggle with, or break through a habit which the practice of many years has rendered familiar.

2. To avoid such things as they found by experience to have been detrimental to their health in the former part of their lives; for how should they bear, now when they are feeble, what in their full strength they could not support?

3. Let their food and drink be such as will give no disturbance either to their stomach or to their head. Or, in case they have exceeded

exceeded by accident, let the excess be immediately discharged.

4. Let their appetite be kept as good, and their secretions as regular as possible.

5. Let their minds be easy and chearful: But this charming serenity is obtained by those only whose age, after a life spent in doing good, affords a retrospect of complacency, and a prospect of happiness.

Dr. Burton's book of the *Non-naturals*, in which " the great influence they have on " human bodies is set forth," was published *anno* 1738. And tho' the author's principal scope is to shew the subserviency of a thorough acquaintance with the nature and properties of air, aliment, *&c.* to the successful practice of physick, and particularly to the cure of epidemical distempers; yet those who study to preserve health are much obliged to him for several useful precepts and judicious reflexions on that subject, which are to be met with in his treatise. He observes,

1. For instance, that " in the spring the " air being impregnated with the salubrious
" effluvia

" effluvia of opening flowers, will be more
" refreshing than the autumnal air loaded
" with steams of putrifying vegetables,
" which, unless dispersed by winds frequent
" at that season, would soon produce fatal
" effects."

2. Speaking of aliment, he takes notice of the error of those " who drink too small
" a quantity of cooling diluting liquors in
" proportion to their solid food; by which
" mistake the blood becomes thick, the se-
" cretions are diminished, and the saline par-
" ticles, for want of a watery fluid to sepa-
" rate them, cluster together, and corrode
" the capillary vessels." And

3. He recommends exercise, from the common observation, that the parts, or limbs of the body, which labour most, are larger and stronger than those which have less exercise. Thus the legs and feet of a chairman, the arms and hands of watermen and sailors, the backs and shoulders of porters, by long use grow thick, strong, and brawny.

Near

Near the same time was written an *Essay concerning the effects of air on human bodies*, compofed by the learned and ingenious Dr. Arbuthnot. After having, with great judgment and accuracy, given us a moſt curious account of the *contents, properties, qualities,* and *nature* of *air*, in *different ſeaſons* and *ſituations;* and of the influence it has on human conſtitutions and diſeaſes; our author draws many uſeful practical aphoriſms from the whole; of which the following well deſerve the attention of thoſe who are ſtudious to preſerve their health.

1. Every human creature, whoſe manner of life demands, and whoſe conſtitution can bear it, ought to inure himſelf to the outward air in different ſorts of weather.

2. In the choice of habitations for mankind, the wholeſomneſs of the air is a principal conſideration, and is as much a particular in the purchaſe of a ſeat as the ſoil.

3. The

3. The local qualities of the air depend upon the exhalations of the soil, and of its neighbourhood, which may be brought thither by the winds: For a gravelly situation may be rendered sickly by a neighbouring marsh.

4. The qualities of the springs are a mark of those of the air; for the air and water imbibe the saline and mineral exhalations of the ground; therefore where the water is sweet and good, it is probable that the air is so likewise. But the best mark of the wholesomeness of the air is the customary longevity of the inhabitants.

5. Dampness of wainscot, rotting of furniture, tarnishing of metals, rusting of iron, efflorescence of salts upon bodies, discolorations of silks and linen, are marks of salts of an unusual nature or quality in the air.

The air of cities is unfriendly to infants and children: For every animal being by nature adapted to the use of fresh and
free

free air the tolerance of air replete with sulphureous steams of fuel, and the perspirable matter of animals (as that of cities) is the effect of habit, which young creatures have not yet acquired.

7. The first care in building cities is to make them airy and well perflated; because infectious distempers must necessarily be propagated amongst mankind living too close together. The air is also extreamly tainted by having *burial places* within the precincts of great cities.

8. Private houses ought to be perflated once every day, by opening doors and windows to blow off the animal steams. Houses, for the sake of warmth, fenced from wind, and where the carpenter's work is so nice as to exclude all outward air, are not healthy; for people who pass most of their time in air tainted with steams of animals, fire, and candles, are frequently infected with nervous distempers.

The

The next performance relating to our subject, that has come to my hands, is Dr. Barnard Lynche's *Guide to health through the various stages of life*, printed 1744. In the first part of his book, besides clearing up the different changes in the life of man, and the unavoidable causes of decrepitude and death, our author has given us, from the sacred scriptures, from Pliny, and other historians, a well attested account of the longevity of several sober and regular persons in various ages of the world; which examples teach those, who desire long life, the necessity of temperance more effectually than they can be taught by precepts.

And in the second part, his *Analysis of air, aliment, and the other non-naturals*, is full and perspicuous. He has explained their respective natures and properties according to the theory of the most celebrated modern physicians; and has given us several useful precepts of health, together with the reasons for enjoining them, in a distinct and
ingenious

ingenious manner, which merit our particular attention. He shews, for instance, "that the more of a sulphureous or chymical oil any distilled spirit contains, the more pernicious it proves to the human body, because it is harder to be washed away by the blood; therefore brandy * is more easily carried off than rum; and Geneva, than anise-seed water."

2. To recommend moderate sleep, he observes that we may look upon the time of waking as the time of wearing out the animal fabric; and the time of sleep as that in which it is repaired and recruited; for, in action, something is continually abraded from the fibres, which cannot otherwise be restored than by their rest from tension, and by the regular and steady course of the blood in sleep, which is proper for nourishment, or an apposition of parts to the wasted vessels.

* This opinion must rest upon the experience of those who accustom themselves to such liquors, which if frequently used, are all pernicious.

3. In describing the just measure of exercise, he says, that those who are lean should continue their exercise only *ad ruborem*, or till the body is gently heated, for that will fatten them; but they who are fat, may continue it *ad sudorem*, because sweating will help to extenuate the body.

4. Speaking of the saliva or spittle, he takes notice, that they who, immediately after eating, fall to smoaking or chewing tobacco, commit two destructive errors: 1. In diverting the saliva from its natural office; and spitting out that fluid which so greatly contributes to digestion. 2. In using that stupifying *American Henbane*, or opiate, which numbs the nerves and destroys the appetite. To conclude, this author merits our esteem for his love and recommendation of virtue and piety.

The last of the British authors that has touched this subject is Dr. Mead, who has done honour to our country by his deep knowledge

knowledge in physick, by his refined taste in the polite arts, and by his unbounded benevolence and generosity to men of merit.

This great physician has closed his book entitled *Monita et præcepta medica*, published *anno* 1751, with several excellent rules and remarks concerning the preservation of health, some of which he took from his favourite *Celsus*, and some from his own observation. Of the latter are these:

1. A man who has eat a large meal, especially of high seasoned food, will receive benefit from drinking after it a draught of cold water with some juice of lemon, or elixir of vitriol, to assist his digestion.

2. Old men should retrench a little of their solid food, and make a proportionable addition to their drink.

3. They should also be well rubbed with a flesh brush every morning, to supply that exercise, which, for want of strength, they cannot use though their health requires it.

4. The

4. The frigidity of men advanced in years, is a faithful monitor, that points out to them the folly of forcing themselves to exert a vigour which they have lost, vainly expecting raptures, but finding only an irksome labour* that will shorten their days.

5. Nothing can be more detestable, or more pernicious to health, than for a man to *commit lewdness on himself.*

6. The gifts of providence, which contribute to health, and the real happiness of life, are more equally distributed than we are willing to believe; and perhaps a larger share of them is possessed by men of low degree, than by those of high rank or great affluence. Moderate labour supplies a poor man with wholesome food, and at the same

---

* It should seem that the author had his eye on those lines of Virgil, Geor. 3. v. 97.

———————— fruſtraque laborem
Ingratum trahit: et, ſi quando ad prælia ventum eſt,
Ut quondam in ſtipulis magnus ſinè viribus ignis,
Incaſſum furit.————

time

time gives him an appetite to relish, and strength to digest it; without goading his lust, or inflaming his passions. His sleep is sound and refreshing, undisturbed with corroding cares: And his healthy and hardy offspring nursed up in temperance, soon grows fit to partake of that labour which made the parents happy. How different are the effects produced by sloth and luxury in the rich! To enable them to eat, their stomachs require high sauces which heat and corrupt their blood, pamper their vicious inclinations, and render them obnoxious to various diseases. The excess of the day destroys the sleep of the night. Their children are tainted in their mother's womb, with distempers which afflict their whole lives, and hardly permit them, diseased and decrepid, to arrive at the threshold of old age. Besides, an anxiety to obtain honours and titles perpetually harrasses their weak minds, and the felicity of enjoying what they possess is forfeited by the restless desire of getting more.

7. NEXT

7. Next to temperance, the surest means to keep the affections of the mind in due subjection to reason is, to associate with wise* and good men, whose conversation and example is very prevalent in regulating the passions, which, unless they are taught to obey, will be sure to grow headstrong and imperious.

* Euripides was of the same opinion: " The wise (said he) will become more wise, by frequently conversing with the wise."

PART II.

Containing a succinct review of the most important rules recommended by physicians and philosophers for the preservation of health: Together with a sketch of the reasons whereon these rules are founded, drawn from the mechanism of the human body.

CHAP. I.

Exhibits a short view of concoction, or the mechanism by which our aliment is digested; and of the circulation of the blood; from which it will be obvious to perceive the ground and reason of the rules laid down for the preservation of health, and the expediency of observing them.

THE art of preserving health promises three things: *First,* To secure or maintain the health which a man enjoys at present. *Secondly,* To prevent approaching distempers. *Thirdly,* To prolong life. Of all which I shall treat in the order here mentioned.

The first of these, in a great measure, includes the other two, because a diligent observation of the rules proper to preserve health, will, for the most part, prevent approaching distempers; and dispose the body to longevity. The first, therefore, requires to be treated of more largely than either of the other articles. But to set it in a clear light we must previously describe some parts of the animal structure and oeconomy, from which we may readily perceive the reason of the rules recommended to preserve health, and the necessity of putting them in practice.

And here we may, with pleasure, remark a surprizing agreement and harmony between the successful practice of the antients, directed only by their assiduous observation of nature, and the mechanical theory of the moderns, founded upon the wonderful structure of our solids, and the perpetual rotation of our fluids, with which the ancients were unacquainted.

Anatomy discovers ten thousand beauties in the human fabrick, which I have no room to mention here; nor is it possible, in a performance of this kind, to describe the geometrical accuracy with which the author of nature has formed every part of the body to carry on the animal oeconomy, and answer

the

the various purpofes of life. All I propofe in this place is, by touching upon a few particulars, to give thofe, who are unacquainted with our profeffion, a general idea of the ftructure of their own bodies, from which they will eafily apprehend, that intemperance, floth, and feveral other vices and errors, have a neceffary and mechanical tendency to deftroy health. To this end it will be indifpenfably requifite to give fome account of concoction, or the mechanifm by which our aliment is digefted; and then to take notice of the circulation of the blood, with fome of its neceffary confequences.

Of CONCOCTION.

Among all the wife contrivances obferved in the human fabric, none can excite our attention and admiration more than the difpofition and mechanifm of thofe parts, by which our aliment is concocted, or fitted for our daily fupport and nourifhment. To have a clear idea of the manner in which concoction

tion is performed, we muſt diſtinguiſh it into three ſtages. The firſt ſtage is performed in the progreſs of the aliment from the mouth down to the lacteal veins*. The ſecond is performed in the paſſage of the milky liquor, called chyle, through the lacteal veſſels to the loins, and then up to where it mingles with the blood, under the collar-bone. The third or ultimate concoction is performed by the circulation of the blood and chyle together, through the lungs, and the whole arterial ſyſtem. In all theſe ſtages, the deſign of the great architect has evidently been to grind and diſſolve the aliment, and to mix and incorporate it with a large quantity of animal juices already prepared, in ſuch a manner as to reduce it at laſt to the very ſame ſubſtance with our blood and humours. How wonderfully and completely this deſign has been executed, we ſhall ſee preſently.

In the firſt ſtage of concoction, by a curious configuration of parts, and action of

---

* The lacteal, or milky veins, are ſmall veſſels, that receive the chyle from the inteſtines.

muſcles,

muscles *, adapted to their respective functions, our food is ground small by the teeth, and moistened by a copious saliva † in the mouth. It is in the next place swallowed, and conveyed down the gullet, where it is farther mollified and lubricated by a viscid unctuous humour, distilled from the glands of that canal. From thence it slips into the stomach, where several causes concur towards its more complete dissolution. It is diluted by the juices, it is swelled and subtilized by

---

* Vid. Boerh. instit. sect. 58. et seq.

Boerhaave has given a fuller and clearer view of the animal oeconomy than any other man ever did. His institutions contain an accurate description of all the principal actions performed in the human body, deduced in the most consequential order that can be imagined; and intelligible to those who are previously acquainted with all the branches of anatomy. But his book was calculated for physicians only: and no man, probably, of any other profession will ever take the pains to understand it perfectly.

N. B. A muscle is a mass or collection of fibres, of different dimensions, by which all the motions of every part of the body are performed.

† The saliva, or spittle, is a pure, pellucid, penetrating humour, containing oil, salt, water, and spirit, strained from the arterial blood, and very useful in digestion; and therefore the habitual and immoderate discharge of it, in chewing and smoking tobacco, must be of bad consequence.

the

the internal air, and it is macerated and diſ-
ſolved by the heat which it meets with in
that cavity. It is alſo agitated and attenuated by the perpetual friction of the coats of
the ſtomach, and the pulſation of the arteries
there; by the alternate elevation and de-
preſſion of the diaphragm* in breathing;
and by the compreſſion of the ſtrong muſcles
of the belly. And after a proper ſtay, it is
gradually propelled into the inteſtines, in
the form of a thick, ſmooth uniform, aſh-
coloured fluid.

When our aliment, thus prepared, ar-
rives at the inteſtines, it is there mixed with
three different ſorts of liquor. It receives
two ſorts of bile †; the one thick, yellow,
and extremely bitter, from the gall-bladder;

---

* The diaphragm or midrif, is a very large tranſverſe muſcle, which ſeparates the thorax or cheſt from the abdomen or belly, and ſqueezes the contents of the ſtomach and inteſtines.

† The bile or gall is the principal diſſolvent of the aliment, and when it is vitiated or defective, there can be no good digeſtion.

the other scarce yellow, or bitter, but in a much larger quantity, from the liver. The third liquor, that falls here upon the aliment, issues plentifully from a large glandular substance, situated beneath the stomach, called the pancreas or sweet bread, and is a limpid, mild fluid like the saliva, which serves to dilute and sweeten what may be too spiss and acrimonious. The two saponaceous biles resolve and attenuate viscid substances; incorporate oily fluids with aqueous, making the whole mixture homogeneous; and by their penetrating and detergent qualities render the chyle fit to enter the lacteal veins, into which it is conveyed partly by the absorbent nature of these veins, and partly by the peristaltic* motion of the intestines.

If we now consider the change which our aliment has undergone in the mouth,

---

* Peristaltic (from περιϛέλλω, *contraho*) is that vermicular motion of the intestines, produced by the alternate and progressive contraction and dilatation of their spiral and orbicular fibres, which presses the chyle into the lacteals, and answers many other good purposes.

gullet,

gullet, and ftomach, together with the large quantity of bile and pancreatic juice poured upon it in the inteftines: And if we reflect alfo on the inceffant action of the mufcles, blending, churning, and incorporating the whole, we fhall readily perceive, that their united agency muft alter the particular taftes, flavours, and properties of our different kinds of food, in fuch a manner as to bring the chyle nearer in its nature to our animal juices, than to the original fubftances from which it was formed. Our aliment thus changed into chyle, conftitutes the firft ftage of concoction; and we fhall find the fame affimilation carried on through the fecond.

THE fecond ftage of concoction begins with the flender lacteal veins, where they arife from the inteftines by an innumerable multitude of invifible pores, through which the fine, white, fluid part of the chyle is ftrained or abforbed; while, at the fame time, the grofs, yellow, fibrous part, conveyed flowly forward, and farther attenuated in the
long

long inteſtinal tube, is perpetually preſſed and drained of its remaining chyle, until the dregs, becoming at laſt uſeleſs, are ejected out of the body.

These lacteal veins iſſue from the inteſtines in various directions, now ſtreight and now oblique, often uniting and growing larger, but preſently ſeparating again. They frequently meet at ſharp angles, and enter into ſoft glands, diſperſed through the meſentery*, from which they proceed larger than before, and more turgid, with a fine lymphatic fluid. In moſt places alſo they run contiguous with the meſenteric arteries, by whoſe pulſation their load is puſhed forward. And thus, after various communications, ſeparations, and protruſions, the lacteal veins pour their chyle into a ſort of ciſtern † or reſervoir formed for that purpoſe

---

* The meſentery is that ſtrong double membrane within which the inteſtines are convolved, and is interſperſed with innumerable glands, nerves, arteries, lacteal and lymphatic veſſels.

† This ciſtern (as anatomiſts call it) is often found to conſiſt only of ſome large branches of the lacteal veins.

between the lowest portion of the diaphragm and the highest vertebre of the loins*. It is very remarkable that these veins are furnished with proper valves which permit the chyle to move forward, but effectually stop its return; and that a great number of veins purely lymphatick, as well as the lacteal, empty themselves into the same cistern.

In all this contrivance it is evident that the chyle, being more and more diluted and blended with abundance of lymph † from the glands through which it passes, and from other sources, approaches still nearer to the nature of our animal juices, and consequently becomes fitter for nutrition.

From its reservoir the chyle is pushed into a narrow transparent pipe, called the *thoracic duct*, which climbs in a perpendicular

* The several bones which compose the chine are called vertebres, of which five belong to the loins.

† The lymph is the most elaborated and finest part of the blood, which is continually flowing into the chyle throughout its whole course.

direction

dirction by the side of the back-bone, from the loins up to the collar-bone, and opens into the subclavian vein*; where, by the peculiar arrangement of several small valves, the chyle mingles gently with the blood, after it has been thorougly elaborated, churned, and attenuated with lymph from every part of the thorax †, and is from thence soon conveyed to the heart.

Thus, by a wonderful mechanism, we may plainly perceive, that a large quantity of chyle and lymph is forced upwards, in a perpendicular course, through a thin slender pipe, if we attend to the following particulars: *First*, To the progress of the chyle, urged forward and continued from the antecedent action of the intestines, and the beating of the mesenteric arteries. *Secondly*, To

---

* Most commonly into the left, but sometimes, tho' very rarely, into the right. Nay, sometimes, as that accurate anatomist Dr. Monro observes, it divides into two under the curvature of the great artery; one goes to the right, and the other to the left subclavian vein.

† By thorax is meant the great cavity of the breast.

the

the motion of the diaphragm and lungs, in respiration, pressing this thoracic duct that lies under them, while the thorax rising and falling resists their action, whereby the duct is squeezed between two contrary forces, and the liquor which it contains pushed upwards. *Thirdly*, This duct runs close by the side of the great artery, (called by anatomists the superior portion of the descending aorta) whose strong pulsation presses its yielding sides, and compels the chyle and lymph to mount in an upright ascent. *Fourthly*, We are to observe that this duct is accommodated with valves, which permit its contents to move upwards by every compression, but never to fall back again. Thus terminates the second stage of concoction, when the chyle falls into the heart. And we see that, in its progress through these two stages, our aliment has been accurately mixed with all the nourishing juices of the body, and with all the substances or principles that compose the blood, *viz.* saliva, mucus, lymph, bile, water, salts, oil, and spirits.

But

But here we must take notice, that the most fluid and subtile part of our aliment, before and after it is elaborated into chyle, passes into the blood by certain absorbent veins dispersed all over the mouth, gullet, stomach and intestines. This is evident from the sudden refreshment and strength communicated to weary, faint and hungry people, immediately upon drinking a glass of good wine; or eating any cordial spoon meat; and from the flavour which different sorts of food give to the urine, much sooner than it is possible for the chyle to reach the heart in its common windings.

The third stage of concoction begins where the chyle mingles with the blood, and falling soon into the right ventricle of the heart, is from thence propelled into the lungs. It will appear that the lungs are the principal instrument of sanguification, or converting the chyle into blood, if we consider their structure, first with regard to the air vessels of which they are composed, and secondly,

with

with regard to their blood veſſels; for we ſhall then clearly perceive the change which their fabric and action muſt neceſſarily produce on the chyle. The wind pipe is compoſed of ſegments of cartilaginous rings on the fore part, to give a free paſſage to the air in reſpiration; and of a ſtrong membrane on its back part, to bend with the neck, and give way to the gullet in deglutition. This pipe is lined throughout with an infinity of glands, which perpetually diſtil an unctuous denſe humour to lubricate and anoint the paſſages of the air. Soon after the wind pipe has deſcended into the cavity of the breaſt, it is divided into two great branches, and theſe two are ſubdivided into innumerable ramifications called Bronchia*, which grow ſmaller in their progreſs, (not unlike a buſhy tree inverted) until at laſt they terminate in millions of little bladders, which hang in cluſters on their extremities, and are inflated by the admiſſion of the air, and ſubſide at

* From Βρογχος, *guttur*.

its expulsion. These clusters constitute the lobes of the lungs. The blood vessels of the lungs next deserve our attention. The branches of the pulmonary artery run along with those of the windpipe, and are ultimately subdivided into an endless number of capillary ramifications, which are spread, like a fine net-work, over the surface of every individual air bladder. And the pulmonary vein, whose extreme branches receive the blood and chyle from those of the arteries, run likewise in form of a net over all the air bladders of the Bronchia.

From this admirable structure of the lungs, it is obvious, that the crude mixture of the blood and chyle, passing through the minute ramifications of the pulmonary artery and vein, is compressed and ground by two contrary forces, *viz.* by the force of the heart, driving the mixture forward against the sides of the bronchia and air bladders; and by the elastic force of the air equally repelling this mixture from the contrary side.

By these two opposite forces, the chyle and blood are more intimately blended and incorporated; and by the admission and expulsion of the air in respiration, the vessels are alternately inflated and compressed (and probably some subtile air or æther is received* into the blood) by which means the mixture is still further attenuated and dissolved; and after various circulations through the lungs, and heart, and the whole arterial system, is at last perfectly assimilated with the blood, and fitted to nourish the body, and answer the different purposes of animal life.

When the blood thus prepared from the aliment is by repeated circulations gradually drained of all its bland and useful parts, and

* This seems, at least, probable from the following simple experiment: Some physicians at Worcester laid bare the crural artery of a fowl, and made two firm ligatures on the artery, at the distance of an inch one from the other. They then cut out the artery above and below the two ligatures, and put it immediately into an air pump, and upon exhausting the air, the section of the artery between the ligatures, which was full of blood, swelled instantly to a considerable degree.

begins

begins to acquire too great a degree of acrimony, it is carried off by fenfible and infenfible evacuations, through the feveral channels and diftributions of nature. By thefe evacuations the body becomes languid, and requires a frefh fupply of aliment; while at the fame time the faliva, and juices of the ftomach and inteftines, growing thin and acrid by multiplied circulations, vellicate the nerves of thofe paffages, and excite hunger, as a faithful monitor, to remind us of that refrefhment which is now become neceffary.

From this fhort view of concoction it follows, firft, that the immenfe variety of aliments, which the bounty of heaven has provided on the earth and in the waters, for the fuftenance of man, is by this divine mechanifm, reduced at laft to one red, uniform, vital fluid, proper to nourifh and fupport the human fabric.

It follows in the next place, that when we take in a larger quantity of aliment than our digeftive faculties are able to conquer and affimilate, fuch a quantity can never turn to good nourifhment.

Thirdly, when by the arts of luxury our food is rendered too high and rich, and confequently too much faturated with pungent falts, and oils; fuch mixtures with the blood will contribute rather to deftroy than maintain health.

It follows, fourthly, that exercife is neceffary to affift the folids* in rubbing, agitating, and levigating our aliment, to mix it intimately with our animal juices, and make it pafs with eafe through thefe narrow pipes and fubtile ftrainers, which it muft pervade, in order to nourifh the body. And here we may obferve, that moderate riding on horfeback, accommodated to a perfon's ftrength, is, of all exercifes the moft proper to promote a good digeftion, by means of that infinity of gentle fuccuffions which it gives to

---

* By folids here I mean the mufcular fibres of the body, or the action of the feveral mufcles concerned in concoction.

the bowels; whereby the stomach is assisted to dissolve the remains of the aliment; the chyle is forwarded in passing from the intestines into the lacteal veins; the lymph and chyle together are pushed briskly through the thoracic duct into the heart; and the circulation is invigorated to assimilate that mixture into good blood and healthful nourishment; and to throw all superfluities, through the natural drains, out of the body. From this corollary may be clearly deduced the reasonableness of every argument advanced by Sydenham, Fuller, and others, to recommend riding.

Fifthly, people in health should not force themselves to eat when they have no inclination to it; but should wait the return of appetite, which will not fail to admonish them of the proper time for refreshment. To act contrary to this rule frequently, will overload the powers of digestion, and pervert the purpose of nature.

And

And to add but one confequence more, it is evident from what has been faid, that to facilitate a complete digeftion, our aliment ought to be well chewed.

In fhort, the reafon and expediency of every rule eftablifhed by experience to direct us in the quantity and choice of our aliment, may, with a little attention, be plainly deduced from the mechanifm by which concoction is performed.

Of the Circulation of the Blood, and its Confequences.

Every man talks familiarly of the circulation of the blood, and feems to be well acquainted with that fubject. But when it is thoroughly confidered, it will appear to be one of the moft ftupendous* works of omnipotence,

---

* Ne igitur mireris folem, lunam, et univerfam aftrorum feriem fummo artificio difpofitam effe, neve te attonitum magnitudo eorum, vel pulchritudo, vel motus perpetuus reddat adeo, ut fi inferiora hæc comparaveris, parva tibi videantur effe: etenim fapientiam, et virtutem, et providentiam hic quoque fimilem invenies. Gal. de ufu partium, lib. 3. cap. 10. verf. latin. vulgar.

omnipotence. Tho' the life of the animal abfolutely depends upon it, yet the greateft phyficians and philofophers of antiquity knew it not. To England, and modern times, was referved the glory of bringing this important fecret to light. And even after the immortal Harvey* publifhed his difcovery with all the evidence of a demonftration, it was a long time before Riolanus, and the beft anatomifts of thofe days, could be perfuaded of the truth of it. So great was their attachment to the ancients, that they could fcarce believe their own eyes.

To form a diftinct judgment of the mechanifm and importance of the circulation, it will be neceffary to defcribe the ftructure of the arteries, veins and nerves; and take notice of fome experiments made upon them. We muft in the next place touch upon the cavities of the heart, by means of

* William Harvey was born at Folkfton in Kent *anno* 1557, and educated at Cambridge. He ftudied five years at Padua, was phyfician to Charles I, and lived to fourfcore.

which

which the blood is propelled through the body. And then proceed to obferve the extenfive ufe and benefit of this circulation to every branch of the animal oeconomy. From all which it will be obvious to deduce the congruity of the principal rules eftablifhed by experience for the confervation of health.

The arteries are blood-veffels confifting of a clofe texture of ftrong elaftic * fibres †, woven in various webs, laid in different directions, and interfperfed with an infinity of delicate nerves, veins, and minute arteries. They are divided and fubdivided into numberlefs branches and ramifications, that grow fmaller and fmaller as they recede from the heart, until at laft their extremities become much more flender than the hairs of a man's head, (called therefore capillary arteries) which are found either to unite in continued

* Elaftic bodies (from ἐλαύνω, *agito*) are thofe which have the power of a fpring, or of reftoring themfelves to the pofture from which they were difplaced by any external force.

† By fibres are meant fmall animal threads, which are the firft conftituent parts of the folids.

pipes

pipes with the beginnings of the veins, or to terminate in small receptacles, from which the veins derive their origin. The arteries have no valves but only where their trunks spring from the heart. They throb and beat perpetually while life remains; and their extremities differ in the thickness of their coats, and some other particulars, according to the nature of the part which they pervade. All the arteries in the lungs (except the small ones that convey nourishment to them) are derived from the great pulmonary artery, which issues from the right ventricle of the heart. And all the arteries in the rest of the body proceed from the aorta*, whose trunk springs from the left ventricle of the heart.

The veins resemble the arteries in their figure and distribution, but their cavities are larger, and their branches perhaps more numerous. Their coats are much weaker and

* Aorta properly signifies an air vessel (from ἀηρ, aër, et τηρέω, servo) because the antients thought that this artery contained air only.

slenderer

slenderer than those of the arteries. They are furnished with several valves, contrived in such a manner as to permit the blood to pass freely from the smaller into the larger branches, but stop its retrogression. They neither throb nor beat. Their beginnings form continued pipes with the extremities of the arteries, or arise from some gland or receptacle where the arteries terminate. All the veins in the lungs, from their capillary beginnings growing still larger, unite at last and discharge their blood into the left auricle* of the heart. And all the veins in the rest of the body empty themselves in like manner, into the *vena cava*, which opens into the right auricle of the heart.

THE nerves deduce their oirgin from the brain or its appendages, in several pairs, of a cylindric form, like so many skains of

---

* The right and left auricle are two muscular caps covering the two ventricles of the heart, thus called from the resemblance they bear to the external ear. They move regularly like the heart, but in an inverted order, their contraction corresponding to the dilatation of the ventricles.

thread

thread within their respective sheaths, which in their progress decrease by endless divisions and subdivisions, until at last they spread themselves into a texture of filaments so slender, and so closely interwoven with each other over the whole body, that the point of a needle can hardly be put upon any part or particle of it, without touching the delicate branch of some nerve.

The great Harvey, and others, made several experiments upon the vessels we have described, in order to demonstrate the circulation of the blood. For instance, it has been found by many trials, that when an artery is laid bare, and a ligature made upon it, if you open the artery with a lancet between the ligature and the heart, the blood will rush out with great violence; and this rapid jerking stream will continue (unless you stop it by art) until, through loss of blood, the animal faints or dies. But if you open the same artery between the ligature and the extremities, a few drops only will ouze out from the wounded coats of the artery.

On the other hand, when a vein is laid bare, and a ligature made upon it, if you open that vein between the ligature and the extremities, the blood will gush out, as we see in common venæsection. But if we open the same vein between the binding and the heart, no blood will appear. From these experiments it is obvious to the slightest attention, that the blood flows from the heart, through the arteries, to the extreme parts of the body; and returns again through the veins to the heart.

For the regular performance and continuation of this motion of the blood (called its circulation) through all the different parts of the body, the wise Architect has furnished the heart, which is the *primum mobile, and gives the first impulse*, with four distinct muscular cavities, that is, with an auricle and a ventricle on the right side, and an auricle and a ventricle on the left. Through these cavities, curiously adapted to their respective offices, the blood circulates in the following order:

order: It is received from the veins firſt into the right auricle, which contracting itſelf, puſhes the blood into the right ventricle at that inſtant dilated. The moment this ventricle is filled, it contracts itſelf with great force, and impells the blood into the pulmonary artery, which paſſing through the lungs, and returning by the pulmonary veins, is received into the left auricle of the heart, and from thence it is puſhed into the left ventricle. The left ventricle thus filled, contracts itſelf, and drives the blood with great rapidity to all the parts of the body, and from them it returns again through the veins into the right auricle of the heart as before. It is very remarkable, that we have here a double circulation: One from the right ventricle *through the lungs*, to the left auricle of the heart, in order to convert the chyle into blood, and finally prepare it for the nouriſhment of the animal. The other from the left ventricle *through the whole body*, to the right auricle of the heart, which ſerves to apply that nourishment to every part, besides various other purposes.

But to proceed. Of these four muscular cavities, the two auricles are contracted at the same instant, while the two ventricles are dilated; the ventricles, in their turn, are contracting themselves at the very instant that the auricles are dilated. The arteries, in like manner, beat in alternate time with the ventricles of the heart, that is, when the ventricles are contracted the arteries are distended, and while the arteries contract themselves the ventricles are distended.

The nerves, as well as the veins and arteries, act their part in this rotation of the blood; for if you bind up the eighth pair which proceeds from the brain to the heart, the motion of the heart immediately languishes, and soon ceases intirely.

Thus we have a *perpetual motion* (so vainly sought for by some philosophers and mathematicians) which none but a being of
infinite

infinite wisdom and power could produce; and perhaps its continuation requires the constant aid of the same hand that first gave it existence. The brain transmits animal spirits to the heart, to give it a vigorous contraction. The heart, at the same instant, pushes the blood into the brain to supply it with new spirits; by which means the head and the heart mutually support each other every moment. But this is not all: The action of the heart sends the blood and other vital humours over the whole body by the arteries, and distributes nourishment and vigour to *every part* *, (while perhaps the animal spirits, from the extremities of the nerves, return again into the blood) and the whole refluent mass is conveyed back through the veins into the heart, which enables it, without intermission, to persist in rolling this tide of life.

If we now take a view of the use and importance of the circulation of the blood

---

* The lungs not excepted, which receive their nourishment by the bronchial arteries from the aorta.

to the whole animal œconomy, we shall find it very extensive.

1. When this circulation is duly performed, man continues in good health; when it grows irregular he sickens: and when it ceases he dies. Nay, if but one member should be deprived of it, that member presently corrupts and mortifies. By means of this circulation, every natural secretion is mechanically regulated, the perspiration promoted, all the dregs of the body discharged, and distempers frequently cured without any other assistance.

2. When the circulation is naturally quick and vigorous, the temperament of the body becomes habitually hot; when it is languid and slow, the temperament is cold. When the original stamina of the solids, which press forward this circulation, are compact and firm, the constitution is proportionably strong; when they are lax and delicate, the constitution is weak and tender. When bile or phelgm prevails in the

fluids,

fluids, the complexion corresponds with the prevailing humour, and is accordingly called bilious or phlegmatic. Thus, from the different velocity of the circulation, the different strength of the stamina, and the different mixture of the fluids in every individual, arises that *peculiar disposition,* or * ἰδιοσυγκρασία, which is the true cause why several things that are hurtful to some are beneficial to others; and why the same person finds some things agree with him at one time, which have disagreed at another.

But further, a moderate and calm circulation of the blood is necessary even towards the right government of our passions, and the true use of our reason. We know by daily experience, that the influence of the mind upon the body, with respect to health, and of the body upon the mind, with respect to the intellectual faculties, is very

† This word cannot be accurately translated into our language, but it means *that singular disposition of the solids, and mixture of the fluids which exist in every individual.*

great.

great. Sudden terrors have killed some, and diſtracted others. Anger and grief impair health, chearfulneſs and contentment promote it: Inflammations, and other diſorders of the brain, ſuſpend the right uſe of our reaſon: Many arguments induce us to believe, that the nerves ſerve for *ſenſation and muſcular motion,* and that by means of theſe two, the mind carries on its correſpondence with external objects. We know alſo that the nerves are ſupplied with ſpirits from the brain, and the brain with blood from the heart. From all which it is evident, that the circulation muſt be gentle and regular, in order to prevent the paſſions from growing boiſterous or headſtrong; and that conſequently it is the ſource of that rational correſpondence and harmony, which ſhould ſubſiſt between the human mind and body.

I shall conclude this article of the uſes of the circulation, with obſerving that the ſame circulation which ſupports life ſo long, and

and preferves it in vigour, does at laft, by a mechanical neceffity, ftop its own courfe, and deftroy the animal. From the perpetual friction and attrition of the parts one against another, the ftamina or fibres in a courfe of years become rigid, and lofe their fpring; the larger pipes grow hard, and the fmall ones, contracting gradually, become at laft impervious; the body is fhrivelled, and the motion of the fluids firft languifhes, and then ceafes: And thefe caufes gradually bring on old age and death, which approach fooner or later, as the attrition of the parts has been either rafhly hurried on with the violence and impetuofity of excefs and riot, or gently led with the calmnefs of moderation and temperance.

From what has been faid, it fhould feem manifeft that health confifts in a moderate, equable and free circulation of the blood, and other vital fluids of the body, through their correfpondent canals. It is no lefs certain, that a proper degree of ftrength and elafticity in the ftamina of thefe cavities and pipes, is neceffary, to enable them to pufh on the fluids with vigour, and that the fluids muft be of a proper confiftence and quantity, to make them yield to the impulfe of the folids. Let us now apply this idea of health to the *fix inftruments of life,* and we fhall fee the reafonablenefs of the rules laid down with regard to every one of them. It will be fufficient to give one inftance of the moft important precepts of each; and firft, as to the air:

1. THE principal rule in reference to the air is, that we fhould chufe fuch as is pure, and free from all pernicious damps and redundant mixtures, and known by experience to be falubrious. The reafonablenefs of this rule will appear, when we confider, that the air is indifpenfably neceffary to expand the lungs, and that it mingles not only with our aliment, but alfo with our blood and juices, and confequently that it ought to be pure and elaftic, becaufe any pernicious qualities in it would foon taint the blood, and difturb the

the circulation, or which is the same thing in other words, would afflict or destroy the life of the animal.

2. An important rule with respect to aliment is, that it should be used just in such a quantity as we find by experience to agree with us, and sufficient to invigorate, but not to load the body. The expediency of this rule will be evident, when we reflect that aliment was appointed to supply what is thrown off by the continual attrition of the solids, and dissipation of the fluids, and that consequently too rigid abstinence will render the solids languid, and unfit for action; and too great excess will increase the fluids so as to choak up, or burst the tubes thro' which they pass; and it is plain that either of these errors would in a short time stop the circulation.

3. We are advised to use moderate exercise, adjusted as exactly as we can to the quantity of our aliment, that so an equipoise may be maintained between what is thrown off, and what is taken into the body. Now since

since moderate exercise is known to give strength to the solids, and motion to the fluids, it is obvious to the slightest consideration, that too much would over-heat the fluids, and render the solids stiff; and too little would relax the solids, and make the fluids stagnate; both which extremes are inconsistent with a free circulation.

4. As sleep was intended by nature to cherish the body after the action or fatigue of the day, by a new and refreshing apposition of parts, which work requires an adequate proportion of time, that differs in different constitutions; it follows, that too little sleep must waste and dry the animal, and too much would render it dull and heavy.

5. In reference to repletion and evacuation; since the quantity and quality of the fluids should bear an exact proportion to the strength and elasticity of the solids, it is certain, that all superfluous recrements and hurtful humours must be discharged out of the body,

body, left they should disturb or destroy the necessary equipoise between the solids and fluids; and that all useful humours must be retained, in order to preserve this balance.

6. LASTLY, as the passions and affections of the mind, by creating disorders in the blood, have so great an influence on health, it is evident that a habit of virtue which can govern these passions, and make them subservient to reason, is the first and principal rule in which mankind ought to be trained up, to secure a good state of health in all the periods of life.

CHAP. II.

A summary of the rules of health proper to be observed, with regard to every one of the six things necessary to human life, as air, aliment, exercise, &c. together with some other general maxims.

OF the rules requisite to preserve health, some are general or common to all ages and conditions of men; and some are particular, or adapted to different periods and circumstances of life. Under the general rules are comprehended those which relate to the *six instruments of life*, as air, aliment, &c. together with some other useful maxims. Under the particular rules are reckoned, *first*, Those which are peculiar to different temperaments, namely, the bilious, sanguine, melancholic and phlegmatic. *Secondly*, Those rules that belong to different periods of life, as infancy, youth, manhood and old age. *Thirdly*, Those that are appropriated to different conditions and circumstances of men,

con-

considered as active and indolent, wealthy or indigent, free or servile.

I shall mention all these in order, beginning with the general rules which relate to Galen's *Six Non-naturals*, viz. air, aliment, exercise and rest, sleep and wakefulness, repletion and evacuation, together with the passions and affections of the mind.

Of AIR.

Air, by its extreme subtilty and weight, penetrates into, and mingles with every part of the body; and by its elasticity gives an intestine motion to all the fluids, and a lively spring to all the fibres, which promote the circulation. As it is therefore the principal moving cause of all the fluids and solids of the human body, we ought to be very careful in chusing a healthy air, as far as it is in our power.

1. That air is best which is pure*, dry and temperate, untainted with noxious

---

* By pure and dry is not meant an air absolutely clear from any heterogeneous mixture, for that is impossible, nor would such be fit for animals, but an air not overcharged with any steams,

damps,

damps, or putrid exhalations from any cause whatsoever; but the surest mark of a good air, in any place, is the common longevity of its inhabitants.

2. A house is healthy which is situated on a rising * ground and a gravelly soil, in an open dry country; the rooms should be pretty large but not cold; the exposure prudently adapted to the nature of the climate, but so contrived that your house may be perflated by the east or north winds, whenever you please, which should be done, at least once every day, to blow away animal steams, and other noxious vapours. But especially let the air of your bed chamber be pure and untainted, not near the ground, or any kind of dampness.

3. Evident marks of a bad air in any house, are dampness or discolouring of plai-

---

* See Columel. de re rust. lib. 1. cap 4. Petatur igitur aër calore et frigore temperatus, quem medius fere obtinet collis, loco paululum intumescente, quod neque depressus hieme pruinis torpet, aut torret æstate vaporibus.

fter or wainscot, mouldiness of bread, wetness of spunge, melting of sugar, rusting of brass and iron, and rotting of furniture.

4. THERE is nothing more apt to load the air with putrid steams, or breed bad distempers, than the general and pernicious custom of permitting *common and crowded burial places* to be within the precincts of populous cities.

5. THE air of cities being loaded with steams of fuel and exhalations from animals, is unfriendly to infants* not yet habituated to such noxious mixtures.

6. SUDDEN extremes of heat and cold should be avoided as much as possible; and they commit a most dangerous error, who, in the winter nights, come out of the close,

* Founded upon experience, is mentioned a calculation in the bishop of Worcester's excellent sermon, (page 18, 19.) preached for the benefit of the Foundling Hospital *anno* 1756, shewing that many more children die in proportion, which are nursed in a populous city, or brought up by hand, than if they were nursed in the country, and nourished at the breast.

hot rooms of public houses into a cold and chilling air, without cloaks or surtouts.

Of ALIMENT.

1. The best food is that which is simple, nourishing, without acrimony, and easily digested; and the principal rule to be observed with regard to aliment in general, is to eat and drink wholesome things in a proper quantity. But, you will ask, how shall the bulk of the people distinguish wholesome aliment from unwholesome? And how shall they measure the quantity proper for them? I answer, that almost all the aliment in common use has been found wholesome by the experience of ages, and a temperate healthy man need not be under great apprehensions of danger in partaking of such. But there is an obvious rule which will direct every individual aright in the choice of his aliment. Let him observe what agrees with his constitution, and what does not, and let his experience and reason direct him to use the one and avoid the other.

ther. And as to the proper quantity of aliment, the rule is, to take juſt ſuch a proportion as will be ſufficient to ſupport and nouriſh him, but not ſuch as will overload the ſtomach, and be difficult to digeſt; yet in this meaſure alſo, every individual has a a ſure guide, if he will be directed by a natural undepraved appetite; for whenever he has eat of any good food, as much as his appetite requires, and leaves off before his ſtomach is cloyed*, or finiſhes his meal with ſome reliſh for more, he has eat a proper quantity. But to prevent any deception, he may be ſtill farther convinced that he has committed no exceſs, if immediately after dinner he can write or walk, or go about any other neceſſary buſineſs with pleaſure; and if after ſupper his ſleep ſhall not be diſturbed, or ſhortened by what he has eat or drank; if he has no head-ach next morning, nor any uncommon hawking or ſpitting, nor a bad taſte in his mouth; but

* Vid. Hippoc. aph. ſect. 2. aphor. 17. Ubi copioſior præter naturam cibus ingeſtus fuerit, id morbum creat.

rises, at his usual hour, refreshed and chearful.

2. ANOTHER useful rule is, that we should not indulge ourselves in a discordant variety of aliments at the same meal. Tho' a good stomach, for example, may make a shift to digest fish, flesh, wine and beer at one repast; yet if one adds salad, cream and fruit to them (which is too frequently done) the flatulent mixture will distend the bowels, and pervert the digestion.

3. THE quantity and solidity of a man's aliment ought to bear a just proportion to the strength of his constitution, and to the exercise which he uses: For young, strong, labouring people will turn to good nourishment any kind of food in common use; and they can digest with ease a quantity that would oppress or destroy the delicate and sedentary.

4. BREAD, made of good wheat flour, properly fermented and baked, is the most valuable

valuable article of our diet, wholefome and nourifhing by itfelf, mixing well with all forts of aliment, and frequently agreeable to the ftomach when it loaths every other food.

5. It is to be obferved, that liquid aliments, or fpoon meats, are moft proper, when immediate refrefhment is required after great abftinence or fatigue, becaufe they mingle fooner with the blood than folid aliments.

6. As drink makes a confiderable part of our aliment, it may not be amifs here to inquire which fort of common drink, generally fpeaking, is the moft proper to preferve health. "Pure water (fays Frederick Hoff-
"man *) is the beft drink for perfons of all
"ages and temperaments. By its fluidity
"and mildnefs, it promotes a free and equa-
"ble circulation of the blood and humours
"through all the veffels of the body, upon
"which the due performance of every ani-

* Differt. phyfico-med. vol. 2. differt. 5.

"mal

" mal function depends; and hence water
" drinkers are not only the moſt active and
" nimble, but alſo the moſt chearful and
" ſprightly of all people. In ſanguine com-
" plexions, water, by diluting the blood,
" renders the circulation eaſy and uniform.
" In the choleric, the coolneſs of the water
" reſtrains the quick motion, and intenſe
" heat of the humours. It attenuates the
" glutinous viſcidity of the juices in the
" phlegmatic, and the groſs earthineſs which
" prevails in melancholic temperaments.
" And as to different ages, water is good for
" children, to make their tenacious milky
" diet thin, and eaſy to digeſt: For youth
" and middle aged people, to ſweeten and
" diſſolve any ſcorbutic acrimony, or ſharp-
" neſs that may be in the humours, by which
" means pains and obſtructions are prevent-
" ed: And for old people, to moiſten and
" mollify their rigid fibres, and to promote
" a leſs difficult circulation through their
" hard and ſhrivelled pipes. In ſhort, (ſays
" he) of all the productions of nature or art,
" water

"water comes nearest to that universal re-
"medy or panacea, so much searched after
"by mankind, but never discovered." The
truth of it is, pure, light, soft, cold water,
from a clear stream, drank in such a quantity
as is necessary to quench their thirst, dilute
their food, and cool their heat, is the best
drink for children, for hearty people, and
for persons of a hot temperament, especially if they have been habituated to the use
of it: But to delicate or cold constitutions,
to weak stomachs, and to persons unaccustomed to it, water without wine is a very
improper drink *; and they will find it so,
who try it under such circumstances.

Good wine † is an admirable liquor, and,
used in a moderate quantity, answers many
excellent

---

* See Hippocrates's opinion on this article, page 106. &c.

† Plutarch, in his life of Cæsar, tells us, that when he had taken Gomphi, a town in Thessaly, by assault, he not only found provisions for his army, but physick also: For there they met with plenty of wine, which they drank freely. Warmed

excellent purposes of health. Beer well brewed, light, clear, and of a proper strength and age, if we except water and wine, is perhaps the most antient, and best sort of drink in common use among mankind.

7. It is necessary to observe, that water or small beer, or some other weak liquor, should be drank at meals, in a quantity sufficient to dilute our solid food, and make it fluid enough to circulate through the small blood vessels, otherways the animal functions will grow languid, and obstructions must follow.

8. Tea, to some, is a refreshing cordial after any fatigue. To some it is useful, and seems to assist digestion, drank at a proper distance of time after dinner: But to others it occasions sickness, fainting, and tremors at all times; so that the experience of every in-

---

ed with this, and inspired with the god, they jollily danced along, and so shook off their disease contracted from their former crude and scanty diet, and changed their whole constitution.

dividual muſt determine not only the uſe or forbearance, but alſo the ſtrength and quantity of this exotic beverage.

As the nature of coffee is more fiery and active than that of tea, and the frequent uſe of it may conſequently be more dangerous, every man's own experience ſhould direct him how and when to uſe or forbear it; but the trial ſhould be fairly made with care and caution.

Chocolate is nouriſhing and balſamic, when freſh and good, but very diſagreeable to the ſtomach when the nut is badly prepared, and is greaſy, decayed or rancid.

9. Persons of tender conſtitutions ſhould be careful to chew their meat well, that it may be more eaſily digeſted.

Of EXERCISE.

As the human body is a ſyſtem of pipes, through which fluids are perpetually circulating; and as life ſubſiſts by this circulation, contrived by infinite wisdom to perform all the animal functions, it is obvious that exercise must be necessary to health, because it preserves this circulation by assisting digestion, and throwing off superfluities. Besides, we see every day that the active * are stronger than the sedentary; and that those limbs of labouring men which happen to be most exercised in their respective occupations, grow proportionably larger and firmer than those limbs which are less employed.

1. Three things are necessarily to be considered with regard to exercise. *First*, What is the best sort of exercise. *Secondly*, What is the best time to use it. And, *Thirdly*, What is the proper degree or measure to be used. As to the first, tho' various exercises suit various constitutions, as they happen to be robust or delicate, yet in general that

* Julius Cæsar was of a weak and delicate constitution, says Plutarch, which however he hardened by exercise, and drew even from the incommodities of war a remedy for his indispositions, by inuring himself to all sorts of fatigue, and turning even his repose into action.

fort

sort is best to which one has been accustomed, which he has always found to agree with him, and in which he takes the greatest delight.

2. In the second place, the best time to use exercise is when the stomach is most empty. Some cannot bear it quite fasting, and therefore to them exercise is proper enough after a light breakfast, or towards evening when dinner is pretty well digested, but should never be attempted soon after a full meal, by such as are under no necessity to work for their daily subsistence.

3. Lastly, The measure or proportion of exercise fit for every individual, is to be estimated by the strength or weakness of his constitution: For when any person begins to sweat, or grow weary, or short breathed, he should forbear a while, in order to recover himself, and then resume his exercise again, as long as he can pursue that method with ease and pleasure: But if he persists until he turns pale, or languid, or stiff, he

has

has proceeded too far, and muſt not only forbear exerciſe for the preſent, but ſhould alſo uſe leſs next day. In general it is to be obſerved, that children and old people require much leſs exerciſe than thoſe who are in the vigour of life.

Exercise may properly be divided into three ſorts. *Firſt*, That which is performed by the intrinſic powers of our own body only, as walking, running, dancing, playing at ball, reading * aloud, &c. *Secondly*, That which is performed by the powers of ſome other bodies extrinſic to us, as geſtation in wheel machines, horſe litters, ſedan chairs, ſailing, &c. And *thirdly*, That which partakes of both the former, as riding on horſeback, wherein we exerciſe our own

* Dr. Andry obſerves, that ſinging is a moſt healthful exerciſe, and ſubjoins the following words: " Tanta denique eſt " vocis et loquelæ in exercendo corpore præſtantia, ut id for- " taſſe cauſa ſit, cur fœminæ non tanto aliàs exercitio indigent " quanto indigent viri, quoniam ſcilicet ſunt illæ loquaciores. " Quæſt. medic. An præcipua valetudinis tutela exercitatio? " In ſchol. medic. Pariſ. diſcuſſa, an. 1723, Præſid. Nic. " Andry."

powers

powers by managing our horse, and holding our bodies firm and upright, while the horse performs the part of a vehicle.

WITHOUT entering into the ancient disputes of philosophers, about the most healthful of all these sorts, we may venture to affirm in general, that what is performed by our own powers, is the most proper for persons of a strong and healthy constitution; that what is performed by external helps only, is most proper for the infirm and delicate; and that the exercise performed partly by ourselves, and partly by foreign assistance, is most suitable to such as are neither very robust, nor very tender: And as to the particular benefits which arise from riding on horseback, they have been set forth in so rational and lively a manner by Sydenham and Fuller, that nothing material can be added to their arguments; and it has been already observed, that whatever advantage can be received from a good digestion, may in an eminent degree be expected from

this

this exercife, adjufted accurately to the ftrength of the rider.

After exercife, we run a great risk of catching cold, efpecially (if we have been in any degree of fweat) unlefs we take care to prevent it, by rubbing our bodies well with a dry cloth, and changing our linen, which fhould be previoufly well aired: But of all the follies committed immediately after exercife, the moft pernicious is that of drinking fmall liquors of any fort quite cold, when a man is hot; whereas if we drank them blood warm, they would quench our thirft better, and could do us no injury.

Lean people are fooner weakened and wafted by too much exercife than thofe who are plump: And every man fhould reft for fome time after exercife, before he fits down to dinner or fupper.

Of SLEEP and WAKEFULNESS.

1. Sleep and wakefulness bear a great resemblance to exercise and rest; as wakefulness is the natural state of action, in which the animal machine is fatigued and wasted, and sleep the state of ease, in which it is refreshed and repaired. The vicissitude of sleeping and waking is not only necessary but pleasing to our nature, while each is confined within its proper limits. But you will ask what limits should be assigned to sleep? The answer is, that tho' different constitutions require different measures of sleep, yet it has been in general observed, that six or seven hours are sufficient for youth or manhood, and eight or nine for infancy, or old age, when they are strong and healthy, but the infirm are not to be limited; and the weaker any person is, the longer he ought to indulge himself in such a measure of sleep as he finds by experience sufficient to refresh him.

2. Mo-

2. Moderate sleep increases the perspiration, promotes digestion, cherishes the body, and exhilarates the mind; and they whose sleep is apt to be interrupted by slight causes, should nevertheless keep themselves quiet and warm in bed, with their eyes shut, and without tossing or tumbling, which will in some degree answer the purposes of a more sound sleep.

3. Excessive sleep, on the other hand, renders the body phlegmatic and inactive, impairs the memory, and stupifies the understanding. And excessive wakefulness dissipates the strength, produces fevers, dries and wastes the body, and anticipates old age.

4. He who sleeps long in the morning, and sits up late at night, inverts the order of nature, and hurts his constitution, without gaining any time; and he who will do it merely in compliance with the fashion, ought not to repine at a fashionable state of bad health, or a broken constitution.

5. A man should forbear to sleep after dinner, or indeed at any other time of the day in our cold climate, except where a long habit has rendered such a custom almost natural to him, or where extraordinary fatigue, or want of rest the preceeding night, obliges him to it; in which case he should be well covered to defend him against catching cold.

6. Two hours or more should intervene between supper and the time of going to bed: And a late heavy supper is a great enemy to sleep, as it disturbs that sweet tranquillity of the body and mind which is so refreshing to both, and produces restlesness and anxiety.

Of REPLETION and EVACUATION.

1. THE whole art of preserving health may properly enough be said to consist in filling up what is deficient, and emptying what is redundant, that so the body may be habitually kept in its natural state; and hence it follows, that all the supplies from

eating and drinking, and all the discharges by perspiration, and by the other channels and distributions of nature, should be regulated in such a manner that the body shall not be oppressed with repletion, or wasted by evacuation. Of these two, one is the cure or antidote of the other; every error in repletion being corrected by a seasonable and congruous evacuation; and every excess in evacuation (if it has not proceeded too far) being cured by a gradual and suitable repletion.

2. When any repletion has been accumulated, it requires a particular and correspondent evacuation, well known to physicians. Repletion, for instance, from eating or drinking, requires a puke or abstinence. A fulness of blood requires immediate venæsection. A redundancy of humours requires purging. And a retention of any excrementitious matter, which should have been discharged by sweat, urine, or spitting, requires assistance from such means as are found by experience

experience to promote thefe feveral evacuations. And if thofe cautions are neglected, there will fucceed an oppreffion of the ftomach or breaft, a weight of the head, a rupture of the blood veffels, or fome other troublefome diforder.

3. It is to be obferved that a perfon in perfect health, all whofe fecretions are duly performed, ought never to take any medicine that is either evacuating or acrimonious, becaufe it may difturb the operations of nature without any neceffity; and Hippocrates exprefly declares*, that thofe who are of a ftrong and healthy conftitution are much the worfe for taking purges ‡. But as to external ablutions of the skin, by wafhing, bathing, or fwimming, they are proper for healthy people, provided they are not carried to excefs.

4. It alfo is to be obferved, that chewing or fmoaking tobacco foon after meals, generally deftroys the appetite, and hurts the

---

* Sect. 2. aphor. 36, 37.

‡ It is to be obferved that the purges ufed in Hippocrates's time were all fomewhat violent.

constitution, both by weakening the springs of life, (as other opiates do) and by evacuating the saliva which nature has appointed to fall into the stomach to promote digestion.

5. Nothing exhausts and enervates the body more, or hurries on old age faster than premature concubinage; and hence the ancient Germans* are extolled by Tacitus for not marrying before they arrived at their full vigour.

Of the PASSIONS and AFFECTIONS of the mind.

1. He who seriously resolves to preserve his health, must previously learn to conquer his passions, and keep them in absolute subjection to reason; for let a man be ever so temperate in his diet, and regular in his exercise, yet still some unhappy passions, if indulged to excess, will prevail over all his regularity, and prevent the good effects of his

* Tarda illis venus, et pares validique miscebantur. De mor. German.

tempe-

temperance; it is neceffary therefore that he fhould be upon his guard againft an influence fo deftructive.

2. FEAR, grief, and thofe paffions which partake of them, as envy, hatred, malice, revenge, and defpair, are known by experience to weaken the nerves, retard the circular motion of the fluids, hinder perfpiration, impair digeftion, and often to produce fpafms, obftructions, and hypochondriacal diforders. And extreme fudden terror * has fometimes brought on immediate death.

3. MODERATE joy and anger, on the other hand, and thofe paffions and affections of the mind which partake of their nature, as chearfulnefs, contentment, hope, virtuous and mutual love, and courage in doing good, invigorate the nerves, accelerate the circulating fluids, promote perfpiration, and affift digeftion; but violent anger (which differs from madnefs only in duration) creates bi-

See Valer. Maxim. who mentions feveral fuch inftances.

lious

lious, inflammatory, convulsive, and sometimes apoplectic disorders, especially in hot temperaments; and excess of joy destroys sleep, and often has sudden and fatal * effects.

4. It is observable, that the perspiration is larger from any vehement passion of the mind when the body is quiet, than from the strongest bodily exercise when the mind is composed. Those therefore who are prone to anger, cannot bear much exercise, because the exuberant perspiration of both would exhaust and waste the body. It is also remarkable, that a disorder which arises from any vehement agitation of the mind, is more stubborn than that which arises from violent corporal exercise, because the latter is cured by rest and sleep, which have but little influence on the former.

5. A constant serenity, supported by hope, or chearfulness arising from a good conscience, is the most healthful of all the affecti-

---

* Vid. Plin. hist. nat. lib. 7. cap. 53. Aul. Gell. Noct. Attic. lib. 3. cap. 15.

ons of the mind. Chearfulnefs of fpirit, (as the great lord Verulam obferves) is particularly ufeful when we fit down to our meals, or compofe ourfelves to fleep; becaufe anxiety or grief are known to prevent the benefits which we ought naturally to receive from thefe refrefhments: " If therefore, fays " he, any violent paffion fhould chance to " furprize us near thofe times, it would be " prudent to defer eating, or going to bed, " until it fubfides, and the mind recovers its " former tranquillity."

Having thus mentioned the principal rules relating to the *Six things neceffary to life*, confidered fingly, I fhall here fubjoin a very important rule, which confiders two of the fix together, and fhews the mutual influence which they have one upon the other, with refpect to health. The rule is, that our exercife fhould bear an exact proportion to our diet, and our diet in like manner to our exercife; or, in other words, that he who eats and drinks plentifully fhould ufe much exercife; and he who cannot ufe exercife,

cife, fhould, in order to preferve his health, live abftemioufly. Perfons who can ufe moderate and conftant exercife, are able to digeft a large quantity of aliment, without any injury to their health, becaufe their exercife throws off whatever is fuperfluous; but tender people, who can ufe little or no exercife, if they fhould take in a large quantity of food, fome indigefted fuperfluity muft remain in the body, which becomes a perpetual fource of diftempers. Hippocrates looks upon this rule of adjufting our diet to our exercife as the moft important in the whole art of preferving health, and has taken particular care to recommend it, as we have feen before.

BUT one caution I muft here recommend, which is lefs attended to than it deferves, *viz.* when a man happens to be much fatigued and fpent after a hard journey or violent exercife, and ftands in need of immediate refrefhment, let him eat things that are light and eafy to digeft, and drink fome fmall liquor

quor warm; for heavy meat and ſtrong drink will increaſe the artificial fever, (if I may ſo call it) which violent exerciſe raiſes in the blood, and will rather waſte than recruit his ſtrength and ſpirits.

Besides thoſe appertaining to the ſix things already mentioned, there are three other general rules greatly conducive to the preſervation of health, which muſt not be forgotten.

The firſt rule is: Every exceſs is an enemy to nature. Whether it it be in heat or cold, in grief or joy, in eating or drinking, or in any other ſenſual gratification, exceſs never fails to diſorder the body; whereas, to be moderate in every affection and enjoyment, is the way to preſerve health.

Rule the ſecond: It is dangerous ſuddenly * to alter a ſettled habit or an old cuſtom, and to fly from one extreme to another.

* Semel multum et repente vel evacuare, vel replere vel calefacere, vel refrigerare, aut alio quovis modo movere, periculoſum. Hipppoc. aph. ſect. 2. aph, 51.

Even thofe things which are in themfelves bad, as *dram-drinking, chewing tobacco, fitting up late at night, fleeping immediately after dinner, morning whets* as they are called, *&c.* when by long ufe they have unhappily grown familiar to any perfon, muft not be broke off all at once, but fhould be relinquifhed by degrees.

The third rule is, that whatever tends to impair our ftrength, fhould be carefully avoided. To bleed often, for inftance, without an urgent caufe; to take ftrong purges or vomits; to go into a flender and vegetable diet rafhly, and rather from whim than neceffity: All fuch errors as thefe, I fay, change the fmall pipes, through which the circulation is performed, into impervious cords, and impair the ftrength by drying up the conduits of life.

Having thus taken notice of the general rules to be obferved by all, let us in the next place confider the particular rules appropriated to the various temperaments, ages, and conditions of men.

CHAP.

CHAP. III.

Of the different temperaments of the human body, viz. *the choleric, the melancholic, the phlegmatic, and the sanguine, with the rules of health relating to them, and some inferences deduced from them.*

TO be acquainted with the temperaments of men is of no small importance to health. Hippocrates* says, " that
" the human body contains four humours
" very different with refpect to heat, cold,
" moifture, and drynefs, *viz.* blood, phlegm,
" yellow bile, and black bile; which feve-
" ral humours are frequently brought up by
" vomiting, and difcharged by ftool; that
" health confifts in a due mixture of thefe
" four; and that diftempers are produced
" by a redundancy in any of them." Upon this obfervation of Hippocrates, the four principal temperaments of choleric, melancholic, phlegmatic, and fanguine, have been eftablifhed,

* De natur. hom, pag. 225, 226.

established. But Galen*, too fond of subtilties and divisions, has reckoned up nine temperaments, *viz.* four simple, the hot, the cold, the moist, and the dry; four compound, the hot and moist, the hot and dry, the cold and moist, the cold and dry; and one moderate or healthy temperament, consisting in a mediocrity that leans to no extreme.

These two great men, and their respective followers, mean nearly the same thing, tho' they differ in words; for the choleric of Hippocrates and his adherents has a great affinity with the hot and dry temperament of Galen; the phlegmatic with the cold and moist; the melancholic with the cold and dry; and the sanguine of the one with the moderate temperament of the other; it will not therefore be of so great moment to determine which division we should adopt, as it will be to give a just notion of these temperaments, consistently with the laws of circulation,

---

* De temperament. lib. 2. cap. 1.

circulation, to which the ancients were ſtrangers. To form therefore a diſtinct idea of the different temperaments which Hippocrates points out, (for I chuſe to follow him) it will be neceſſary to conſider what change is produced in the whole maſs of fluids, by the prevailing humours from which theſe temperaments take their names, and what effect this change has upon the human body and mind.

In choleric * temperaments, or in bodies abounding with yellow bile, the blood is hot and thin, moves with great rapidity through the pipes, diſpoſes the body to inflammations and acute diſtempers, and the mind to a promptneſs and impetuoſity in all its deliberations and actions. Perſons of this temperament ought to avoid all occaſions of diſpute, ſtrong liquors, violent exerciſe, and every thing by which they are apt to be overheated.

* Vid. Hoffm diſſert. de temperamento, fundamento morum et morborum in gentibus.

In melancholic temperaments where perfons abound with a grofs, earthy, auftere humour, called by the antients black bile, the blood is heavy and thick, moves flowly, difpofes the body to glandulous obftructions, and lownefs of fpirits, and the mind to fear and grief. To fuch perfons a healthy air, moderate exercife, light food, a little good wine, which fhould be mixt with water for common drink, and chearful company, are the beft means to preferve health.

In phlegmatic temperaments, where there is a large proportion of a watery tenacious mucilage, the flimy blood moves languidly, difpofes the body to white fwellings and dropfical diforders, and the mind to ftupidity and floth. In this temperament, a diet moderately attenuating, conftant exercife, and fome warm gentle phyfic at proper times, will prevent bad diforders.

In fanguine temperaments, where there is no redundancy of bile or phlegm, the blood
(except

(except in cafes of fulnefs from high living, or inanition from hæmorrhages) circulates freely and equably through all the veffels, which difpofes the body to health and long life, and the mind to chearfulnefs and benevolence. The principal care of fuch perfons fhould be, by a moderate and prudent ufe of all the neceffaries of life, to avoid the extremes of plenitude and voluptuoufnefs, and every fort of intemperance which may fpoil a benign and healthy conftitution.

It is true, that thefe temperaments are not eafily diftinguifhed at firft fight, in every individual; but a confiderate man may, by obfervation and experience, difcover which temperament he himfelf principally partakes of, and confequently may, by proper precautions, obviate any inconvenience apt to arife from it.

From what has been faid of thefe different temperaments, it will clearly follow, firft, That there can be no fuch thing contrived

trived by man, as an univerſal remedy to prevent, or remove, all ſorts of complaints, becauſe that which would agree with the hot, muſt diſagree with the cold. Beſides, all ſuch boaſted ſpecifics have been found ineffectual from experience, and every pretender to them has at laſt been convicted either of ignorance or diſhoneſty. In a word, none but he who had skill to create the human body, can contrive a ſpecific for all diſtempers; and I am fully perſuaded, that except the *tree of life,* there never was, nor will be an univerſal panacea.

It follows, ſecondly, That we cannot with certainty promiſe for any particular aliment, or any kind of medicine, that it will agree with this or the other individual, until we are acquainted with his peculiar temperament; and conſequently, that it is abſurd to preſcribe a method of diet or phyſic for any man, without ſuch a previous knowledge.

After

[401]

AFTER this short sketch of the temperaments, we come next to take a view of those rules of health which are peculiar to the different periods of life.

CHAP. IV.

Of infancy, youth, manhood, and old age; together with the precepts of health peculiar to each of them.

HAD the philosopher, " whom Aulus " Gellius * introduces declaiming a- " gainst the unnatural behaviour of mothers, " who neglect to suckle their own children," lived in our days, and known that men of rank and fashion frequently chuse their wives not for the graces of their person, or the

* Lib. 12. cap. 1. Oro te, inquit, mulier, sine eam totam integram esse matrem filii sui; quod est enim hoc contra naturam imperfectum atque dimidiatum matris genus, peperisse, ac statim ab sese abjecisse? aluisse in utero sanguine suo nescio quid, quod non videret: non alere nunc suo lacte quod videat, jam viventem, jam hominem, jam matris officia implorantem?

virtues

virtues of their mind, but only for the largeness of their fortune, he would perhaps, in compaſſion to the infant, have preferred a healthy diſcreet nurſe to a weakly capricious mother. Such parents therefore as have not taken care, by their own temperance, good humour and health, to ſecure a vigorous and happy conſtitution to their children, may ſurely be permitted to make up that deficiency as well as they can, in the choice of a proper nurſe.

The firſt care to be taken of the infant, (in caſe the mother ſhould not be fit for the momentous task) is to chuſe a virtuous, healthy, chearful, cleanly, and experienced nurſe. Her milk ſhould be white, ſweet, and of a good flavour, untainted with any foreign taſte or ſmell, between two and ſix months old, and of a thin rather than a thick conſiſtence. The child's other food ſhould be ſimple, and of very eaſy digeſtion; his cloaths ſhould neither be ſtrait nor too warm, and the nurſe ſhould be diſcharged from uſing pins

pins in dressing him, where there can be any danger of pricking his skin; and she must give him as much as he can bear of air and exercise.

To prevent rickets, scrophulous disorders, coughs, and broken bellies, to which children are very liable in this island, the most likely means would be to introduce the custom of dipping their whole bodies every morning in cold water, after which they should be immediately rubbed dry and dressed; deferring nevertheless the commencement of this practice for some months, or to the next summer after the infant is born, lest there should be too quick a transition from the warmth in which the fœtus was formed, to the extreme coldness of the water. If the infant becomes warm and lively upon rising out of the bath, there can be no danger in this immersion; but in case he should remain chilly and pale for a considerable part of the day, the use of the cold bath must be laid aside for some time, and may be tried again when the child grows stronger.

WHEN

When the first dawn of reason appears in children, the parents should take the earliest care possible to make their minds obedient to discipline, and " gradually* instil
" into them that great principle (as Mr. Locke calls it) of all virtue and worth, *viz.*
" to deny themselves their own desires, and
" purely follow what reason dictates as best,
" tho' the appetite should lean the other
" way. We frequently see parents, by
" humouring them when little, corrupt the
" principles of nature in their children, and
" wonder afterwards to taste the bitter wa-
" ters, when they themselves have poison-
" ed the fountain; why should we think
" it strange, that he who has been accu-
" stomed to have his will in every thing
" when he was in coats, should desire it,
" and contend for it, when he is in breech-
" es?"

And in this our judicious author has adopted or confirmed the remark which the

* Locke on education.

admirable

admirable Quintilian made long before him, part of whose words* I have quoted at the bottom of the page; and indeed we frequently see, that those indulgences to the child have grown into settled habits, and proved the ruin of the man, with respect both to his health and his morals.

Of YOUTH.

The diet of youth should be indeed plentiful, as Hippocrates advises †, but simple, and of easy digestion; because food which cannot be well digested breeds gross humours, and imperceptibly lays a foundation for scurvy, stone, rheumatism, and other very bad distempers. Wine also, or strong drink, should never, or very sparingly, be allowed to youth. They should be kept

* Utinam liberorum nostrorum mores ipsi non perderemus, infantiam statim deliciis solvimus. Mollis illa educatio, quam indulgentiam vocamus, nervos omnes et mentis et corporis frangit——Fit ex his consuetudo, deinde natura. Instit. orat. lib. 1. cap. 2.

† Sect. 1. aph. 13.

intirely

intirely from unripe fruit, and from too much of what is ripe. Their exercife fhould be moderate, for too little would bloat them and make them fhort breathed; and too much would wafte their ftrength. Too much fleep alfo (like too little exercife) would ftupify them, and too little would render them thin, and fubject to fevers.

But, above every other care and confideration, youth is the moft proper feafon to inure the mind to the practice of virtue, upon which their future health and reputation muft depend, and without which it will be impoffible to deliver their conftitutions unbroken to manhood and old age. Many vices are abfolutely inconfiftent with health, which never dwells where lewdnefs, drunkennefs, luxury, or floth, have taken poffeffion. The life of the rake and epicure is not only fhort but miferable. It would fhock the modeft and compaffionate to hear of thofe exquifite pains and dreadful agonies which profligate young perfons fuffer under the

the reiterated courses of their debauchery, before they can reach the grave, into which they often hurry themselves: Or, if some stop short in their career of riot, before they have quite destroyed the springs of life, yet these springs are generally rendered so feeble and crazy by the liberties which they have already taken, that they only support a gloomy, dispirited, dying life, tedious to themselves, and troublesome to all about them; and (which is still more pitiable) often transmit their complaints to an innocent unhappy offspring.

The expediency of virtue towards the preservation of health, is no new doctrine with those who studied and recommended that art; it was taught many ages ago by Galen, who, speaking of youth, expresses himself in the manner following: "This* " is the proper season to discipline the

---

* De san. tuend. lib. 1. cap. 12. Vide insuper ejusdem libellum de cogno scend. et curand. animi morbis. cap. 7.

" mind,

" mind, and train it up in virtuous habits,
" especially in modesty and obedience,
" which will prove the most compendious
" method to attain whatever may be necef-
" sary towards the health of the body in
" the future periods of life."

But how shall giddy youth, hurried away by strong appetites and passions, be prevented from running into those excesses which may cut them off in the prime of their days, or at least hoard up diseases and remorse for old age? I answer, that their passions and appetites must be restrained early by proper discipline and example. This is to be done by their parents, whose first care should be to train up their children at home in "the way they should go, that " when they are old they may not depart " from it."

In the next place, such as can afford their sons a liberal education, ought to send them, for instruction and example, to those seminaries of learning where religion and virtue are held in the highest esteem, and practised

with

with the greateſt care and decency; for ſuch an education will not only prove a benefit to the youth themſelves, but a bleſſing alſo to the community, which is always ready to imitate as well the good as the bad example of their ſuperiors.

We have reaſon to felicitate our youth upon the many opportunities which they have of a virtuous education in the excellent univerſities of Great Britain. Oxford is certainly one of the moſt commodious reſidences for ſtudy on the face of the earth. I was never ſo charmed with any place of public reſort as I was with that univerſity. *There* religion, learning and good manners, appear in all their beauty. *There* ignorance, vice, and infidelity are reputed clowniſh and contemptible: And *there* the virtues and the graces are united, or, in other words, the knowledge of the ſcholar is joined with the politeneſs of the gentleman. I never indeed had the good fortune to be at Cambridge, but from the great and good men which that univerſity

univerſity has produced, it is reaſonable to conclude, that ſhe is not inferior to her ſiſter of Oxford. Nor have the ſeveral univerſities of Scotland been at any time deſtitute of maſters or ſcholars, conſpicuous for genius, literature or virtue.

Those gentlemen, therefore, who ſend their ſons abroad for a foreign education, before they are grounded in virtue and learning at our own univerſities, ſeem to have no great value for the *future health and dignity of their children,* or (give me leave to add) for the *proſperity of their country**.

Of MANHOOD.

To this period belong all the general rules of health before mentioned, and, in a word, all theſe rules that are not diſtinctly appropriated to infancy, youth or old age.

---

* " What can be expected from thoſe young adventurers, " but an importation of all the follies, fopperies, vices, and luxu- " ries of the ſeveral countries through which they have paſſed." Sherridan on Britiſh education, book 1. chap. 2. page 32, 33.

THE beſt ſecurity to health in this period is the good habit of temperance and moderation, tranſmitted to it from childhood and youth; for a man arrived to the perfect uſe of his reaſon, is not very apt (unleſs he lays reflexion quite aſide) to indulge any vicious appetites over which he had an abſolute command in the former part of his life.

IT is alſo reaſonable to expect that a perſon will, in this period, attend to the temperament moſt predominant in himſelf, whether it inclines to the choleric, melancholic, phlegmatic or ſanguine, and will regulate his way of living in ſuch a manner that his peculiar temperament ſhall be kept within the bounds neceſſary to the conſervation of health; or (which is the ſame thing) that he will be careful to avoid whatever he finds by experience to be detrimental to his health, and will perſiſt in the uſe of ſuch things as he finds by the ſame experience and obſervation to agree with him; ſeriouſly reflecting how eaſy it is either by a ſupine indolence, or by criminal

criminal excesses, to destroy even a good constitution in the prime and vigour of life, beyond the possiblity of repair: Of this unhappy conduct, too many sad examples fall within the circle of every man's acquaintance.

Of Old Age.

Health is an invaluable blessing in age, when the judgment arrived at full maturity, displays more strength and beauty than ever it did before; and therefore it should be secured, as far as lies in our power, by a diligent observation of the following plain rules, which point out to the aged, first what they ought to avoid; and secondly, what they ought to pursue.

In the first place, old people must be careful to avoid whatever they have by experience found always hurtful to them in the former part of their lives, for age is not the proper season to struggle with new or unnecessary evils. They must also shun every excess cefs that has a natural tendency to impair their remaining ftrength; for tho' men may fometimes efcape the bad effect of thofe exceffes in the vigour of life, old age would quickly be demolifhed by them; fuch are too much care and anxiety about wealth, an over affiduous application to ftudy, habitual fretfulnefs; or, in a word, whatever is known to weaken* a good conftitution.

Secondly, As to what they ought to purfue. Old men fhould be careful to practife the following important rules. *Firft,* To chufe a pure and healthy air for the place of their refidence. In the next place, To adjuft their diet to their exercife; to be moderate in both; to retrench a little in their folid food, and add proportionably to their drink; and to rife from meals always with fome appetite to eat more; but in cafe of any accidental excefs one day, to retrench

* Exceffive venery enervates old men extremely. The Adventurer, in one of his admirable effays, humoroufly applies to them what Virgil reports of his fighting bees, *animafque in vulnere ponunt.*

the

the next, or for a longer space, unless the stomach is quite easy. *Thirdly*, To contrive that their evacuations be regular by nature or by art. *Fourthly*, To study every means that can contribute to make their night's rest sweet, and their sleep sound; for quiet sleep * wonderfully cherishes old people. *Fifthly*, To be clean and neat in their persons, and to keep their bodies well clothed, especially their stomach, legs and feet, without which they cannot enjoy a good state of health: And, *sixthly*, To be of a contented, chearful mind, and endeavour to render their behaviour and conversation agreeable to, and courted by, young people, and to be frequently in their company.

* Pax animi quem cura fugit, qui corpora duris
Fessa ministeriis mulces, reparasque labori. Ov.

CHAP.

CHAP. V.

Of the various conditions and circumstances of men considered as robust or delicate, free or servile, wealthy or indigent; together with the rules of health accommodated to them respectively.

THE several conditions and circumstances of men, supposed to enjoy their usual health, may be reduced to two sorts, *viz.* internal and external. The internal conditions of men are strength, or weakness of constitution. Their external circumstances are either wealth and freedom, which enable them to live as they please; or ambition and poverty, which bind them down to splendid or obscure servitude, and other inconveniencies.

Persons of a healthy and strong constitution, should observe the two following rules. The first is, to avoid a precise and uniform diet, and to diversify their method of living; to be sometimes in the city, and some-

sometimes in the country; to eat and drink sometimes more, and sometimes less than usual, but always within the bounds of temperance; to partake of whatever wholesome food comes in their way, be it ever so ordinary; to use at one time little, at another much exercise; and in short, by a various life, to be always prepared, and ready to fall in with any condition which may be appointed for them by providence.

The second rule is, to be cautious not to destroy in their gay days of pleasure and health, by any great excess or debauchery, that vigour of constitution which should support them under unavoidable infirmities.

On the other hand, persons of a tender and delicate habit of body, (among whom Celsus reckons most of those who live in great cities, and all the studious and contemplative) should endeavour to repair by their temperance, regularity, and care, what is perpetually impaired by their weakness, situation and

and ftudy: And, in effect, we often fee that perfons of a weakly conftitution, who are immediately injured by any excefs, and confequently obliged to be careful in the management of their health, live more comfortably, and longer than thofe of a robuft conftitution, who, from a vain confidence in their vigour, are apt to defpife all rules and order.

As to external circumftances; thofe who, by birth or acquifition, are poffeffed of a fortune which makes them able, and of a difpofition which makes them free to live as they pleafe, having it in their power to put every rule in practice that can conduce to the prefervation of their health, are to blame if they neglect fo great a bleffing, which every man will know the value of and deplore, when once he has loft it.

Those again, who either by choice are engaged to ferve the public, or by poverty obliged to ferve private families, and are not at liberty to beftow much time or care on

their health, muſt make the beſt uſe they can of ſuch opportunities as their engagements will afford them. Every condition has ſome vacant hours, which may be employed to the purpoſe of health. " The emperour Anto-
" ninus, ſays Galen, who diſpatched ſo much
" buſineſs in the day, began his exerciſe al-
" ways about ſun-ſet." It is important for a ſtateſman to obſerve, that " the more buſi-
" neſs he has been fatigued with upon any
" particular occaſion, the more temperately
" he ought to live;" and that he ſhould not at ſuch times, eat any thing hard of digeſti- on, or drink more wine than what is juſt ſufficient to refreſh him.

It is moreover to be obſerved, that per- ſons of all ranks who eat and drink freely, and are at the ſame time ſo much confined by their employments, as to be able to uſe little or no exerciſe abroad, ſhould be ſure to uſe ſome exerciſe within doors, of which a great variety may be contrived to every man's taſte, as ſhittle-cock, billiards, hand-ball,

dumb

dumb bell, &c. and should also frequently chaff his body with a flesh brush in the morning, and now and then take some very gentle physic, to carry off what may remain indigested in his stomach and bowels.

To conclude, the poor, if they are virtuous and cleanly, have great advantages over the rich, with respect to health and long life, as the narrowness of their circumstances prompts them to labour, and withdraws all temptations to luxury.

CHAP. VI.

Of the prophylaxis, or ways to prevent approaching distempers.

IN the beginning of Part II. I observed, that the art of preserving health might be divided into three branches, whereof the first points out the rules calculated to maintain the health we enjoy at present. The second treats of the best method to prevent distem-

distempers; and the third directs the way to long life. I have already spoke of the first branch. The precepts which relate to the two following will be but few.

When distempers are perceived to make their approach, they should be prevented, by removing their causes as soon as possible. " A man, says Galen*, seems to be in a
" middle state between health and sickness,
" when he has some slight ailment that does
" not confine him to bed, or from business,
" such as an inconsiderable head-ach, loss of
" appetite, some unusual weariness, weight
" or drowsiness: but it is the part of a wise
" man to prevent those small disorders from
" growing worse, by correcting without de-
" lay the disposition by which they are
" propagated. If, for example, the begin-
" ning complaint arises from too great a ful-
" ness, that fulness should be diminished
" by abstinence, or (if abstinence is not suf-
" ficient) by bleeding, purging or sweating.

* De medic. art. constitut. cap. 19.

" If

" If it arifes from crudities, and indigeftion,
" the remedy to prevent its growing worfe,
" is to keep one's felf warm, to live abfte-
" mioufly and quietly for fome days, and to
" drink a little good wine to ftrengthen the
" ftomach. And in general we fhould en-
" deavour (continues he) to remove the pre-
" fent flight complaint by purfuing a me-
" thod, in its tendency and effects, directly
" contrary to the caufe which produced that
" complaint; or, in other words, thick hu-
" mours muft be attenuated; acrimonious
" and redundant humours corrected and dif-
" charged; crude humours concocted; con-
" tractions relaxed, and obftructions open-
" ed."

WHEN a beginning cold or cough threatened an impending fever, the fagacious Sydenham frequently* removed the cough, and prevented the fever, by prefcribing air and exercife, and a cooling ptifane for drink, together with abftinence from flefh meat, and ftrong liquors.

* De tuff. epidem. pag. 207. 208.

BOERHAAVE.

BOERHAAVE, who had studied all the ancient and modern physicians of any reputation, and knew perfectly well how to extract what was most useful from their several writings, has, in his Prophylaxis*, recommended the three following excellent precepts to prevent distempers.

1. As soon as we perceive, from certain symptoms, says he, that any distemper is approaching, we should prevent it, by pursuing a method opposite to the cause which is likely to produce it: And this method chiefly consists in using the following means, *viz.*
" We must, in the first place, practise absti-
" nence and rest, and drink several draughts
" of warm water. We ought, in the next
" place, to use some moderate exercise, and
" persist in it until a gentle sweat begins to
" break out; after which we should imme-
" diately go into a warm bed, and there in-
" dulge a free perspiration, and sleep as long

* Instit. medic. sect. 1049.

" as

" as conveniently we can; for it is obvious
" that by thefe means the veffels are relax-
" ed, grofs humours are diluted, and noxi-
" ous humours difcharged; and thus im-
" pending diftempers are prevented by re-
" moving their caufes.

2. " To guard againſt diftempers in ge-
" neral, there cannot be a more ufeful pre-
" caution in our climate, than to keep up
" a free and uniform perfpiration, by not
" laying afide our winter garments before
" a warm May; and by putting them on
" again before a cold November.

3. " In fummer (continues he) our diet
" fhould be light, foft, and mild; our
" drink cooling; and our exercife gentle.
" In winter, on the contrary, our food
" ought to be folid, dry and favoury, warm-
" ed with a little good wine; and the exer-
" cife vigorous. In fpring and autumn the
" aliment and exercife fhould keep a medi-
" um between both, but leaning to thofe of
" fummer

" summer or winter, as one is more or less
" affected with the heat or cold."

To the directions of these great men, I shall subjoin a simple and easy method of preventing impendent distempers, frequently practised with good success, *viz.* When you find yourself indisposed, go directly to bed, and there ly for one, two, or three days, until your complaints are removed; living all the while on water gruel or panada for food; and on water or small warm Negus, or white wine whey for drink. Your gruel or panada may be made more or less substantial as you require them. This is very nearly the advice of Celsus, an author of no mean reputation, whose sentiments* to the same effect,

* Igitur si quid ex his (*notis futuræ adversæ valetudinis*) incidit, omnium optima sunt quies et abstinentia : si quid bibendum, aqua; idque interdum uno die fieri satis est; interdum, si terrentia manent, biduo : proximéque abstinentiam sumendus cibus exiguus, bibenda aqua, postero die etiam vinum, deinde alternis diebus, modo aqua, modo vinum, donec omnis causa metus finiatur. Per hæc enim sæpe instans gravis morbus discutitur.————Neque dubium est, quin vix quisquam, qui non dissimulavit, sed per hæc morbo maturè occurrit, ægrotet. Lib. 3. cap. 2.

effect, expressed with assurance of success, may be seen at the bottom of the preceeding page.

And tho' some may deride the simplicity of this prescription, they will find that where such food agrees with the stomach, and time can be spared to make the experiment, it will prove more beneficial than they may imagine. I have been often told by a lady of quality, whose circumstances obliged her to be a good œconomist, and whose prudence and temperance preserved her health and senses unimpaired, to a great age, that she had kept herself out of the hands of the faculty many years, by this simple regimen. Gruel indeed is a very insipid diet to a person of a nice palate. Plutarch, in his life of Lycurgus, tells that one of the kings of Pontus, who loved good eating, having heard great encomiums made on the *black broth of Sparta*, hired a cook from that city. But when he came to taste this celebrated dish, he called immediately for his cook, and with some warmth told him that it was a vile abominable mess. To which the other modestly replied, *Sir, to make this broth relish well, a man must bathe himself in the river Eurotas**.

Of INOCULATION.

It has been suggested to me by a learned and ingenious physician †, to whose judgment I pay the greatest deference, that, in a *history of health*, the modern practice of *inoculating the small pox*, which appears to have preserved the lives of thousands, ought to be introduced, as a valuable branch of the art of *preventing distempers*. The thought never occurred to me before, but I am sensible that it is just; and shall therefore endeavour to give a short and distinct view of the commencement, progress, utility, and proper management of Inoculation.

---

* A river of Laconia, running by Sparta, so that *to bathe in Eurotas*, means *to imitate the discipline and temperance of the Lacedemonians*.

† Sir Alexander Dick baronet, President of the Royal College of physicians at Edinburgh.

IN the beginning of the eighteenth century*, Dr. J. Pylarini, an Italian phyſician, ſent to the Royal Society from Conſtantinople, the firſt authentic account which we have of this practice.

TWELVE years after Pylarini's account, Timoni (another Italian phyſician) wrote to the ſame ſociety, that the Circaſſians and Georgians had, for the preceeding forty years, uſed a method of communicating the ſmall-pox, by a ſort of inoculation among the Greeks at Conſtantinople. He extolls the ſafety and benefit of this practice, and writes a long and laboured diſſertation upon

* Operationem medicam pandimus, (ſays Pylarini) non a phyſicæ cultoribus, ſed a plebeia rudique gente detectam. Verus ignoratur ejus inventor. In Græcia tamen primum invaluit; hinc in propinqua ſucceſſivè ſerpendo loca, in Byzantinam tandem irrepſit urbem, ubi latuit per aliquot annos, raro quoque et inter humiliores duntaxat recepta. Immaniter autem nuper graſſante variolarum epidemia, latius innoteſcere cœpit. Nunquam tamen ſublimiores auſa eſt ingredi aulas, donec nobilis quidam inter præſtantiores Græcos, anno 1701, ſerio me, quidnam de hac inſitione ſentirem, conſuluit, et an ad eandem in quatuor ſuis propriis filiis celebrandum præberem aſſenſum. Amico me haud alienum, ſub levi tamen hæſitantia, præbui. Phil. Tranſact. abridg. vol. 5. pag. 370, 377.

the Ætiology * of it, comparing the procefs of the diftemper, (as feveral before and fince his time have done) with the fermentation † and defpumation of vinous liquors, which is an hypothefis much more ingenious than folid ‡.

About

---

* Ætiology, from ἀιτία caufa, et λογος ratio, fignifies the real or fuppofed caufe of any fymptoms or appearances.

† " Nec obfcurior eft infitionis modus, (fays Timoni) quam " panificium, aut ars cerevifiaria, in quibus ex admixto fer- " mento maſſæ fermentandæ turgefcunt, &c. Phil. tranfact. " abridg. vol. 5. pag. 370."

‡ We know nothing of the nature of that *miafma* or poifon which produces the fmall pox, and I cannot imagine why we fhould be afhamed to acknowledge our ignorance in unfolding the operations of nature, when every moment prefents the curious enquirer with difficulties impenetrable to his underftanding. This pretty hypothefis of fermentation in the fmall-pox, reminds me of what the famous anatomift Steno faid of the hypothefis of Des Cartes, in which that acute philofopher fuppofes the *glandula pinealis* to be the refidence of the human foul; viz. that Des Cartes's *man* was indeed a very *ingenious fellow*, but happened to be quite different from the man whom God made. See Winflow's anatomy of the head.

It is well known to the Chymifts, that there are three forts, or three degrees of fermentation, diftinguifhed one from another, by their feveral productions: The vinous, the acetous, and the putrid. Macquer's Elem. chym. vol. 1. chap. xii. of thefe the

putrid

About the year 1717, The Honourable Mr. Wortley Montagu, being ambaſſador at Conſtantinople, lady Mary his wife, with particular care, enquired into every circumſtance relating to this practice, and had her ſon inoculated in that city. And in the year 1721, her daughter was the firſt that ever underwent the inoculation in England, under the care of Mr. Maitland, a Scotch ſurgeon, who had attended the ambaſſador, and ſeen the practice in Turkey *.

Soon after this commencement, the experiment was made, with good ſucceſs, on ſix condemned malefactors in Newgate.

putrid alone belongs to animal ſubſtances; but the circulation muſt previouſly ceaſe, and death muſt always precede the courſe of a total putrid fermentation in the human body; for where many other ſigns may be ambiguous, the cadaverous ſmell ariſing from this fermentation, is univerſally allowed to be a certain mark, and an inconteſtible proof of death.

* Here I muſt with gratitude acknowledge, that this little treatiſe on inoculation, has been much improved by the friendly remarks of that accompliſhed gentleman, the Lord Chief Baron Ord, who takes pleaſure in promoting every deſign, as well the ſmalleſt as the greateſt, that can be uſeful to the publick.

Five

Five of the parish children of St. James's were next inoculated, and recovered. A few families of diſtinction had the ſmallpox tranſmitted to their children alſo with the deſired effect. And when after theſe ſuccefsful trials, the inoculation was happily performed on ſeveral of the Royal Family, the practice gained ground every day.

"That inoculation was not ſtifled in
"the bud (ſays the learned Dr. Davies* of
"Bath) by the prevailing paſſions and pre-
"judices of mankind, we owe chiefly
"to two favourable circumſtances, *viz.*
"to the countenance it received from the
"Royal Family, and to the abilities and
"integrity of Dr. Jurin, who undertook
"the office of a candid hiſtorian, putting
"that practice to the fair teſt of experi-
"ence.

* This worthy phyſician gave me two valuable manuſcripts upon inoculation, compoſed by him ſome years ago, the one in Engliſh, and the other in elegant Latin.

THE rapid progress which inoculation made very early, induced several among the clergy and physical faculty, to inquire into the moral and medical objections that might be raised against it. Parties were formed, and a controversy arose which soon grew warm, and was carried on with great animosity for a considerable time: Nor are the consciences of some yet satisfied with regard to the lawfulness of anticipating such a distemper. But the fortunate success of an infinity of experiments hath established the practice, which among people of the best judgment is now become almost universal *.

WHAT shall we say of the first introduction of inoculation among mankind? Could any man in his senses ever form a scheme of preserving life, by mingling a virulent poison with the blood of a healthy person? The inventor seems to have had no such intention. Dr. Mead says, ‡ " that by the best " information which, after diligent inqui- " ry, he could acquire, the practice of in-

---

* Opinionum commenta delet dies, naturæ judicia confirmat, Cic. de nat. deor.

‡ De variol. et morbill. cap. 5. pag. 74.

" oculating

" oculating was invented among the Cir-
" caffians, whofe women are reported to
" be very beautiful, and to be fold for
" flaves by the poorer fort to the neigh-
" bouring nations." It is indeed very reafonable to think that a nation trading in flaves, fhould endeavour to propagate among parents a good opinion of their children's having the fmall-pox very young, that fo they might be difpofed to take the firft opportunity of communicating the diftemper to them as early as poffible. Befides, if the poorer fort among the Circaffians carried on a traffick of felling their handfome young women to the Turkifh officers; and if a different education were given to the plain daughters from that which was beftowed upon the beautiful, (thofe being bred up to hard labour, and thefe to polifh and qualify themfelves for a higher ftation in life,) it was neceffary that all their females fhould have the fmall-pox in their infancy, becaufe that diftemper might fpoil a fine face at any time, and the expence

pence of a polite education might in such a cafe be intirely thrown away.

Supposing parents therefore to have an earneft defire of communicating the fmall pox to their children very young, it was natural that they fhould embrace the firft opportunity of carrying them to places where they might receive the infection early, as they have done for time immemorial, and do at this day, in fome parts of the Highlands of Scotland. Or if the diftemper was not communicated by keeping company, or lying on the fame bed, with the fick; the communication might be rendered yet more certain by rubbing the crufts of the puftules over the skin of the perfon to be infected, which was the practice in Wales. Or in cafe parents were impatient, the tranfplantation might be ftill made more expeditious, dropping the purulent matter into little wounds or punctures made in the skin with the point of a needle, which feems to have been

been the firſt rude method of inoculating among the Circaſſians.

Upon the whole, it is utterly improbable that the firſt inventor had the leaſt notion of preſerving life, or rendering the ſmall pox more favourable by inoculation. But that adorable Being who *can do every thing; who worketh on the right hand and on the left, tho' we cannot behold him;* and *whoſe mercy endureth for ever,* ſeems to have directed this rude and mercenary eſſay, contrary to all human expectation, to be the means of ſaving the lives of multitudes.

While this practice was yet in its infancy among us, the proportion of thoſe who died under the inoculation to thoſe who ſurvived, was in the year 1722, according to Dr. Jurin, as one to ninety nearly: Whereas the proportion of thoſe who died of the natural infection, during that period, to thoſe who eſcaped, was, according to Dr. Nettleton, nearly as one to five. But when experiments

periments were multiplied the practice grew soon more safe, and we are told by Dr. Mead * that scarce one in a hundred was lost under inoculation; and of late in the hands of skilful practitioners, not one of many hundreds has perished by ingrafting this distemper. In a short and judicious manuscript treatise on inoculation, composed by Mr. Ranby † serjeant surgeon to his Majesty, and communicated to me by the ingenious and publick spirited Dr. Baylies of Bath, are the words following. " For my part, I can with " the strictest truth aver that, out of the " many hundreds under my care in thus " transplanting the distemper, during the " course of several years, I have not lost a " single individual."

* Satis manifestum est vix centesimum quemque insitivis variolis perire. De var. cap. v. pag. 79.

† It is worthy of observation, that this gentleman has had more experience in attending inoculation, especially among persons of distinction, than perhaps any other practitioner in England, and that there is no reason to doubt of the truth of his assertion.

MANY

Many and great are the dangers attending the natural infection, from all which the inoculation is quite secure*. The natural infection may invade weak or distempered bodies by no means disposed for its kindly reception. It may attack them at a season of the year either violently hot, or intensely cold. It may be communicated from a sort of small-pox impregnated with the utmost virulence. It may lay hold on people unexpectedly, when a dangerous sort is imprudently imported into any maritime place †. It may surprise debauchees soon after excesses committed in luxury, intemperance, or lewdness. It may likewise seize on the innocent after indispensable watchings, hard labour, or necessary journies. And

---

* The great planters in our islands of America have found by experience, that their stock of slaves is at least 20 or 30 per cent. more valuable since they have practised inoculation than before; as the small pox in the natural way is generally fatal to the negroes.

† This was the case of Irvin in Scotland some years ago, where the small-pox was spread from an Irish beggar who brought her children thither under that distemper. The whole town was immediately infected, and few survived the disease. This account was given to Sir Alexander Dick by Mr. Cummyn a surgeon of reputation then at Irwin.

is it a trivial advantage, that all thefe unhappy circumftances can effectually be prevented by inoculation? By inoculation numbers are faved from deformity as well as from death. In the natural fmall-pox how often are the fineft features and the moft beautiful complexions miferably disfigured, whereas inoculation rarely leaves any ugly marks or fcars, even where the number of puftles on the face has been very confiderable, and the fymptoms by no means favourable! And many other grievous complaints, that are frequently fubfequent to the natural fort, feldom follow the artificial. Does not inoculation alfo prevent thofe inexpreffible terrors that perpetually harrafs perfons who never had this difeafe, in fo much that when the fmall pox is epidemical, intire villages are depopulated, markets ruined, and the face of diftrefs fpread over a whole country. From this terror it arifes, that juftice is frequently poftponed, or difcouraged, at feffions or affizes in cities where the fmall-pox rages. Witneffes and juries dare not appear; and by reafon of the neceffary abfence of feveral gentlemen, our honourable and ufeful judges are

not

not attended with that reverence and splendor due to their office and merit. Does not inoculation in like manner prevent our brave sailors from being seized with this distemper on shipboard, where they must quickly spread the infection among such of the crew as never had it before, and where they have scarce any chance to escape, being half stifled with the closeness of their cabins, and but very indifferently nursed? Lastly, With regard to the soldiery, the miseries attending these poor creatures, when attacked by the smallpox on a march, is inconceivable, without attendance, without lodgings, without any accommodation, so that one in three commonly perishes.

We come now to the most important part of the whole, namely the proper management of inoculation, where prudence and caution are indispensable. Several eminent physicians and surgeons have wrote on this subject, whose works will at all times do them honour. And even those who have written against the practice, or have committed blunders in it, by giving an opportunity to o-
others

thers of anſwering their objections or rectifying their miſtakes, have contributed to convince the publick of the utility of inoculation. I would gladly do juſtice to the various talents and merit of all who have laboured in this field; but the narrowneſs of the bounds within which I am neceſſarily circumſcribed will not permit me to enter into ſuch a diſquiſition. It may not, however, be improper to acquaint the reader with the names of moſt of them, that ſo he may (if he pleaſes) make himſelf acquainted with the real merit of ſuch among them as are not known to him already.

The firſt treatiſe that appeared on this ſubject in Europe, was publiſhed in the Acta Lipſienſia, *anno* 1714, by Emanuel Timonius, who correſponded with, and was himſelf a member of, the royal ſociety. It bears the title of *Hiſtoria variolarum quæ per inſitionem excitantur.* Conſtantinop, *anno* 1713, menſe Decembri.

The next was written by Jacobus Pylarinus, who tranſmitted the firſt account of inoculation

inoculation to the same society, and was published at Venice, *anno* 1715, in 12mo, by the title of *Nova et tuta variolas excitandi per transplantationem methodus, nuper inventa et in usum tracta.* But as the practice of inoculation has been conducted with more caution, and cultivated with greater accuracy and propriety in Britain than in any other nation, it would be needless to mention foreign authors after the practice was once begun in England.

Among our early writers, the most considerable are Jurin, Mead, Nettleton, Scheuchzer, Blackmore, Strother, Dummer, Maitland and Neal. Wagstaffe, Sparham and Howgrave wrote against inoculation; but their arguments have been refuted by Brady, Maitland, Crawford and Williams. This practice has been also treated on since their time by Whitfield, and by Freewin of Rye. But of all the performances published on this artificial disease, Dr. Kirkpatrick's analysis is the most compleat that I have

I have seen, and ought to be in the hands of every practitioner. I have been lately told that Dr. Archer physician to the *inoculating hospital* in London, and Mr. Hawkins a gentleman of great experience and reputation in surgery, intend to publish their observations on the same subject, which I hope will render the practice still more safe, and a prosperous event less doubtful.

From the approved practice of some of the authors above mentioned, and from my own observation, I shall in the most perspicuous order in my power, touch on such rules as have been found most successful in the management, (if I may use that expression) of this salutary distemper.

The most favourable period for inoculation, seems to be that which preceeds the breeding of teeth in children, while the several complaints attending that event are yet unfelt, and the humours are so

mild

mild that an inflammatory diftemper can, at that time, fcarce rife to any great degree of violence. Sometimes indeed the infection cannot be communicated fo early, from the fweetnefs of the juices; but that need not hinder a more fuccefsful trial at any proper time afterwards.

The next favourable period commences, after the accidents that accompany the breeding * of teeth are paft, and reaches from four years of age to feven: The third period ftretches from feven to puberty: And the fourth from puberty to full growth, commonly at one and twenty: Every trial growing thus gradually more dangerous, through all the climacterical afcents, as the folids of the body advance in ftiffnefs ‡, or the fluids in acrimony.

* In tenera ætate, fays Dr. Davies, nervorum convulfiones, leviffimâ datâ occafione, excitantur, quas facile inferat vel febris eruptivæ impetus, vel, dentibus erumpentibus, irritatio membranæ alveolos inveftientis.

‡ We all know that there may be exceptions to this obfervation, fince in the natural way fome have had the fmall-pox favourably at fourfcore.

With

With refpect to the condition of the patients whether young or old: They ought to be in perfect health and ftrength when they receive the infection, for this is one of the principal advantages that recommends inoculation. Adult females fhould be inoculated three or four days after the menfes have gone off.

The fitteft feafon of the year for inoculating with us, is, either the fpring when the weather begins to grow mild, from near the beginning of April to the middle or end of May; or the autumn from the middle of September to the end of October. But in cafes of neceffity one may inoculate at any time of the year, obferving to keep the bed-chamber moderately warm in winter, and cool in fummer.

There is but very little preparation* neceffary for children's receiving the infection, fince their diet is commonly of the moft

---

* Some operators from a fordid defire of ingroffing the whole practice, within their reach, to themfelves, pretend to have

moſt ſimple and wholeſome kind, as milk, water-pap, ſmall broth, bread, light pudding, mild roots, and ſometimes a little white meats, which cannot be changed for the better. Phyſick is ſeldom required oftener than twice, and that with a view only of emptying the bowels, for which purpoſe any mild domeſtick purge, known by experience to agree with the children,

have extraordinary ſecrets or noſtrums, in preparing perſons for inocuation, which never faill of ſuccefs. But to prevent people from becoming the dupes of ignorance or knavery, it will be proper to take notice, that the true reaſons, why the inoculation is more ſafe than the natural infection, ſeem to be the three following: 1. Becauſe the poiſon is communicated by inciſions, from which a great part of its virulence is again diſcharged. 2. Becauſe the infection is (or ought to be) communicated to ſound healthy bodies, properly diſpoſed for its reception. 3. Becauſe a proper regimen is obſerved in diet, and in guarding againſt cold, from the operation, or firſt introduction of the matter, to the time of the eruptive fever, which cannot be obſerved in the natural ſeizure. From theſe reaſons it is obvious, that whatever laboured or fantaſtical preparation changes the mild and natural temperature of the fluids, or renders the patient more feeble than he was before, muſt make him leſs fit and able to ſtruggle with this diſtemper, than a plain ſimple preparation where the ſtrength is preſerved.

will

will be fufficient, among which rhubarb may be generally reckoned the fafeft. Opening a vein in children, unlefs they happen to be of a very florid complexion, is unneceffary, and if they are bled, it fhould be fparingly.

And here I muft beg leave to remark, that, fince it is poffible a child (let him look ever fo healthy) may chance to have a hard ftruggle for his life in this artificial diftemper; parents, who pufh their children to the combat, are bound by all the ties of nature and religion, to give them the beft affiftance, both from the phyfician's and furgeon's art, that they can afford; which affiftance, neverthelefs, fome people of fortune have fhamefully neglected.

The principal preparation for inoculating adults, is great temperance, and a plain diet for fome weeks*, the body being all the

* The length or fhortnefs of the time to be determined, by forming the moft accurate judgment poffible of the patient's conftitution.

while

while in perfect health. They should be purged gently three or four times, and if of a full habit, a vein should be opened a day or two before the operation. If children or adults have issues, care must be taken to promote the discharge from them, during the whole process.

The pus or matter for inoculation, ought to be carefully chosen from healthy persons, and from a distinct kind, with this particular caution, that there be no other sort of eruption* on the skin at the same time, besides the small-pox.

To furnish himself with matter for the operation, Mr. Ranby rolled up a piece of fine lint, to the size of the coarsest sewing thread, and drew it across some well digested pustules (first pricked with a needle) either on a leg or arm, after the pocks were turned on the face. When the thread was

* It has been frequently observed, that through neglecting this caution, the eruption has been transferred, (together with the small-pox) to the person inoculated.

well

well moistened, he put it into a box close stopped, and made use of it within ten hours at the farthest †.

The proper place for inoculating, is that part of each arm ‡, where the Deltoid muscle is inserted, and where issues are always cut, by such surgeons as are acquainted with anatomy. The incisions ought to be longitudinal, about half an inch in length, but superficial, and not so deep as to wound the membrana adiposa. To this wound is applied a piece of cotton thread, or fine lint fraught with the variolous matter, over which is laid a pledget of digestive, and then a snip of the most simple plaister, with a bandage just tight enough to keep on the

† If these threads are dried immediately, with a very gentle heat, they retain their virtue for several weeks, and the matter does not become rancid or corrosive.

‡ I was told by a physician of great reputation and merit, that for several years, he had ordered incisions to be made in both arms, but found afterwards, upon trial, that a single incision made in one arm, equally answered every good purpose of inoculation, and therefore he persisted constantly in that practice.

dressing,

dreſſing. Things may be left in his ſtate for one or two nights, and then the whole may be taken off, and the ſore dreſſed every day with digeſtive, and the ſame ſimple plaiſter.

AND here it will be proper to take notice, that the frequent misfortunes conſequent to inoculation, ſuch as boils and foul ulcers, cannot, in the opinion of ſeveral good judges, be better accounted for, than by imputing their riſe to the inciſions being made quite through the true skin, and wounding the cellular or fatty membrane*.

As to the appearance of the wound after the operation: For the the three or four firſt days, it remains pretty much in the ſame ſtate, but about the fifth day, begins to ſhew ſome ſigns of the approaching dif-

* Membrana cellularis, (ſays Dr. Davies) purulentæ materiæ recipiendæ et generandæ apta nata eſt, et inter muſculos omnes, et ad oſſa ipſa penetrans, humores artuum perniciofos, et apoſtemata in ſpongioſa ſua ſubſtantia formari finit.

eafe. The earlieft intimation of the infection's taking place, feems to be a little itching, and a fmall degree of inflammation about the incifions. Towards the feventh day, and fometimes fooner, the patient is feized with a chillnefs or fhivering, complains of a wearinefs in the limbs, a pain in the fore part of the head, attended with a change of colour, and fome other flight fymptoms of a fever; and, indeed, experience obliges us to admit the feventh or eighth day, as the moft general term of invafion, and the ninth or tenth of eruption. The urine is alfo of a whey colour at the time of eruption.

BLEEDING at the nofe, in a proper quantity, is no bad fymptom in any ftage of the diftemper.

" CHILDREN are apt to doze much, fays
" the judicious and acute Dr. Kirkpatrick*,
" and to have a dewy moifture on the skin

* Analyf. pag. 258.

" previous

" previous to a generally benign eruption.
" They have also a frequent nausea, which
" makes them puke upon drinking, or mov-
" ing out of a decumbent posture, and after
" puking they are easier. And sometimes
" such flushings and redness appear previous
" to, or a little after sickening, as would
" give dreadful apprehensions under the na-
" tural infection, but it is very usual for
" them to vanish, and a placid gentle erup-
" tion ensue.

The next article to be mentioned is the proper treatment of patients from the time of the operation to that of a perfect eruption. In this period great temperance and regularity of diet must be observed. Flesh meat should rarely or never be eaten between the operation and eruption, but rather light bread pudding, or some other mild vegetable food of easy digestion, suitable to the season of the year, and agreeable to the constitution of the patients; unless they should happen to be faint or low spirited, in which cafe, a little light white meat, and wine diluted with warm water, fhould be allowed. A ftool ought likewife to be procured, at leaft every other day during that interval, not by purging phyfick, but by fome gentle opening diet, or mild glyfters. A free and eafy perfpiration fhould be promoted, and every risk of catching cold ought carefully to be avoided. And in cafe of convulfions, it will be very proper to apply blifters, efpecially to children where bleeding is generally detrimental.

We come in the laft place to touch upon the care to be taken of the fick from the time of the eruption to a final recovery. After a perfect eruption, matter begins to ooze from the incifions as the puftules advance towards fuppuration, for the difcharge before that time is very inconfiderable; and it is worthy of obfervation that a plentiful difcharge from the wounds is always a good prognoftick. The ufual management of patients in this period, where the fymptoms are

are generally favourable, is nearly the same which has been recommended in the interval between the operation and eruption. But if the distemper should prove of the confluent or dangerous kind (which rarely happens) a regimen and medicines ought to be directed as if the seizure had been in the natural way; and in such a case Sydenham, Boerhaave*, and Mead are faithful guides. A vein should be opened, for instance, in a

---

* I was favoured with some manuscript notes on Boerhaave's treatise *de variolis* by that publick-spirited and beneficent gentleman Sir Alexander Dick, which give great light and evidence to the author's aphorisms, and which I heartily wish were published, together with his other notes on the same author, for the benefit of the community. It is astonishing that the industry of one man should be able to collect into so small a volume, as *Boerhaave's aphorisms of knowing and curing diseases*, all that is valuable among the antients and moderns on that subject; yet as far as I am able to judge, there is scarce any precept omitted in those aphorisms, which is necessary to give the young physician a clear insight into the nature and cure of almost every distemper incident to the human body. This unrival'd abridgment of all that is useful in the practice of physick, ought to be taught in every university, and is annually explained, and elucidated with suitable remarks and observations, by that ornament of his profession, the learned and humane Dr. Rutherford, in the university of Edinburgh.

great

great ſtraitneſs of breath. Bliſters ſhould be applied in convulſions. If the fever runs high, it might be proper to procure one ſtool every day either by glyſter or an opening cooling diet. And in a bad concoction of the puſtules, or where purple ſpots appear on the skin, the Peruvian bark becomes neceſſary, which may be given with or without acids, as circumſtances direct the attending phyſician. When painful inflammatory tumours appear or continue after the turn of the diſtemper, plentiful bleeding may be uſeful in facilitating a ſuppuration when the patient is plethorick; but when he is weak or exhauſted, the Peruvian bark will anſwer the ſame purpoſe better.

AFTER the puſtules become quite dry, the patient ſhould take ſome gentle phyſick, which, at the ſucceſſive intervals of a few days, ought to be frequently repeated. And laſtly, the country air, under a proper regimen of diet and exerciſe, is of great uſe towards recovering the ſtrength of ſuch as are brought low by this diſtemper.

CHAP.

CHAP. VII.

Of longevity.----The natural marks of it.----The means of attaining it.----The rise and fall of the transfusion of blood from one animal into another. The conclusion.

I Have already observed, that when the continual attrition of the solids and fluids of the human body against each other, is hurried on with violence, death must advance hastily, and arrive early; but when it is performed with moderation, the springs of life last longer, and death is more slow in its approaches.

LONGEVITY may proceed either from nature or from art; but chiefly from their happy conjunction.

THE natural marks by which we discern

that

that a man is made for long life, are principally as follows:

1. To be descended, at least by one side, from long lived parents.

2. To be of a calm, contented, and chearful disposition.

3. To have a just symmetry, or proper conformation of parts; a full chest, well formed joints and limbs, with a neck and head large rather than small in proportion to the size of the body.

4. A firm and compact system of vessels and stamina, not too fat; veins large and prominent; a voice somewhat deep; and a skin not too white and smooth.

5. To be a long and sound sleeper.

THE great assistance which art affords towards attaining long life, arises from the benefit

benefit of good air * and good water †, from a frugal and simple diet, from the wise government of our appetites and passi-

* Brasiliæ salubritatis fama non paucos olim senes, aliosque minus prosperâ utentes valetudine, ex Hispania, et Indiis, aliisque dissitis locis, excivit ad aërem et aquas has cælo datas, tanquam ad duo validissima præsidia vitæ et valetudinis. Perquam maturè enim pubescunt incolæ: senescunt tardè, idque sine canitie aut calvitio. Quo fit, quod longè ultra centesimum ætatis annum, viridi senectâ, non Americani tantum, sed et ipsi Europæi fruantur, totumque adeo territorium *Macrobium* dici mereatur. Guil. Pisonis hist. nat. et medic. Brasiliæ continentis.

† Audio in Ægypti locis homines vivere longiorem vitam quam alibi, (dicit Melchior Guilandinus) quando ipsorum permulti annos plus centum vivunt: communis fere omnibus iis habitatoribus vita annorum nonaginta solet esse.—Aquæ Nili fluminis clarefactæ, dulces, tenuissimæ, splendidissimæ atque levissimæ existunt, ita ut celerrimè corporis viscera permeent. Audio etenim (quod olim, cum Cayri moram facerem, etiam observavi) in singulis fere corporibus ab ipsis epotis aquis statim vel copiosas urinas, vel sudores, vel per alvum dejectiones observari, atque in hypochondriis nullam fluctuationem ab ipsis ostendi: loquor de iis quæ Cayri habentur et potantur, quando Alexandriæ aquæ constent substantiâ crassiori, quæ pessimæ existunt, tardissiméque viscera permeant. Confirmo tuam sententiam, (respondet Alpinus) atque me in omnibus corporibus observasse, citissimè illas aquas Cayri clarefactas, vel per alvum, vel per urinam, vel sudorem exiisse. Prosper Alpinus de medic. Egypt. lib. 1. cap. 11. et 12.

ons,

ons, and, in a word, from a prudent choice and proper use of all the instruments of life and rules of health, of which we have spoke before.

But some of the moderns have gone farther, and recommended new and bold methods to prolong life, which the antients either had not perspicacity to discern, or wanted resolution to practise. The comprehensive and exalted genius of lord Verulam was not to be limited by common rules. He advises old people " once every " two years to change their whole juices, " and render themselves very lean by a course " of abstinence and proper diet-drinks, in " order to sweeten their blood and renew " their age." And Boerhaave*, who like the industrious bee collected honey from every flower, adopts his lordship's opinion with some small amendment; for, speaking of the most proper diet to attain longevity, he expresses himself in the manner follow-

* Instit. med. num. 1059—1062.

ing:

ing: "Great abstinence, or an extremely "slender, drying and emaciating diet now "and then, but very rarely put in practice, "is of wonderful use to attain longevity." And a little lower he explains his meaning more perspicuously, by telling us, that "a "radical, or almost total change of the "humours by resolvent medicines, and a "succeeding discharge of them out of the "body, such as happens under a course of "mercury, or under a course of attenua- "ting, drying, and sudorific decoctions, of- "ten dispose the body in an admirable "manner, to expel old distempered hu- "mours, and to fill the vessels with fresh vi- "tal juices." And thus art, conducted with prudence, may effectually lead to long life.

But how far this method of renewing their age may be safely practised by old peo- ple, I will not take upon me to determine, since the success must, in a great measure, depend upon the goodness of their stamina, the strength and perseverance of their resolu- tion,

tion; and the skill of the artist who conducts the regimen. And though this and the following brave but unsuccessful effort to prolong life, discover a quick penetration and a laudable boldness of the human mind; yet a sure and easy road to longevity, different from the general rules of health already mentioned, seems to be among the desiderata in our art, the discovery of which is reserved, perhaps, for a more meritorious generation.

About a hundred years * ago, a new and gallant effort was made to mend distempered constitutions, and consequently to prolong life, by supplying the human body with young and healthy blood from other animals.

The first hint of this great attempt was given at Oxford *anno* 1658, by Dr. Christopher Wren, Savilian Professor of astronomy there, who proposed to the honourable Mr.

* See the original transactions of the royal society, vol. 1.

Boyle,

Boyle, a method of *transfusing* liquors into the veins of living animals.

In 1666 his hint was farther improved, at the same perennial source of ingenuity and learning, by Dr. Richard Lower, who invented the method of *transfusing* blood out of one animal into another.

He was followed by several ingenious men at London, and particularly by Dr. Edmund King, who rendered Lower's method of transfusion still more easy and commodious. And as it was intended by the royal society that those trials should be prosecuted to the outmost variety which the subject would bear, by exchanging the blood of old and young, sick and healthy, fierce and timid animals; various experiments were accordingly made with surprising effects upon lambs, sheep, dogs, calves and horses, &c.

From England this invention passed into France and Italy, where after old, decrepid

and

and deaf animals had their hearing, and the agility of their limbs, reſtored by the tranſfuſion of young and healthy blood into their veins, and other wonderful cures had been atchieved, J. Denis, doctor of phyſic at Paris, with the aſſiſtance of Mr. Emerez, ventured to perform the operation on men in that city: And Johann. Gulielm. Riva*, a ſurgeon of good reputation, made the ſame experiments at Rome.

After ſome trials, Monſieur Denis publiſhed one account of a young man that was cured of an uncommon lethargy, (ſubſequent to a fever in which he had been blooded twenty times) by *transfuſing* the arterial blood of a lamb into his veins: And another account of the cure of an inveterate and raging phrenzy performed on a man thirty-four years old, by *transfuſing* the arterial blood of a calf into his veins, in the preſence of ſeveral perſons of quality and learning.

This daring enterpriſe having ſucceeded ſo well at the firſt ſetting out in France, it

---

* Vide Merklin de ortu et occaſu transfuſ. ſang. edit. Norimberg, *anno* 1679.

was also practised in England from the arteries of a young sheep, into the veins of one Mr. Arthur Coga, November the 23d, *anno* 1667, at Arundel-house, before a splendid company, by Dr. Edmund King, and Dr. Richard Lower. And Coga published, under his own hand, an account of the great benefit which he received from the operation. But unfortunately this *transfusion* happened to be soon after performed in France and Italy with bad success on some persons of distinction*; by which unhappy accidents the practice (being yet in its infancy, and unsupported by a sufficient number of experiments) fell into discredit, and was prohibited by the king's authority in France, and by the pope's mandate at Rome.

Thus was defeated a noble essay, begun with prudence in England, but rashly pursued in foreign countries, which, had the first trials on the human species been conducted

---

* It was imprudently and fatally tried in France on baron Bond, son to the first minister of state in Sweden, after he was given over by his physicians, and his bowels began to mortify; and had the same ill fate at Rome, being injudiciously tried on a person just worn out with a consumption. Vide Merklin de ortu et occasu transf. sang.

with care and caution, might in time have produced moſt uſeful and ſurpriſing effects.

But after all, I am of opinion, that the greateſt efforts of the human mind to extend a vigorous longevity much beyond fourſcore, will generally prove ineffectual; and that neither the total alteration and diſcharge of old diſtempered humours, by a courſe of reſolvent medicines, nor the ſubſtitution of freſh vital juices in their room, preſcribed by the great lord Verulam and Boerhaave; nor the transfuſion of young blood into old veins, tho' performed with the utmoſt precaution and dexterity, will ever avail to beſtow ſtrength and vigour on the bulk of mankind, for any great number of years, beyond the limits marked out by the Pſalmiſt, and much leſs to produce rejuveneſcency. Though I am perſuaded, at the ſame time, that theſe methods proſecuted to accuracy, and reduced, if poſſible, to a general and eaſy practice, would make the life of man hold out, free from the uſual complaints of decrepitude, longer than it does at preſent, ſince we ſee every day, that an extraordinary ſtrength of
con-

constitution, managed with common prudence, often exceeds an hundred years *

LET us in the mean time make the best use of those advantages which we can easily compass. Let us, by a virtuous course of life, and by the practice of such rules as the experience of ages has established, endeavour to preserve health of body and soundness of mind, until we arrive at the boundaries which providence (unless we are our own enemies) seems to have nearly marked out for our respective constitutions. And then let us chearfully submit to have the curtain drawn for a little while between our friends and us; and be ready and willing to enter into that happy state for which we were originally intended, and where we shall be secure from the approach of age and infirmities.

* See the diligent and good bishop of Bergen's natural history of Norway, where he relates from credible vouchers, that in the year 1733, four married couple danced in the presence of Christian VI. king of Denmark, whose ages joined together, amounted to more than eight hundred years, none of the four couple being under an hundred. Part. 2. chap. 9 sect. 8.

FINIS.

AGING AND OLD AGE

An Arno Press Collection

(Armstrong, John). **The Art of Preserving Health.** 1744

Canstatt, Carl. **Die Krankheiten des Hoheren Alters Und Ihre Heilung.** 1839

Carlisle, Anthony. **An Essay on the Disorders of Old Age, and on the Means for Prolonging Human Life.** 1818

Cavan, Ruth Shonle, et al. **Personal Adjustment in Old Age.** 1949

Charcot, J(ean) M(artin). **Clinical Lectures on Senile and Chronic Diseases.** 1881

Cheyne, George. **An Essay of Health and Long Life.** 1724

Child, Charles. **Sensecence and Rejuvenescence.** 1915

Cicero, M(arcus) T(ullius). **Cato Major.** 1744

(Cohausen, Johann Heinrich). **Hermippus Redivivus.** 1771

Cornaro, Luigi. **The Art of Living Long.** 1917

Cowdry, E. V., ed. **Problems of Ageing.** 1939

Cumming, Elaine and William E. Henry. **Growing Old.** 1961

Day, George E. **A Practical Treatise on the Domestic Management and Most Important Diseases of Advanced Life.** 1849

Department for the Aging, City of New York. **Older Women in the City.** 1979

Floyer, John. **Medicina Gerocomica.** 1724

Gruman, Gerald J., ed. **The "Fixed Period" Controversy.** 1979

Gruman, Gerald J., ed. **Roots of Modern Gerontology and Geriatrics.** 1979

(Hufeland, Christoph Wilhelm). **Art of Prolonging Life.** 1854

Jameson, Thomas. **Essays on the Changes of the Human Body at Its Different Ages.** 1811

Kirk, Hyland Clare. **When Age Grows Young.** 1888

Kleemeier, Robert W., ed. **Aging and Leisure.** 1961

Lessius, Leonard and Lewis Cornaro. **A Treatise of Health and Long Life With the Future Means of Attaining It.** 1743

MacKenzie, James. **The History of Health, and the Art of Preserving It.** 1760

Martin, Lillien J(ane) and Clare de Gruchy. **Sweeping the Cobwebs.** 1933

Minot, Charles S. **The Problem of Age, Growth, and Death.** 1908

Nascher, I(gnatz) L(eo). **Geriatrics.** 1914

Pearl, Raymond and Ruth DeWitt Pearl. **The Ancestry of the Long-Lived.** 1934

Ramon y Cajal, S(antiago). **El Mundo Visto a Los Ochenta Anos.** 1934

de Ropp, Robert S. **Man Against Aging.** 1960

Stieglitz, Edward J. **The Second Forty Years.** 1946

Sweetser, William. **Human Life.** 1867

Thoms, William J. **Human Longevity.** 1873

Tibbitts, Clark, ed. **Living Through the Older Years.** 1949

Tolstoy, Leo. **Last Diaries.** 1960

Vercors (pseud. Jean Bruller). **The Insurgents.** 1956

Warthin, Aldred Scott. **Old Age.** 1929